THE BIRTH OF ELECTRIC TRACTION

the extraordinary life and times of inventor Frank Julian Sprague

By Frank Rowsome, Jr.

Copyright © 2013 John Sprague

All rights reserved.

ISBN:1490955348

ISBN 13:9781490955346

Library of Congress Control Number: 2013920777
CreateSpace Independent Publishing Platform
North Charleston, South Carolina

INTRODUCTION

When Frank J. Sprague died in 1934, he was renowned in electrical circles around the world as "The Father of Electric Traction". However, to the U. S public he remained an obscure and little known inventor. His most successful businesses had been sold to Edison General Electric, Otis Elevator, and General Electric, and the only enterprise that bore the Sprague name was an increasingly successful electronic component manufacturer founded in 1926 by his son, Robert (my father).

In 1947 his second wife, Harriet Sprague, published an important monologue, *Frank J. Sprague and the Edison Myth* (The William-Frederick Press, New York, 1947). She had become increasingly concerned about the lack of public appreciation of the pioneering work her deceased husband had done in electric motors, street railway electrification, and urban transportation, both vertical (electric elevators) and horizontal (electric rail and subways). Well researched, and its brief 24 pages packed with facts and figures, in it she argued persuasively that, as great an inventor as Thomas Edison was, he was often being credited with inventions that were the work of others, including Frank J. Sprague. Today this small volume is repeatedly referenced in the growing literature about her husband.

Then in the mid-1950s, along with her two sons, Robert and Julian, she contracted with historian E. S. Lincoln to write a biography of Frank J. Sprague. The manuscript was completed in the fall of 1958 and search began for a publisher. It was rough going. Most publishing firms returned queries with a polite "no", adding something like, "such a biography is outside our current publication guidelines". However, by 1959 the family had reached an accommodation of sorts with The Bobbs-Merrill Company. There were two issues. First, how much of the publication costs was the family willing to underwrite? After lengthy negotiation, agreement on this was reached that seemed to satisfy both parties. However the second issue was more intractable as the B-M editorial staff insisted that the manuscript required a major rewrite. They felt, and the family agreed, that while the manuscript did an excellent job of portraying Frank J. Sprague as an inventor, it was much less successful in doing so as a man. So Lincoln was scrapped, and in the spring of 1960 the family turned to Frank Rowsome, Jr. for a major revision, which quickly became a complete rewrite.

Although today Rowsome is probably best remembered for his book on the Burma Shave roadside ads

(*The Verse by the Side of the Road,* Stephen Greene Press, 1970), at the time he was managing editor of Popular Science Monthly and a fine technical writer (he later became NASA's chief of technical publications). He also was familiar with Frank J. Sprague and had included a chapter on him in his 1956 *Trolley Car Treasury.* Armed with the Lincoln manuscript and numerous other sources, he quickly formed a close and warm relationship with the Sprague family, and by mid-1961 a preliminary manuscript was complete. Although factually similar to Lincoln, Rowsome's Frank Sprague was not only an extremely important inventor and entrepreneur, he was also a fascinating and complex human being. In addition the author also vividly brought to life the times in which Sprague lived and worked.

However, Rowsome had no better luck with publication and by 1963 copyright had been returned to the Sprague family and reluctantly both Lincoln and Rowsome disappeared into a box full of Frank J. Sprague papers where they languished undisturbed for the next 30 years. Rowsome died in 1983.

I was only four years old when my grandfather died, and I have no personal remembrance of him. Within the family archives there is a photograph of him holding a chubby baby that apparently is me. From our expressions one can conclude that, at least at the time, neither of us was particularly impressed by the other. He is regarding me somewhat quizzically, while I am staring off in space, completely oblivious of the importance of my companion. He had little time to change his mind, but I have had my entire life. On the other hand Harriet lived another 35 years after Frank and died in Williamstown in 1969. I used to visit her regularly, but to me she was just a nice little old lady who was slowly losing her memory. I only wish that I had recognized what an extraordinary woman she was, both as a well recognized woman of letters and as a huge contributor to Frank Sprague's life and success.

Although as I grew up there was never a lot of discussion in our house about my grandfather, we all knew he was an important, if relatively unknown, inventor. Over time I read Harriet's short monologue, Harold Passer's *The Father of Electric Traction,* and in 1980 for my 50th birthday my father gave me the six volume collection of letters that Frank Sprague received for his 75th birthday. While it would be more than another 10 years before I read them in detail, my obsession with his genius was slowly beginning to simmer. A few years later I learned of the retirement of metro line 14 in Paris, *Le Sprague,* which had run from 1903 until 1983, and on a later trip to Paris I was invited to the opening of the new RATP headquarters. Deep in the basement there is a fascinating collection of Sprague-Thomson rolling stock that had run on line 14 (some are still in use today for maintenance runs, and on special by appointment only midnight excursions through abandoned metro stops under Paris). Then in 1991, shortly after my father died, in the dark corner of my parents' large storage garage, I found a small, dirty, and rusty electric motor with the date 1884 etched into its casing, one of Frank Sprague's very early models. Completely refurbished, it now happily hums away in a special room of the Shore Line Trolley Museum in Branford, CT.

While my own technical background is in electronic devices, especially semiconductors, I was now hooked on trying to better understand the electrical world and why there were no biographies of my grandfather. This was especially true after finally reading the Lincoln and Rowsome manuscripts. I even considered trying to resurrect Rowsome, but there were major related obstacles. First of all, I really had no contacts in the publishing world. More important, however, was the fact that the manuscript lacked any references or footnotes. From my own research I was certain that what was written was correct, but how could I prove it? Therefore to ensure credibility, I felt that such a biography should be peer-reviewed and published by an academic press. This didn't happen until 2009, 75 years after his death, when *Frank Julian Sprague, Electrical Inventor and Engineer,* by W. D. Middleton and W. D. Middleton, III, was published by the Indiana Press. This was followed a year later by *Frank J. Sprague and the U. S. Electrical Industry,* by F. Dalzell (MIT Press). Although I was the author of neither, I contributed in many different ways to both (especially Dalzell), and wrote the Foreword to Middleton and Afterword to Dalzell. Since both biographies vindicated what Rowsome had written, I began to wonder if there was room for yet another biography of Frank J. Sprague, especially one that contains interesting anecdotes and material absent in other publications. Unusual for a technology writer, Rowsome's prose is also laced with some truly unforgettable imagery, making it even more enjoyable to read.

So at the suggestion of two friends and associates, transit historian Joseph C. Cunningham and Carl Sulzberger, associate editor of the IEEE Power & Energy Magazine, I contacted Robert Colburn at the IEEE History Center and sent him a sample chapter. After review he replied that he and his colleagues believed that the Rowsome manuscript could be an important addition to the history of electric power and transportation.

The manuscript that follows is the original Rowsome text, with some modest editing, to which have been selectively added photographs and images that compliment what the author has written. Also added are two appendices which tell the Frank J. Sprague story through the eyes of people who knew him or about his work, including friends, associates, employees, competitors, and his immediate family. The included letters and images are taken from the previously referenced "birthday books" and provide an unusually intimate look at this extraordinary man.

John L. Sprague

I: NOT WITHOUT HONOR

"Sprague was an engineer-entrepreneur. He gave economic worth to scientific advance by using newly discovered scientific principles to solve economic problems."

— Prof. Harold K. Passer

Monday, 25 July 1932, was a sticky day in Manhattan, with the temperature reaching up to the nineties. The newspapers reported that President Hoover had chosen to stretch the weekend in his mountain camp at Luray, Virginia. Governor Roosevelt of New York was conferring privately in Albany with Democratic chieftains, but his son Jimmy announced that his father, if elected, would call a special session of Congress to repeal the Volstead Act. International news was mixed: a British expert announced that Italy was undoubtedly building secret warships; in Geneva a disarmament conference was in the doldrums; and from Berlin the New York Times correspondent was reporting on the upcoming German election, the fourth to be held that year. (He felt that Adolf Hitler and his weird National Socialist Party would win only another stalemate but predicted that "the Nazis' denunciation of Jews, bankers, and capitalists generally becomes more ferocious than usual in the closing days of the campaign. That, however, is for campaign purposes only.").

Much of the news that day was Depression-oriented. Salary cuts for city employees were in the offing. The advertisements reflected the times. You could get a suit for $19, or a seat for *Showboat*, with Helen Morgan and Paul Robeson for 50 cents to $3. An Essex Terraplane ("the lowest priced six in America, featuring suave six-cylinder pneumounted power") listed for $425.

On West 39th Street in Manhattan at the Engineering Societies Building, a neoclassic limestone pile where electrical, chemical, mechanical, and mining engineers were accustomed to gather for the ventilation of professional views and prejudices, it became evident by late afternoon of that muggy summer day that something out of the ordinary was about to take place. Technicians in the comparatively cool dim auditorium were setting up and checking the public address system. In the lobby downstairs, the marble columns and their adjoining bas-reliefs had been vacuumed and mopped and wiped to a decorous gleam. Caterers' men were setting up on trestles the gear for a fruit punch reception. It was easy to hear the question asked and answered by one of the men who worked for the building superintendent: "Damned if I know... some kind of a testimonial for a guy named Sprague. They got a big bunch of people coming in here tonight. Later, they got some admiral making a talk about it on the radio. Which is why we got to get a radio feeding those p.a. speakers."

By seven-thirty, when summer dusk was softening the long shadows on West 39th Street, the first taxis and limousines began to draw up before No. 29. To casual idlers and passers-by in the third year of the Depression, any function that brought limousines and their well-dressed occupants would also attract a silent sidewalk crowd. This must have seemed an impressive but anonymous turn-out. The faces were not readily identifiable to tabloid readers, not movie or theatrical people, not instantly recognizable personalities like Mae West or Mayor Jimmy Walker or Governor Franklin D. Roosevelt.

To most of the onlookers, attracted by the possibility of wholly free sidewalk entertainment, the arrivals were oddly anonymous. Who among the silent watchers would be likely to recognize Dr. John H. Finley, the editorial page panjandrum of *The New York Times* and the celebrant— in numerous polished essays—of the peculiar joys of walking? Who would be likely to spot Dr. Gano Dunn, the president of the multimillion-dollar engineering and construction firm, J. G. White Company? How easy would it be for a street corner apple vendor to identify the faces of the top executive brass of General Electric, Westinghouse, and New York Edison?

What was the probability, for that matter, that the name of the guest of honor— Frank J. Sprague—would communicate any special meaning to random sidewalk observers? For the thin old gentleman getting out of a car in front of No. 29 was one of the most distinguished—if little-known—scientist-inventor-engineers in the entire history of American technology.

Sprague was among the first men to bring rigorous mathematical discipline to replace cut-and-try research. He was a life-long rival of Thomas A. Edison, and—by no coincidence— a man who detested the word "wizard." For all that he might not have been identifiable to sidewalk observers that summer night, he was a man who had earned a distinguished place in the country's technical and social history. Forty-five years earlier, he had helped change electricity from a laboratory and lecture platform oddity to a vital part of the modern world. Almost single-handedly he had wired electricity into the second industrial revolution as a basic source of power and transportation.

Frank Sprague invented many things, most of them inventor's inventions. He was the first to design electric motors capable of earning their way in industry. He helped perfect the high-speed electric elevators that make skyscrapers possible. He created the basic circuitry that ran, and still runs, subways, elevateds, and electrified railroads. But of all the socially influential and highly profitable inventions that he fathered, the one that would be spoken loudest to the public in 1932 was the trolley car.

It is apparently difficult for people today to envision what street cars meant in the recent American past. Few lines survive for them to see, and those that do are running chiefly in protected enclaves. The whole concept of street cars can seem improbable and a little bizarre: rails embedded in the public streets and a web of charged wires strung overhead, all for the sake of what obviously was slow and inconvenient transportation. The answer lies in a fuller awareness of what the United States was like prior to the trolley. Trolley cars arrived in a rush in the 1890s, and very little in the nation was ever precisely the same again. They modified and accelerated patterns of city growth. They created "ribbon communities" that reached out fifteen or twenty miles away from the places where men earned their livings. Far more than the steam railroads and horse cars ever had, trolleys stimulated the rapid growth of suburbs. And they provided mobility to other members of the family beside the wage earner.

Taking an "electric" now became a convenient way for women to get to downtown shops; for youngsters to attend high schools miles from home; for sports to get out to the racetrack or ballpark; and for courting couples to ride out by open car to the Trolley Park at the end of the line, with its band concerts, fountains, ice-cream parlors, and breathtaking displays of fireworks on Saturday nights.

In the 1880s, before trolleys, mobility for the daily occasion was mainly limited to the range of human muscle, or to the only slightly greater radius provided by horse cars. Then, quite suddenly, trolleys brought an abrupt increase in personal freedom and scope.

It was an increase that speedily affected everything from land values and merchandising to the theater and the support of local baseball teams. (Today one big league team still honors the debt in its name. So thickly did street cars swarm along the streets of Brooklyn that its citizenry became known as "Trolley Dodgers".)

Nor is it evident today, when the few trolleys that survive mainly trundle about in big cities, how widely they once reached out to smaller communities and even rural areas. One of the astonishing things about the "electrics", in their great growing years, was the way in which they could make money in unlikely spots. By linking together strings of small towns they supplied a cross fertilization that not only made trolley bonds a joy to bankers (for a time) but also reflected a golden glow on building construction, retail trade, and property values. The fanciful network of the American interurbans, now almost entirely vanished, had for three decades a luxuriant flowering. (This, too, seems as hard for the young to comprehend today as are the vogue for egret feathers, or the concept that hot passions could be engendered by the improbable corsetry of 1900.) Improbable or not, interurbans grew so rapidly in the years before the First World War that they threatened even the rich and lordly railroads. To hundreds of sleepy rural areas that had changed little for generations, interurbans brought new and easy access to the city, new markets, and new life. In fact it was not until the automobile created still more mobility for Americans that electric cars began the sloping decline that has brought them to being the technically quaint collection items they are today.

In his early twenties Sprague had been preeminently a scientist: a gifted and highly- trained young man—wholly unknown—who applied intuition, imagination, and mathematics to explore electromagnetism. Beginning a little later and continuing for the rest of a long life, Sprague became dominantly an inventor. (And a highly successful one; though never a multimillionaire in the gaudy tradition of the times, Sprague was comfortably prosperous by the time he was twenty-nine, and a few years later sold just one set of patents for more than $1,000,000.) Finally, from his youth to his death at seventy-seven, Sprague was an exceedingly competent engineer. The graceful sketches in his notebooks reveal machinery that could be built economically and efficiently, that could be oiled, adjusted, and repaired. Sprague never needed to have his work redesigned; it was eminently practical to begin with. In a technical frame of reference, it was often esthetic, for this was a man who wanted the machinery and circuitry he created to be clean, simple, and elegant.

*Frank J. Sprague on his 75th birthday
(courtesy of John L. Sprague)*

In the big auditorium of the Engineering Societies Building, Chairman Gano Dunn rapped for order at

8:15. Next to him on the platform was the guest of honor, nervous, a little solemn, blinking behind his rimless glasses. Three well-primed main speakers, and an array of greats from the worlds of electricity, transportation, and engineering were also on the platform. Facing them in the first rows of seats were scores of the movers and shakers of the day, men like Nicholas Murray Butler, Charles M. Schwab, Michael Pupin, Gerard Swope, and Owen D. Young. In one group near the front were members of Sprague's family: his brother Charley, his wife Harriet, his daughter and three grown sons. In all nearly a thousand people gathered for this birthday tribute to Sprague, a considerable turnout in view of the fact that several of the speakers were mentally rehearsing speeches that would touch on the theme that Sprague had never won the fame properly due him.

The chairman first introduced Dr. Finley of The New York Times, a remarkably urbane and polished speaker. His erudite quotations from Latin and Greek were, at the very least, ornamental, and his sallies (laughter) and elaborate but graceful apostrophes (applause) must have made many members of the audience feel that they were in good hands.

But how did it go with the guest of honor, shy and fidgeting on the platform? What goes on in a man's head when he finds himself tendered a public tribute for his career? Much is unknowable and yet some things can be inferred. Some, too, are a matter of record. Sprague had gotten wind of the surprise two days in advance, and hurried home in alarm. "Do you know what Frank Shepard and the others have done?" he asked Harriet anxiously. "Why, it's the middle of summer and nobody will come!" Mrs. Sprague, who had been confided in by the group of old friends that had spent months in organizing the tribute, managed to reassure her husband, at least temporarily. Sprague used the advance warning to rough out a graceful speech of thanks and reminiscence.

But surely no man looks back on a long and often turbulent lifetime without recapturing vivid images of people and days long dead, of bitter struggles lost and won, of high excitement and bitter despair. Some at least of Sprague's memories must have centered on the dramatic technical developments that his brain had sired and that had succeeded only after months and even years of threatened failure. These were the big milestones, sure to win laudatory mention this night.

There must also, however, have been personal memories that were almost as vivid, maybe from earlier days. Perhaps there was a memory of the almost magical effect that the Centennial Exposition of 1876 had had upon an ambitious nineteen year old, with its glittering vision of the excitements that the new world of electricity offered. Perhaps there was a glimpse of a sixteen year old, his anxieties concealed from the aunt who brought him up, setting out to travel hundreds of miles from home for the first time to go to Annapolis. And perhaps there was a recollection of a far-off boyhood, seventy years distant, bathing in a warm and lamp-lit kitchen after rolling a hoop through dusty small town streets.

If so, it was a memory of a world that Sprague himself had done much to change.

II: TO ANNAPOLIS BY INADVERTENCE

"I was not born with a silver spoon in my mouth, nor even a pewter one... in 1857, the year of a great panic, and of the first unsuccessful attempt to lay the Atlantic cable."

— *Frank J. Sprague*

The year 1857 is today almost inconceivably remote. Thomas Jefferson and John Adams had been dead for only thirty-one years, and the way of life was little changed from that of 1757 or even earlier. Candles and whale-oil lamps lighted village houses, fireplaces and Franklin stoves heated them, and if there was running water in the kitchen, it most likely splashed out from a wooden or cast-iron hand pump. Bathrooms were wholly unknown, their duties being divided between the kitchen, where wash water could be warmed from a kettle, and the outhouse which—because of New England's weather— was often prudently linked by roof with woodshed and barn or stable. There were no refrigerators nor—except among the rich—any iceboxes; butter and milk were kept in the springhouse or cellar and, in thunderstormy weather, expected to spoil. And of course there were no telephones – most news and gossip had to be delivered in person – and no rural free delivery of mail. Such letters as were dispatched from a village were most often presented directly to the postmaster with the pennies to pay for them: few people kept a supply of those newfangled gummed stamps that the Government had been trying to introduce.

If serious illness struck a family and a doctor was needed, it was necessary to hitch up the rig, saddle up a horse, or send a small boy on the run (he had no bicycle to pedal). When the doctor arrived, the chief contributions that he could provide were laudanum, calomel, and consolation. Bleeding and cupping were growing out of favor, though by no means unknown; and surgery, usually performed without anesthesia and always without antisepsis, was resorted to only in extremis. Illness and accident caused a grim mortality that is hardly imaginable today; diphtheria and scarlet fever were often death sentences for the young, while consumption, cholera morbus, and pneumonia carried off their elders. And yet, saving a certain dirge note observable in the tombstone verse of the times, this was not held to be a peculiar and somber misfortune. It was the way life was, and had always been.

Away from small villages and rural areas, life in 1857 was also drastically different from what it would become just one lifetime later. It was, to begin with, difficult to get away from the rural countryside. The easy mobility that we take for granted was unknown. It was in no wise uncommon for people to live out their lives without ever traveling more than fifty miles from their birthplace. Railroads were just beginning to spread a net over the eastern and central parts of the United States. But they were still thought of as the "steam cars" – wood burning, uncertain, and, considering their frequent shattering boiler explosions, supplying scant peace of mind for the prudent. In midcentury a trip by the steam cars was fully as memorable for most people as a transoceanic jet flight would be today, and vastly less comfortable. Away from the single-track railroad lines, public transportation was by stage — iron-tired, leather-sprung coaches that rocked over un-surfaced roads – or by river and coastal packets. Once within a city, one could travel by omnibus or perhaps by the new horse cars, excitingly modern city railroads that could take you faster than you'd be likely to walk. But the shape and the size of cities was altogether different then. Restricted transportation held down growth because workers could only live within a radius that could be travelled at the start and end of a twelve or fourteen-hour workday. Skylines were modest too, not just because iron was only beginning to come into use as a structural building material, but also because five or six stories were the effective limit of most people's stair-climbing muscles.

North Adams in the early 1800s (courtesy of North Adams Historical Society)

It would be a mistake, nonetheless, to underrate the technology of the mid-19th Century, nor to neglect the fact that people quite accurately believed then that they were seeing new pinnacles of human achievement. It was a golden age of steam and iron. Great steam engines were freeing factories and mills from their ancient dependence on water power. Steam locomotives were threatening the huge and laboriously constructed canal systems in New York and Ohio, and steam-powered sternwheelers had become kings of the rivers. On the oceans paddle and screw steamers had already started to displace sail. Even the lordly and sophisticated clipper ships were past their peak of glory. Science as well as technology had been making exciting advances. Biology and geology were undergoing drastic change. Astronomy had become mathematical as well as observational, and human minds were reaching beyond the solar system. In medicine nitrous oxide and chloroform were ready to provide the immense gift of relief from surgical pain. All over the world, the etiology of disease was under study by fresh and questioning brains; and even ill-trained and hard-working general practitioners were beginning to make correlations between polluted water, say, and cholera and various mortal fevers.

Electricity in 1857 had a special and peculiar position. For a decade or more it had won marvelous attention by way of the electric telegraph, an invention that—by permitting instantaneous communication over long distances—had brought revolutionary changes in business, railroading, politics, and war. It had already demonstrated, to alert members of the commercial community, the enchanting prospect of making money on a monopolistic scale. The true course of electricity's future development, however, was imperfectly perceived. (Only a few solitary originals cherished the notion that there might be a future for electricity in power or transportation.) For the most part, the strange "electric fluid", that could travel invisibly through metal and that arose from the alchemy of primary cells (the dynamo was of no consequence until after mid-century), was devoted to the agitation of pith balls and to the creation of small blue sparks and exhilarating shocks. During the 1850s electricity grew to be a fad or rage, not unlike a similar fad of the time for Mesmerism. It was often felt that—before long—the learned electricians would find a way to enhance a man's physical and mental powers, and perhaps even to revive the recently dead. This was an article of faith that may well have arisen from wide-eyed watching while the proud electricians touched frogs' legs with wires from voltaic cells, a rite guaranteed to produce an awesome and presumably meaningful twitch.

Frank Julian Sprague was born on July 25, 1857, in the village of Milford, Connecticut. He was the eldest surviving son of David Cummings Sprague and Frances Julia King Sprague, both New Englanders of English descent. His father worked as superintendent of the local hat-making factory, which used water power and steam to drive its machines. The little family— both parents were in their twenties in the 1850s—seems to have lived in modest but not straitened circumstances. A younger brother, Charley, came along in 1860, almost three years after Frank.

Early in 1866 the mother, after whom Frank Sprague had been named, died suddenly, and in a few weeks the family broke up. Perhaps an eight-year-old could not understand or forgive a father's unwillingness in that first restless postwar year, to try to keep a home going for his two small children. An echo of resentment could still be discerned sixty-eight years later when Sprague observed that he had been "shunted to the care of a maiden aunt, while my father sought fortune in the West." Fortune permanently eluded David Sprague. He later returned empty-handed from Colorado, made a precarious living as a travelling salesman in a number of different jobs (which got better after his son became influential), and was killed in a railroad-crossing accident in 1896.

All his life, Frank Sprague looked back on the time of the family break-up as a low point of despair. Certainly the eight-year-old was burdened by an uncommon sense of responsibility toward five-year-old Charley, who had already begun his lifelong habit of looking to his brother for guidance. Frank was startled in 1932 when someone sent him a clipping from a Milford newspaper that seemed to provide independent confirmation of his memory. It was a feature story on the early days in the Milford schools, based on interviews with an elderly resident named Susan Amelia Shove. Miss Shove remembered it this way:

> "One day word came that sudden death had taken the mother of one of our little boys. Soon after, the father decided to move the family from Milford, and the little fellow came for his books. I can see him now, a pathetic figure standing in the doorway, with spelling book, reader, and slate under his arm, while we at the teacher's bidding all shouted in unison: 'Goodbye, Frank.'. That boy was Frank J. Sprague."

Aunt Ann (courtesy of John L. Sprague)

It turned out that Aunt Ann was a complete blessing to Frank and Charley Sprague. A handsome intelligent woman, Elvira Ann Sprague was thirty-eight and unmarried when her nephews came to live with her. She made a living as a schoolteacher in North Adams, Massachusetts, and she was soon loved by her

II: TO ANNAPOLIS BY INADVERTENCE

two small charges. They found her a strict disciplinarian, formidable in those matters of politeness and cleanliness that are such burdens to the young, but always tempering her sternness with love. In years to come Frank Sprague always thought of North Adams as home, and of Aunt Ann as a foster mother who had opened her home and heart to two mischievous small boys.

During his years in Drury Academy in North Adams, Frank began to display uncommon gifts at mathematics and science, then called natural history. Knowing that there was no money for college, the school's principal advised the youngster to take the competitive examination for West Point, where he could get an education for nothing. Sprague felt no particular call for the military life (he worked for the local paper after school, and had vaguely thought of being a newspaperman), but the principal's advice seemed to make sense. The exams were to be given in Springfield, several hours away by train. When Sprague, all scrubbed and alert, arrived and met his several dozen rivals, he was distressed to find that through some mix-up the exams were not for West Point but for the Naval Academy at Annapolis. The idea of a career afloat had no more appeal than that of being an Army officer, but he took the exams anyway – one didn't travel the seventy-five miles between North Adams and Springfield for no purpose in those days. Sprague was shortly notified that he had won an appointment.

The choice of Annapolis, although by default, or at least by accident, was—like Aunt Ann—another blessing in disguise. At West Point he would have received a general technical education, but any specialized training given him then would have qualified him—in the context of peacetime—for some such pursuit as civil engineering or railroading. The U.S. Navy in the 1870s however was growing interested in electricity (it promised to be handy, someday, for shipboard lighting and signaling). The Navy had more of the early experimental dynamos than were available at any other institution in America. That a boy who could become an inventive genius in electrical circuitry should go to the best school in the nation to learn electricity, and should do it by accident, seems a remarkable coincidence.

There is a glimpse or two of what this seventeen year-old was like when he set out from North Adams in 1874. He was thin to skinniness, of medium height, with sandy coloring. Although Aunt Anna's training had provided him with a civility and good manners that would last his life, Sprague was not the timid and bookish lad that one might expect of an orphaned and gifted child, brought up by a maiden aunt. He was instead an oddly self-confident youngster, one who'd had his full share of juvenile pranks and scrapes. He had a coolly detached attitude toward Annapolis. He wasn't sure it would be what he wanted, but at least he'd try it for a time and see. Borrowing $400 for travel and expenses from several of the town's more fatherly citizens, he bade good-bye to Aunt Ann and Charley and set-out for college. Often in the years to come Sprague would display a calm confidence when under pressure, and this quietly poised departure may have been a first example of the trait. On the way there was a chance to inspect New York City for the first time. Writing as an old man, he told it this way:

> "The New York of that day was not the great metropolis of the present. There were no bridges, no river tunnels, and no subways. There were no telephones, electric lights, or electric cars... On the corner of 42nd Street and Fifth Avenue was a great stone reservoir, and the vast territory north of 72nd Street was largely barren, the home of goats and squatters.

> "I little dreamed that I should ever in any way be a factor in the city's growth; but, determined to make the most of this, my first visit, I climbed halfway up Trinity steeple to get a panoramic view of the city. Now that territory is occupied by a forest of skyscrapers, and all that one can see from that vantage point is across the cemetery."

It is an oddity of technology that, from the perspective of history, many of man's most important machines took a remarkably long time to get invented. Afterward it often looks as if they could have been built years before, if only someone had chanced on the right combination. Those strange hot-water-powered Newcomen engines that drained English collieries in the 18th Century were steam engines of sorts; but the following century was a third gone before powerful, practical steam engines really took up man's work. There was a similar lag with the automobile. Otto's engines began to sputter and bang in the 1860s, complete vehicles first ran in the 1880s, but it wasn't until the turn of the century that the automobile arrived.

This perplexing time spread seems to have been particularly true with electric power. Oersted, Henry, and Faraday had made most of the underlying discoveries in the years before 1830; and in 1831 Faraday announced the fundamental principles that would make generators and motors possible. Yet for thirty-odd years virtually no progress was made toward electric power. It took another twenty in total, a half century after the point of theoretical possibility, before Sprague and others achieved their brilliant successes. What on earth, one is tempted to inquire, had all those people been doing for fifty years?

It was a tragedy of the generations following Faraday's 1831 announcement that most investigators chose blind alleys. Because the convenient way to create electricity at the time was by decomposing zinc in primary cells, almost all work was devoted to the limited (and, except for the telegraph, trivial) uses that could be achieved by weak, chemically generated currents. For thirty-odd years there were no practical electric generators (dynamos, the 19th Century preferred to call them) that could translate mechanical power into powerful current. Nor, for that matter, were there any practical ways of converting electricity back into useful power.

But the blind-alley years did produce some remarkable electrical inventors. One of the earliest in this country was an eerie original, Thomas Davenport, an upcountry Vermont blacksmith. In 1834 he chanced to see an electromagnet—it was only four years after Henry had first defined the phenomenon—and the little device utterly enchanted him. At home in Brandon, Vermont, Davenport set about making electromagnets of his own. (He won awed fame from historians for his temerity in tearing up his wife's silk wedding dress to obtain insulation.) It came to Davenport that the straight pull of an electromagnet could be converted into rotary movement by rigging curved magnets to switch themselves on and off automatically. Soon he created an electric motor, one of the very first in history. By 1835 he had one installed in a model locomotive that circled a table-top, for all the world like a toy train. Davenport's was not remotely a practical invention, but it was, in its time and place, a dazzlingly brilliant contrivance.

A few other originals reached toward the goal of electric transportation in those early days. A Scot named Robert Davidson built in 1839 a primitive electric locomotive that weighed five tons. It was controlled, in theory, by ropes that raised or lowered the battery plates: dip the zinc in the acid and you went, hoist it up and you stopped. Once or twice this touching monster managed to move at 4 mph. Then it was wrecked at Perth by a gang of stokers who believed, in beery befuddlement, that it threatened their jobs.

In 1847 a New Hampshire professor, Moses Farmer, revealed an electric car that could, when all went well, carry two people along a short length of demonstration track. The professor, whom we will meet again, contributed a brilliant notion: why bother to carry the batteries along? He stored them at one end of his track, a wire from the battery connected to each rail. This was a fine fresh idea, though one that would cause endless difficulties when the first halting street cars were to use it thirty years later.

A far more ambitious try at electric transportation followed in three years. In 1850 a Professor Charles G. Page wangled a $30,000 appropriation from Congress for the construction of a working electric railway to run the 5 1/2 miles from Washington to Bladensburg, Maryland. Page was a Patent Office examiner and a popular lecturer on the mysteries of magnetism. He had no engineering or railroading experience, although he did have a liberal supply of self-confidence. It was his conviction that magnetic engines should carefully follow the trails that had been blazed by the highly successful steam engine. He built a number of gawky iron oddities that imitated steam engines as closely as possible. They had solenoids —hollow electromagnets—that took the place of steam cylinders, and were complete with walking beams, crossheads, and flywheels. When Page's locomotive first rolled out in the spring of 1851, it proved to be a boxy wooden structure that looked as if it had been nailed together for the professor by a house carpenter, as indeed it had.

Inside was Page's latest magnetic engine, along with a power plant of 100 acid-filled cells (to save weight, the cells had been very lightly constructed). But the Government's $30,000 was gone, along with Page's life savings of $6,000, and his whole supply of self-confidence. Secret trials indicated that the magnetic engine was so badly balanced that it threatened to shake itself to bits; the battery acid had already begun to eat through the thin cell walls; and Congress was deaf to the idea of more money without a successful public showing. This took place on 29 April 1851, and it was a black day for the professor. True, the locomotive did manage one trip to Bladensburg and back, and on one brief stretch with the help of a grade, actually managed a dizzy 19 m.p.h. But the day was a disaster, for the locomotive returned home wrecked, with its seven distinguished guests barely speaking to Page. From the beginning of the trip, speed had fluctuated mysteriously between an almost imperceptible creep to a shuddery gallop. The distinguished guests were repeatedly compelled to climb out to lighten the load, and then run along behind at full tilt to catch up.

Congress refused to vote more money and the project was soon forgotten. Its failure was not rooted in Page's innocent electromagnetic engine, nor even in his casual approach to engineering design. The failure was preordained by Page's attempt to draw substantial power from his zinc-and-acid cells. But in the Sixties the blind-alley era drew to a close. In Germany, England, and France men were working to perfect the dynamo, the machine that creates electricity from mechanical power. By 1870 a truly satisfactory one appeared, invented by a Belgian-born Frenchman named Zenobie Theophile Gramme. It was the first of the electrical machines that would change the world, and the fulfillment of the promise that had existed ever since Faraday's discovery of 1831. Two years after Gramme's dynamo came a discovery of nearly equal importance, made quite by chance by one of Gramme's workmen. To his startled alarm this man discovered one day that a dynamo could be made to run all by itself. Feed electricity to this machine that ordinarily made electricity, and it would spin its shaft powerfully all by itself, without steam engine or water wheel. The dynamo was, in fact, also an electric motor. The news of this exciting "reversibility of function" spread all over the world, and set the stage for the many rapid developments in electricity that came from the mid-seventies on.

It was an exciting time everywhere on the frontiers of electricity. The telegraph had grown into a complex and reliable network, of considerable electrical sophistication. In 1876 Alexander Graham Bell's "speaking telegraph" first appeared, to set off a newer revolution. In Menlo Park, New Jersey, Thomas Edison, with many valuable telegraphic patents under his belt, as well as a strange "talking machine" that was the wonder of all, had just begun intensive work on his incandescent light bulb. He was late in starting; several British inventors were under way with somewhat similar bulbs. And the electric power available from the Gramme-style dynamos was already lighting flaring arc lamps all over the world. There were electric arcs in lighthouses along the English coast, and hanging from tall poles along the Avenue de l'Opera in Paris, known there as the "electric candles of Jablochkoff." In 1876 at the Centennial Exposition in Philadelphia three blinding arc lamps were on display, powered by a dynamo along Gramme principles that had just been perfected by that celebrated New Hampshire electrician, Professor Moses Farmer.

It was an exciting, fast-changing period, surely an almost perfect time for a youngster of Frank Sprague's gifts to be starting his technical education.

III: ANNAPOLIS AND THE WORLD

"An electric-light and magneto-electric machine, built to a view of its usefulness aboard ship for signaling purposes, searching for torpedoes, and preventing collisions or surprises."

— *description of a dynamo made for the Navy in 1874 by Prof. Farmer*

His college years were not entirely easy for Sprague. It took him a while to learn to get along with his classmates, and to persuade them to tolerate him. At first his lot was not eased by a tendency toward jaunty assurance of the sort not relished in a lowly underclassman. Decades later, after Sprague had won a reputation as an inventor-engineer, one classmate searched his memory and recalled a pert but not dangerously muscled lad who, in the privacy of quarters and for the improvement of his character, could be knocked flat with comparative ease. He also recalled, though, that the youngster from North Adams displayed so pronounced a tendency to bounce back up fighting that the sport soon grew tiresome. It began to dawn on his colleagues that Sprague was actually not, as he seemed, cocky and conceited. It was just that he displayed the trait, often so aggravating in the young, of usually being right. Sprague's own recollection, perhaps softened over the years, was concise: "Four years of hard study and drill took some of the New England freshness out of me."

Sprague's phrase is interesting for what it did not say. A major factor in his first-year difficulties at the Academy was his deep involvement in a question of principle. In that Reconstruction period the Academy had, for the first time in its history, admitted a black man. But the strain was too much for that always conservative school, and he was not made welcome by most of the under-classmen. When Sprague, articulate and brash, protested this treatment, he was himself "sent to Coventry" and not spoken to over a period of many weeks. (He also got into a fist fight that was remembered with awe sixty years later.) But the black cadet flunked out, and the issue blew over, in the manner of undergraduate tempests. Sprague rarely mentioned it afterward. On the occasions when he did, it was evident that his indignation was not so much caused by egalitarianism, though that was a fine youthful fire, as it was in his annoyance at illogical behavior. If the Academy was going to admit blacks, he argued sharply, it was simply irrational not to do it wholeheartedly.

*Midshipman Frank J. Sprague
(courtesy John L. Sprague)*

The academic side was little problem to him. He did well in all subjects, and particularly so in mathematics, physics, and chemistry, the latter a subject that in the 1870s included electricity. The teaching in the Academy then was mainly done by the "problem method." It was a system under which the instructor did very little lecturing, but instead chiefly propounded a series of problems, in the solution of which students were supposed to perceive general principles. The value of the problem method is something that educators can wrangle over with fine professional obscurity, but there is no question that it was a form of training almost ideally suited to Sprague's sharp and inventive mind.

By the time Sprague was nineteen he knew beyond a shadow of doubt that he wanted to devote his life to electricity. The field was excitingly new, full of great cloudy opportunities for fame and riches. (It was perhaps the frugal years in North Adams that led him to the conclusion that making at least a comfortable amount of money was one highly acceptable objective.) What seems to have tilted his choice toward electricity was an eye-opening visit with some classmates to the Philadelphia Centennial Exposition in 1876. Here the nineteen-year-old's imagination was captivated by everything that he saw: the 1,600 horsepower giant Corliss steam engine that was the most efficient and sophisticated prime mover in the world; and the fantastic Jacquard power loom, that outperformed the best-trained human fingers. There were the excitements of the latest

Krupp guns, the Hoc web press, and the new Ingersoll jackhammer. But it was the electrical exhibits that hypnotized Sprague. There were the newest telegraph repeaters and multiplexers, so ingenious in their use of pulses and polarized currents. There were daily demonstrations of Bell's fantastic speaking telegraph, already modified and improved by clever variations from Gray and Edison. And there were those blindingly bright arc lamps running on heavy current from Professor Farmer's thrilling Gramme-type dynamo. Sprague spent his time at the Centennial in wide-eyed scrutiny of these new marvels, wholly unwilling to join those classmates who had sought out earthier entertainments.

It wasn't a passing enthusiasm. Two years later, as Sprague was finishing his last year, he wrote to Edison at Menlo Park. Could he, perhaps, be permitted to borrow briefly certain pieces of telephone apparatus? He would be very grateful for the favor, which would allow him to test out certain modifications in telephone circuitry that had occurred to him. Edison returned a courteous refusal, "Western Union won't allow me to", but invited the young man to drop in sometime. This Sprague did on his way to North Adams for leave before his final cruise. Edison, who was only ten years older than the midshipman, but already a world famous inventor and favorite of newspaper feature editors, received him at Menlo Park and took him on a tour of the laboratory. It was the first meeting between two gifted and stubborn men whose later relations were not always to be so amiable.

Sprague finished his studies at Annapolis in the spring of 1878, ranking seventh overall in a class of fifty and winning honors in mathematics, physics, and chemistry. In those days midshipmen did not technically graduate until they had first completed a two-year cruise and then returned to the Academy for a final rating. Sprague's cruise was on the *U.S.S. Richmond*, sailing for station with the Asiatic Squadron and one of the ships assigned to escort General Grant on part of his tour around the world. Through a friend in North Adams, Sprague managed to wangle an appointment as a part-time correspondent for the Boston Herald on the cruise. He mailed back a number of dispatches that reported to newspaper readers in his home state on the beauties of the Gulf of Pechili and the inland sea of Japan, and on the enthusiastic reception that the warrior ex-president was receiving on his tour.

This pallid part-time journalism didn't begin to absorb Sprague's energies in his off-duty hours. Though there was no electrical equipment aboard the *Richmond* then, not even a call-bell system, he contrived to collect enough wires, wet cells, and other oddments to conduct experiments in the ship's workshop. While other midshipmen were on their shore leaves acquiring worldly airs and—at the very least—tattoos, Sprague was industriously filling notebooks with proposed inventions to be worked up when he had access to an experimental shop. Several such notebooks survive, making fascinating reading today. There is typically

III: ANNAPOLIS AND THE WORLD

a title, a beautifully drawn pen-and-ink sketch, a few descriptive details, followed by the date, location at sea or in port, and often the signature of a witness.

Leafing the yellowing pages, one sees:

X Proposed electric light; Yokohama
X Electric gas lighter; at sea
X Water cooler and filter; at sea
X Marine governor
X Double circular brake
X Duplex facsimile telegraph; Singapore
X Refracting telescope
X Electric motor, reversible and adjustable
X Vibratory Telephonic Octoplex
X Ice machine
X Manufacture of nitro-glycerin
X Make-and-break armature; Hong Kong

Sometimes this enchanting notebook——so evidently the work of a gifted, intensely creative, and perhaps lonely boy——had signatures and doodles, Gothic-lettered and bizarre, or fine-lined drawings where armature circuit drawings are subtly changed into demon's heads or dragons. A companion notebook, kept simultaneously, records the day-to-day log of a cadet midshipman:

X Exchanged colours with Danish brigantine
X Passed large school of blackfish

X Took aboard 20 natives
X Prisoner escaped
X Scraped spars

Leafing through the pages of his invention notebook years later, with the judgment of an experienced engineer, Sprague showed little of the amused horror that most men accord their juvenile visions. It seemed to him that "a pretty fair number" of the sixty inventions would have been well worth developing at the time.

For more than a year after he received his commission it seemed to the new ensign as if the Navy had no concept at all of what he and electricity could do for it. His first temporary assignment was to the Brooklyn Navy Yard, and he plunged delightedly into electrical work, only to be reassigned to the training ship *Minnesota* where his duties were to teach novice sailors the elements of seamanship. This, as he wrote Aunt Ann, was "particularly distasteful." Then an inspiration of a way to make duty on the *Minnesota* palatable came to him. Like all ships in the Navy then, the *Minnesota* was illuminated by kerosene lamps. But lying unused in one corner of her engine room was an old reciprocating steam pump. An exciting vision appeared to the twenty-three year old ensign. On his off-duty hours he would rebuild the decrepit pump into a regular steam engine. He would try to buy from Thomas Edison a dynamo for it to drive, and he would assemble a number of those dazzling arc lamps and then the stodgy old training ship would shine with the most exciting and modern refulgence of any vessel in the entire American Navy. That a bright light would also shine on Ensign F. J. Sprague must also have occurred to him, though there was little enough Walter-Mittyism in the carefully worked-out proposal that he presented to his superiors. The response from Edison jarred Sprague: "no, the pump wouldn't serve". It seemed inconceivable to Sprague that so worthwhile a project could be turned down. His disappointment was so evident that a kindly superior officer took him aside. The old pump *really* couldn't have been made into a satisfactory engine and the dynamo couldn't have been driven smoothly and reliably. Not even Ensign Sprague would like that, for some of those old mossbacked captains and admirals would have seized on the results as proving that electricity was no good on shipboard. Recalling this explanation fifty years later, Sprague could feel nothing but agreement with the conclusion, and affection for the officer who had handled him so gently.

During most of his duty on the training ship, Sprague was restricted to pencil and paper for his electrical experiments. But once the *Minnesota* put in at Newport, Rhode Island, it was heaven. Newport, the Navy's Torpedo Station, afforded extensive experimental shops. Better, it was where Professor Moses Farmer had served as government electrician, that same man who, thirty-three years before, had built a two-man electric locomotive, and who had designed the arc-light dynamo at the Centennial that had directed the course of the youngster's career.

Sprague's enthusiasm soon won over the old man and he was given the freedom of the shops. In addition to his government duties, Farmer had recently been branching out as a manufacturer of electric lights, perhaps the first in America. With his partner, William Wallace, a brass manufacturer in Ansonia, Connecticut, he was already selling arc-light systems for street lighting and illuminating factories. It consisted of an eight horsepower Farmer dynamo that supplied current for eight 500-candlepower arc lamps. A chance to meet and work with a man like that made Sprague almost deliriously happy. He hurriedly searched his notebooks for the most promising idea to work up first, and finally chose an unconventional dynamo design. Technically it was the first to use series-parallel armature circuits. The little machine worked well, and under Farmer's guidance Sprague ran careful tests on its behavior both as a dynamo and a motor. Although the younger man was concentrating then on the idea of improving dynamo design (he had dropped his earlier preoccupation with telephone circuitry), Moses Farmer seems to have implanted a seed that would germinate a few years later. This was Farmer's conviction that electric motors might someday be designed that would be ideally suited to rail transportation, a conviction that had remained with the old man ever since his first experiments years before.

It was during his short stay at Newport that Sprague learned of a large electrical exposition scheduled to be held in Paris during the fall of that year, 1881. The first solely electrical exposition ever held, it would attract as exhibits the newest and best developments from all over the world. He immediately applied for orders to be sent there as assistant to the officer representing the Navy. To his sharp disappointment the Navy turned down his request. Resourcefully, he then applied for temporary duty aboard the *Lancaster*, a ship sailing to join the Mediterranean squadron. Since he had a good deal of unused leave accumulated, he figured he would be able to get away from the *Lancaster* long enough to make his way to Paris and, on his own hook, study the latest wonders of the electrical world.

USS Lancaster (image courtesy of the Chapin Library, Williams College)

But this piece of enterprise miscarried too. His orders to the *Lancaster* came through but the ship's sailing was delayed. Sprague didn't arrive in Europe until the spring of 1882, long after the Paris Electrical Exhibition had closed. The only alleviation of this disappointment was essentially trivial: on the transatlantic trip, he had persuaded the ship's officers to let him install the first electrical call system ever used in the U.S. Navy.

Being so near to a chance of learning what European scientists were up to in electricity was exasperating to Sprague. When he learned that there was something called the Crystal Palace Electrical Exhibition which would open shortly in London, he resolved to play his hand very carefully. Obviously there was technique to managing the Navy. He put in for orders to go to Germany, for the purpose of making a technical inspection of the Krupp works at Essen. On the way, he added casually, it might be valuable to the Navy for him to stop in at the London exhibition. (Chuckling over it later, Sprague defined Essen as the bait and London as the hook.) Sure enough, the orders came through promptly. Ensign Sprague's request to go to Essen was denied; instead he would proceed at once to London. He was off like a shot. In London he found, for the first time in his life, a chance to eat, sleep, and drink in the world of electricity. He introduced himself to the exhibition authorities, made a good impression, and was delighted when they appointed him secretary to the awards jury. This provided a chance to meet and indeed to work with the distinguished savants who made up the jury. Much better, from Sprague's point of view, it gave him an ideal excuse to study minutely every piece of equipment at the Exhibition, and to run extended tests on its performance and efficiency.

Wholly engrossed in what he was doing, Sprague spent months in recording performance figures on dynamos and distribution systems. He also helped settle an argument that had been raging about the comparative merits of two new three-wire systems. One had been designed by Edison, to save copper on the feeder circuits of his new lighting system, while the other had been almost simultaneously invented by a brilliant Englishman named Hopkinson. Considerable controversy raged over which was the better. Sprague tested both carefully, finding them almost identical in efficiency and economy, and settled the argument. He also began to conduct tests that may perhaps have been not entirely the province of a very junior member of the awards jury: private investigations into the comparative merit of series, shunt, and compound dynamo windings, and similar arcane topics. At the exhibition there were some strange new prime movers from Germany called "gas engines" and Sprague didn't hesitate to run all the tests he could think of on them too.

It was the happiest time in his life so far, and the months went racing past. He grew friendly with several Americans he met there, including two young Edison employees, William J. Hammer and Edward H. Johnson. Johnson was then the head of Edison's

British subsidiary and was a fine flamboyant figure of the sort Sprague had never known before. He had been a young telegrapher in Colorado, had come to New York to help work on a new automatic system, and there met Edison. Johnson's breezy western ways impressed Edison as being useful for promoting inventions, and he hired him to push the phonograph. Soon Johnson had become Edison's chief businessman-promoter.

At the Crystal Palace, Johnsons' job was to tout Edison's new incandescent lamp and to prove its superiority to all rivals, especially the arc lamps. Sprague watched open-eyed when Ed Johnson rounded up a covey of notables, including the Prince of Wales, and staged a series of electrical stunts calculated to suggest that Edison's lamps were far superior. One stunt was to wrap a lighted bulb in a handkerchief and then smash it, without harm to the handkerchief, in contrast to the flames that ensued when a handkerchief was even brought near an arc lamp. To Sprague's logical mind such charades indicated no more than that the lamps worked by totally different principles, but he did note Johnson's plausibility and effectiveness. Johnson in his turn marked down this calm and intelligent young naval officer who was so intense about the world of electricity.

One day Sprague was riding to the Crystal Palace at Sydenham on a train of the Metropolitan District Railway. This was a steam-powered line that, during its frequent plunges into tunnels, nearly asphyxiated its passengers with smoke and coal gas. It came to him that this was really unnecessary: all that you would have to do is to discard the smoky steam engines and propel the cars by the clean and quiet power of electricity. Sprague had already noted that not one true electrical motor had been shown at the Exhibition. It was the practice then, on the rare occasions when shaft power was called for, simply to use a dynamo as a motor. But the idea of electric rail transportation, using specially built and efficient motors, kept popping back to his mind. He amused himself during his London stay by designing such a system in his head. At first he thought he would feed current to the motors as old Professor Farmer had, though the two rails, or through both and one insulated third rail. But this would obviously make complications at switches, to say nothing of the problem of protecting people and animals from shocks if the car tracks should run on the street. He concluded that the cheapest and most practical method would be to have a single "hot" wire overhead (the rails could be used to complete the circuit), with some kind of under running contact pressing upward against it from the roof of the car. Although Sprague was later able to show that he had had this idea during his stay in London, he did not apply for a patent on it until sometime later, and this proved to be a mistake.

The happy, busy days in London came to a halt one day early in 1883 when Sprague received an abrupt communication from the Navy. Preliminary inspection of the records indicated that Ensign Sprague had overstayed his orders by approximately six months. He was to report back to the *Lancaster* immediately. The question as to whether he should be court-martialed would be taken up at the proper time.

This sent Sprague hurrying to rejoin his ship at Le Havre in March, 1883. She was due in New York in May of that year. He spent the intervening weeks in preparing a report that might avert the court-martial, if it could prove that he hadn't been AWOL and roistering in the British capital.

The report was 169 text pages plus original illustrations, circuit diagrams, and charts. It summarized his tests on dynamos and dynamo windings; on arc and incandescent lamps; and on the comparative efficiency of various electrical distribution circuits. For shipboard use in the Navy in the immediate future, he recommended consideration of direct-connected, compound-wound dynamos, for these would be suited for use with either arc or incandescent lamps, whichever type carried the day. Then he added reports on new devices shown at the Exhibition. One was an electrochemical device called an "accumulator", a new type of battery that didn't generate electricity but did have an ability to store it in considerable amounts. Another special report was on the new German gas engines, strange benzene-fueled internal combustion engines that were like nothing known before. He described one curious finding he had made; he had gotten a gas engine well warmed up and discovered that, in certain circumstances, it would actually keep itself going with its electrical ignition system turned off. (This seems to have been the first demonstration of the principles that Rudolph Diesel would later make famous.)

The effect of this work, titled Report on the *Exhibits at the Crystal Palace Electrical Exposition, 1882*, was to torpedo any plan to court-martial Sprague. The Navy responded to it by promoting him to lieutenant, and by reprinting the gas-engine section of his report for distribution to all scientific and technical personnel.

But the months in London had been too exciting and too happy to allow Sprague to think of going back to routine Navy service. He remembered an offer that Ed Johnson had passed along to him in London: any time he wanted to work on exciting new electrical projects all day long, and most of the night, he should go to see Thomas Edison. So in June 1883, Frank Sprague resigned from the Navy and went to work at Menlo Park. He was to last there for just eleven months.

IV: THE BEGINNING OF THINGS/ WORKING AT ELECTRICITY/THE PRACTICE OF ELECTRICITY/INTERLUDE AT MENLO PARK/WORKING FOR THE WIZARD

> "...I worked backward and soon had it by the tail. The method took two to four hours versus six or seven days. In doing this I proved the Menlo Park work all wrong, and generally I made a pretty good hit. This made me pretty solid with Edison."
>
> — *Sprague to W. J. Hammer, December 27, 1883*

Menlo Park in 1883 was a strange institution. It was one of the world's first invention factories. There was an element of similarity to the research and development "teams" cherished by some modern corporations. It had its own confident and successful boss (Edison); its resident genius (Edison); its own practiced and skillful press agent (Edison); and its own pipelines to sources of capital beyond that of Edison's already considerable personal fortune, that flowed from a syndicate of financiers of which the key member was J. Pierpont Morgan. It had a laboratory that was as well-equipped as any in the world, for Edison never stinted himself in buying equipment that just might, someday, be handy or useful. There were more than a dozen men whose skills at pattern making, foundry work, machining, and glassblowing were among the best that could be hired. There were also skills that matched or exceeded Edison's own, contributed by men like John Kreusi, originally a Swiss clockmaker and now an artist at designing brass instruments; or Francis R. Upton, a quiet young scientific aide whose skill at juggling differential equations Edison learned, rather grudgingly, to lean upon.

But for all the facilities and skills available, Menlo Park remained very much a one-man show. Upton's problems when he first went to work with Edison were rather like those that faced Sprague in his turn. Partly because Edison's own perceptions were so often intuitive, and partly because he was defensive about the gaps in his education, Edison often found great glee in flicking his abrasive tongue over those of his associates who had had technical training. It was young Upton who had won Edison's scorn for innocently trying to calculate the volume of a pear-shaped lamp bulb, rather than by filling it with water and then measuring the volume of the water. It was generally understood at Menlo Park that technically trained young employees would do well to refrain from parading their skills before Thomas Edison.

Sprague's instruction on such matters began on his first day. "When I reported for duty to Mr. Edison," he recalled years later, "I remember the surprise with which he received the news that Johnson had promised me the munificent salary of $2,500, and how, inferentially, his manner betokened doubt of my earning capacity." It was a fitting beginning for a wary, thorny relationship that would last as long as the two men would live, and more typical than the casual courtesy with which Edison had shown the young midshipman candidate through the laboratory five years before. In 1883 Edison was thirty-six and world-famous, a self-taught inventive genius and self-made millionaire; and Sprague at twenty-six, though unknown and virtually penniless, was also an inventive genius as well as a highly trained engineer. The two men immediately learned mutual respect, though nothing could ever make them like each other.

During his stay at Menlo Park Sprague must have examined with fascination the work that Edison had intermittently devoted to electric locomotives. This project had begun in 1880, more or less as a recreational change from the main effort of the period, an intense concentration on the electric light and the generating and distributing systems to go with it. Edison's electric railway began with a loop of narrow-gauge track that extended a third of mile around the grounds. Two dynamos were wired to supply current to the rails, technically, across the rails, one lead of an ll0 volt, 75-ampere circuit running to each rail. On the track went a little four-wheel truck, about six feet long, that bore a third dynamo lying on its side and rigged to serve as a motor. It powered the wheels, which of course had to have electrically insulated axles, through a friction drive system that broke down so regularly that it was replaced by a semi-satisfactory belt drive. On this rig, over the next few years, Edison was delighted to give exhilarating rides to important visitors to Menlo Park. Samuel Insull, newly arrived from London to take up his job as Edison's private secretary, could remember vividly forty five years later that his initiation ride, careening at forty miles per hour over a rickety trestle while holding on white-knuckled, "was enough to scare the life out of me." This at least must have been one aspect of the little electric line that pleased Sprague, since he and other Edison aides shortly learned a cordial dislike for the brassy young Britisher.

Some of Edison's visitors took the little show road seriously. One who did so was Henry Villard, a speculating financier who had just won control of the Northern Pacific Railroad. In 1881 he advanced Edison

IV: THE BEGINNING OF THINGS ...

$40,000 to pay for experiments on electric locomotives that could replace steam power on major railroad systems. For reasons that are unclear now, Edison saw little future for electricity as a replacement for horses or cables on street railways, or on city elevated lines. It was his idea that electricity would either drive mainline locomotives or, failing that, power temporary, portable branch lines that could be used to carry ore in mines or imaginatively bring in the crops on large farms.

A combination of circumstances brought Edison's electric railroad efforts to nothing. For one thing, the patents that he applied for were carelessly drawn and, because they claimed too much and disregarded prior work, were legally dubious. Soon Edison was enmeshed with suits filed by a rival designer of electric locomotives, Stephen D. Field, and his lawyers persuaded him it would be wiser to join Field than to try to fight him. This took much of the edge off Edison's zest for electric transportation; it was hard for him to be a co-inventor.

A second difficulty arose when Villard came upon hard times in the financial world and could no longer supply money for the work. A third factor was that electric transportation did not need inventing in the early Eighties (it had already been invented in a dozen places in Europe and America) half as much as it needed engineering development and this was an area where Edison was not so regularly a leader. His dominant personal interest at the time was in spreading the growth of his lighting system; the little locomotive that circled Menlo Park seems more to have been a plaything than a serious project. But there is no question that it must have fascinated Sprague, and its crudities of design and construction must have provided him with a vivid awareness of matters to be avoided in his future efforts.

In July of 1883 Edison took Sprague with him to help on the construction of a new lighting system to be installed at Sunbury, Pennsylvania. This was exciting work, a form of technological pioneering that is difficult to visualize today. It was not enough to install a dynamo that created current or lamps that would last for forty hours before burning out. It was also necessary to design, install, and operate a complete, working system, at a time when there was no prior experience or background on the hundreds of problems raised by insulation, fuses, switches, fixtures, meters; by the effect of wind, rain, and lightning on outside wires; and by the need to discover how a powerhouse should be run in order to supply so unstorable a commodity as electricity at the instant it was needed.

The installation of lights at Sunbury was historic because, although it followed Edison's larger city-type system at Pearl Street in New York by almost a year, it was the first time that an overhead three-wire distribution system had been attempted. Some of Edison's backers had been shocked by the cost of the copper wires needed in the New York installation, and by the limited area covered. The three-wire system was therefore to be built in Sunbury, to show its comparative economy in copper, and to prove that lights were practical even in a small community.

The three-wire circuitry to be used was the same one that Sprague had tested in the Crystal Palace the year before, and his familiarity with it was undoubtedly the reason why Edison had agreed with Ed Johnson's suggestion of hiring him. In the classic pattern of pioneering developments, difficulty after difficulty developed. One of the first was in determining the correct diameter of the wire to be used in the feeders and branches of the system. This was important: if the wire was not thick enough, subscribers' lamps would be too dim and yellow, whereas if it was of heavier gauge than it needed to be, the copper cost would skyrocket and spoil the point Edison was trying to demonstrate, as well as add unnecessarily to the costs.

Realizing that this was not something that could be accurately determined by cut-and-try, Edison sent several of his young men, Sprague among them, back to Menlo Park to see if they could work out a satisfactory way of predicting the proper wire size.

Edison's own preference was for a method that the Menlo Park group had used before. This was, in effect, to construct an electrical scale model of the community. First an enlarged map of the installation was traced on a big panel, and a peg was inserted at the site of each subscriber who had signed up for electric lights. On each peg was put a spool wound with a number of turns of resistance wire that corresponded to the number of lamps that the subscriber had contracted for.

Then tiny branch-line feeders were strung along the model streets, leading to heavier mains that marched to the site of the powerhouse. When the model of the community had been completed (it took several men almost seven working days to build the Sunbury model), voltmeters were used to measure the current drop existing in the system. If the figures were too high or too low, the model branch and feeder wires were changed and the model remeasured.

This laborious approach to the problem amazed Sprague. There seemed to him to be no advantage in building an analogue when mathematics would serve. So he pulled out a pencil and devised a set of formulas for the calculation of ideal wire gauges under varying circumstances of length and load. Using the formulas, the proper wire for all parts of the Sunbury installation could be calculated in an afternoon.

At first this bookish approach was regarded with suspicion. It went against the grain of the old-timers in the group, and for Edison in particular, to accept the idea that anything figured out on paper could possibly be as accurate as an expertly made scale model, especially when figured out by a fresh-faced youngster who couldn't have had much practical experience as an electrician. But before long it became evident that the formulas worked beautifully; not only did they predict what the model would later show, but they also could be worked back to show some known mistakes that had been made in earlier installations. So Sprague's methods were taken up by the Menlo Park group, and were later used generally by the growing electric-utility industry.

The curious cult of empiricism by Edison and his associates was noted by others than Sprague. Nikola Tesla, who also worked for Edison during part of 1883, thought that "the chief" sometimes took an anti-intellectual approach. "If Edison had to find a needle in a haystack," he once observed uncharitably, "he would proceed at once with the diligence of a bee to examine straw after straw until he found the object of his search. I was a sorry witness of such doings, knowing that a little theory and calculation would have saved him ninety percent of his labor." Back at Sunbury to help with the new system, Sprague found that each week brought its new crisis. One of them was of his own doing.

For several days before the new lights were to be officially turned on, the young engineers had been running private tests, and all seemed ready. The night before the opening ceremonies, Sprague was so busy that he forgot something that had been in the back of his mind for several days: he really ought to study the complicated and unconventional new lubricator on the Armington-Sims steam engine that drove the dynamos. But the electrical tests were most exciting and the lubricator was forgotten, until a terrible knocking clatter from the steam engine announced that its main bearings had burned out. Feverishly, Sprague and a master mechanic worked almost the entire night before the opening in fitting new bearings. When Edison arrived for the ceremonies and learned what had happened, he blew up. Years later, Sprague remembered wryly that "he dressed me down with remarks that would not look well in print". The next crisis came soon after, though here Sprague's trait of calmness under pressure helped out. The biggest single installation of lamps in Sunbury was in the town hotel, an institution that was highly proud of its modern electric lights. But a sharp thunderstorm one afternoon changed that. Guests complained of receiving shocks from the fixtures, and in the lobby a series of terrifying flashes and sparks had spouted from one of the electrical candelabra. With indignant disappointment, the hotel proprietor summoned Edison's young men and ordered that the perilous and untrustworthy wires and lamps were to be taken out immediately, before the building was burned down.

Sprague left the angry scene and checked over the installation in the hotel. He noted that the wires were attached in many places to the older gas fixtures, and he theorized that the sparks had probably been from static charges leaping to the ground of the gas pipes. He came back and told his colleagues of his findings. "You may not realize it," the hotel man was told, "but your building may well have been struck by lightning yesterday. Without the wiring, you might well have been the proprietor this morning of a heap of ashes! Those sparks were probably the lightning being shunted to ground." This ingenious, if possibly inexact argument, and these assured young practitioners of electrical mysteries, persuaded the proprietor to allow electricity to stay in his building.

A second small city installation of electric lights followed in the fall, this one in Brockton, Mass. It also was a three-wire system, though with the wires experimentally installed underground rather than up on poles. Here Sprague stayed on for several months as superintendent after the plant began operation (Edison was discovering that he needed men who knew something about electricity, not just steam engineers, to run his plants). The first super at Brockton, although an experienced locomotive engineer, had been a distinct disappointment. One night when a heavy short circuit had developed in the wires of the dynamo room, he had become so alarmed that he grabbed his hat and departed forever.

The stay in Brockton pleased Sprague because he had discovered a machine shop a few doors down the street where he could have experimental electric motors made to his designs. Already it was evident that Edison had, at the time, little interest in electric power; the entire motivation behind the electric systems he was so busily installing was to provide a use for his lamp bulbs. Some private systems were also being installed, ranging from one on a ship to another at one of the homes of J. Pierpont Morgan. There were also a number of private installations being made in factories, mostly at large New England textile mills, where the proprietors were putting in electric lamps on the theory that the help would be able to turn out more work than they had been able to do under gas lamps. But even in these places there was no evidence of interest in electricity for other purposes than illumination. The attitude exasperated Sprague. He believed that electricity was a convenient and flexible source of power, better adapted for many jobs than the standard big steam engine arranged to drive individual machines through a network of overhead shafts and belts. Sprague's initial idea was to power looms by electricity, a motor for each loom. Many other applications occurred to him: hoists, pumps, blowers, and individual machine tools. And still very much in his mind, though clearly one step farther off, was his London idea of applying electricity to urban rail transportation.

The problem was to design a good motor. The small dynamos of the day were motors of a sort, to be sure, but hardly able to do the jobs Sprague envisioned. They were inefficient and costly. Worse, they ran at widely varying speeds, fast when under little or no load, very slowly when work was demanded of them. And finally, they needed to be tended by an experienced electrician who would adjust the position of their brushes for minimum sparking under each condition of load and speed. They were, in short, so unsatisfactory as to mask the potentialities of motors that didn't have such inconvenient traits.

Through the winter and early spring of 1884 Sprague spent all his spare time on designing an improved motor. His notes of the time are instructive, for they afford a picture of an original mind considering and discarding possible solutions. Although the constant speed might be achieved by a mechanical governor, following steam-engine practice, he dropped this approach very quickly: it would be costly, cumbersome, and, worse, inelegant. Then it came to him, an idea quite contrary to the general conceptions of 1884, that a motor could be electrically governed by a reverse winding, arranged to vary the field strength inversely with the speed/load variable. This was the ideal solution, automatic, inexpensive, and elegant, even if it seemed heretical by the conventions of the period.

The second problem, how to set the brushes backward under heavy load and forward under light, also responded to Sprague's strangely fastidious and almost esthetic approach to circuit design. It might be possible to rotate the brushes mechanically, but when he built such a motor he rejected it almost at once, also as cumbersome, costly, and graceless. Again, unconventionality brought the solution. Since one had to move the brushes, and at the same time didn't want to move them physically, it followed that the proper thing was to rotate the electromagnetic field in the opposite direction. He devised a series field winding that "would automatically create a corrective resultant" and, presto, there appeared the first of the capable, efficient electric motors that would revolutionize the world.

Not that everything went smoothly. One of Sprague's colleagues in Brockton, Charles Clark, remembers one dismal day when Sprague hurried back from the machine shop with the parts for yet another experimental motor. Working with suppressed excitement, he spent hours in winding on wire according to his latest ideas. With the windings liberally daubed with insulating varnish, Sprague sat back to wait for the varnish to dry before he could test the motor. When, impatiently, he "put it on the line," the motor immediately gave off such dense clouds of acrid smoke that the room became almost uninhabitable, and it was necessary to throw the motor right through the glass of the nearest window. The varnish had not dried out, the motor was a complete short circuit, and the blueness of the air was not solely caused, Clark recalled, by the smoking and ruined motor.

Then, in early April 1884, a difficult crisis arose: Edison asked Sprague to begin work on transmitting power through the lighting systems. This meant, in effect, that he would work on motors in his Edison-employed hours, and it posed a set of ethical problems. After considerable thought, he sent off this long letter to his employer:

April 24, 1884

My dear Mr. Edison:

Since you have asked me to take up certain problems relative to the transmission of power, my reluctance to do which you may have noticed, it becomes necessary for me to enter into some explanation and to define my future position.

Before entering your service, in which I hope I have satisfactorily performed whatever duties you have assigned me, I had become interested in this subject, and while I had not had as much opportunity for experimental work as I should desire, I have lost none of my interest in it and have advanced far enough to keep it entirely apart from whatever duties are owning you and to make it my special study, that is, to retain intact my individual title to its development.

I desire to go into a course of work to settle practically the theories I hold, and to compare whatever results I may get with the best work of Desprez, Aurton, Perry, and Hopkinson. Such work must be largely mathematical, and a system of distribution for power requires the best work of this character. I feel that I can, and to a great extent in my own mind have solved the question of this transmission. To take up the subject in response to your request would be simply to make over my own work without due consideration, and due regard for my future makes it impossible for me to do this.

You, surely, will understand me when I say that I desire to identify myself with the successful solution of this problem and when I also say that I am actuated by the same spirit with which you attacked the electric light, with the result of making yourself world-famous. You believed that you could solve that problem and you did it. But with all the responsibilities that solution brought you, and with the question of thermoelectricity still remaining, you have stated that you have not the time necessary to give to the transmission of power. Surely it is enough for anyone, and I will have to devote the best of whatever knowledge I possess to make it a success. As your subordinate I cannot work with the same freedom as if I take the future into my own hands. Personal reasons, and my relations with others, make it necessary that I should look well to the future, and with the confidence I feel and the example of your own perseverance, I am willing to take upon myself whatever responsibility attached to my action.

I am aware that the future of the Edison system of lighting must be allied with the transmission of power, and I hope it may be my good fortune to be instrumental in such alliance.

In taking this position, I of course know that you may feel that the salary you are paying me does not warrant you retaining my services as an electrical expert, but I am ready to relieve you of this burden by tendering you my resignation, if you so desire, to take effect on the 1st proximo.

Lest you think me influenced by other electric light interests, I will say that I have had absolutely no negotiations with any other company, that I have the same unbounded confidence in the soundness of the principles and successful development of the Edison system that I have so long had, and that I look forward to that development with the same hopes and interest I now feel.

Should it be desirable that I continue with your work, I can only consent to do so in a purely consulting capacity, with a perfect freedom to the time and title of my own inventions. In regard to the dynamo now being added to the Pearl St. Station, the rewinding of the 50-light machines, and the reducing of the speed of the S, Y, and H machines, I will do what I can and do it willingly.

In closing, let me express my sincerest personal esteem for yourself, and my personal regret that the highest duty to myself and those related to me make it necessary that I should take this step.

Very truly yours,
Frank J. Sprague

It is now only possible to guess at the pen chewing and redrafting that this letter cost; at the extraordinary tug-of-war within it between pride and resolution on one side and tact and perhaps a measure of wishful dreaming on the other. During its composition, it now seems likely, Sprague may have forgotten, for a moment, the man he was addressing. If so, the answer the next day reminded him.

> Sprague: As the construction department is about to be given up, I think the better plan would be for you to resign.
>
> Edison

V: THE FIRST SPRAGUE COMPANY

The night the Franklin Institute Exposition closed, a dozen or twenty of us were drinking beer at a saloon and we got into an argument in which Sprague was on one side and all the rest of us were on the other. We all decided that while Sprague had a very good motor, the theory on which he built it was scientifically wrong. Later events proved that all the rest of us were scientifically wrong.

—*Admiral Bradley Fiske, USN*

The break with Edison did not mean a break with any of the friends that Sprague had made during his eleven months with the Menlo Park Group. Of these the most important for the next few years was to be Ed Johnson, the kind of person who, a generation later, would be described as a "live wire", and who was enterprising, energetic, and a mixture of administrator and promoter. Ambitious and keenly aware of the possibilities for making a fortune that were latent in the new world of Electricity, Johnson had risen in the Eighties to be Edison's principal business manager. But by 1884 he had also become restively aware that Edison's announced policy of "taking care" of his associates did not show prospects of helping him build a personal fortune. Some instinct, a very sound one as it turned out, told Johnson that this quiet young Yankee he'd met in London might be worth linking up with when he struck out on his own.

Sprague's own account of the informal partnership was characteristically precise; writing in The Century Magazine twenty years later he put it this way:

> "On resigning from Mr. Edison's employ in 1884, I formed the Sprague Electric Railway and Motor Company, of $100,000 nominal but no cash capital, with which I made a contract by which virtually all its capital stock was assigned to me, on my agreement to assign patents and inventions, conduct experimental work, and pay myself $2500 a year salary. Two friends took, I think, about sixteen shares of stock, the proceeds of which quickly went for personal needs; and being without means, I made an agreement with Mr. E. H. Johnson, then president of one of the Edison lighting

companies, by which he was to meet my financial obligations for a portion of the profits. I was vice-president, electrician, treasurer, and general factotum. One small room sufficed for our needs, and much of the mechanical and electrical work I did myself."

Ed Johnson's business-wise experience was reflected in the way that the little company was able to function on almost no capital. He pointed out to Sprague persuasively that not much cash would be needed to begin the manufacture of electric motors. It should be possible to sell them, assuming that they were as good as Sprague said they would be, through commission agents in various parts of the country. Which meant that the company would have no selling cost and little or no cash tied up in inventory. Nor would money have to be spent for machinery; manufacturing could be farmed out to the Edison Machine Works, which had both the capacity and skill, and which would make the motors on a reasonable cost-plus basis. As for the limited amount of cash that would be needed, Ed Johnson went on, he'd advance that himself in small amounts, as necessary.

The total amount that Johnson paid in seems to have been less than $20,000, spread over the next two or three years. It turned out to be quite the most lucrative investment that shrewd Ed Johnson ever made, paying off liberally in profits and also giving him an interest in the firm that he was able to sell, five years later, for $400,000. Characteristically, Johnson blew most of this sum on a baronial chateau in Connecticut that had belonged to Andrew Carnegie.

By the late summer of 1884 Sprague was satisfied with the performance of his constant speed motors, and he sent off several to Menlo Park. (Whether this was a gesture of pride or simply a request for independent checking is impossible to determine now.) To his astonishment, in view of the laconic request for his resignation a few months earlier, Edison responded with an indirect but handsome endorsement. On September 21, replying to an interviewer's inquiry about the "transmission of electrical force", Edison said:

> "That problem has been pretty well worked out. A young man named Sprague, who resigned his position as an officer of our Navy to devote himself to electrical studies, has worked the matter up in a very remarkable way. His is the only true motor; the others are but dynamos turned into motors. His machine keeps the same rate of speed all the time, and does not vary with the amount of work done, as the others do."

Later in the fall of 1884 the Franklin Institute in Philadelphia opened a large exposition at 33rd Street and Market, the first solely electrical exhibition ever held in America. It drew wide attention from the press as well as from the business and financial world, now sensitive to the commercial possibilities of electricity. Large crowds turned out in the evenings, attracted by the awesome beam of light in the dark sky that came from the Navy's brilliant new 36-inch searchlight. There were brisk complaints from the Pennsylvania Railroad at the Navy's habit of demonstrating its searchlight by using it to track passing trains, a practice that, the Pennsy complained testily, was blinding its locomotive engineers.

The Exposition was a perfect way to launch the new little company, and Sprague and Johnson made the most of it. Newspaper reporters covering the show wrote that Edison's was the largest exhibit, and the Navy's drew the most public attention. However, the electrical cognoscenti appeared most impressed by the "constant speed motors" unveiled by a quiet young fellow named Sprague. The impression was confirmed when a bearded dignitary, named Professor Sylvanus Thompson, solemnly informed the reporters that, "By far the most important of all exhibits of their class is that of Mr. F. J. Sprague, which shows a very great advance on anything hitherto accomplished". And then Edison confirmed the triumph (and again startled Sprague) by repeating and expanding to the press his earlier approval.

With the help of these testimonials and publicity, the little company soon began to prosper. Some 250 motors were sold in the first year of business, most of them going to drive pumps, blowers, and individual machines like lathes and looms. A few were put to work running factory hoists. In the last months of 1884 in the Pemberton Mills at Lawrence, Mass., the first electric elevator in America was installed under Sprague's supervision.

Because of the way Johnson had set up the little company, with both manufacturing and selling farmed out to others, the business did not take all of Sprague's time and energies. It left him with enough leisure to pursue two goals that were much in his mind. One was to build an electric railroad. The other was to marry a Southern belle named Mary Harned Keatinge.

Sprague met Mary Keatinge in New Orleans early in 1885 when he had been on a vacation there. She was then 22, six years his junior, and gay and vivacious. Her family was unusual. Her father was an artist and engraver, her mother one of the first women physicians in the south and her sister also a practicing doctor. But Mary shared none of these interests; she seemed to Sprague to be gay, sociable, and utterly captivating with her strong Southern accent. The two were married in the spring of 1885 and, after a brief honeymoon, returned to New York to live.

V: THE FIRST SPRAGUE COMPANY

Mary Keatinge (image courtesy of John L. Sprague)

THE BIRTH OF ELECTRIC TRACTION

* * *

Sprague was far from the first man to dream of electric powered transportation. (Although, as we will see shortly, he seems to have been the first to bring sound engineering concepts, as well as an inventive and original mind, to bear on the problem.) By the mid-Eighties, electric rail cars had been tried out all over the world. In Berlin Werner Siemens had built a fairgrounds line a few hundred yards long in 1879, and followed it with a public street car in 1881. (Its two rails were electrified, stimulating skittish horses into gloriously showy runaways.) Edison and Field, first separately and then together, had been working on electric locomotives in desultory fashion from 1880 on. In 1883 a tireless man named Leo Daft turned up in New York with a locomotive that he called the "Ampere." (Daft, who was gifted as well as indefatigable, though without much technical grounding, named his later creations the "Volta," "Faraday," and "Ohm". He managed to keep an electrified branch of a Baltimore horse car line running for a few months, electrocuting one horse and a large number of chickens and dogs before the line went out of business.)

Also in 1883 Charles J. Van Depoele (who for a time would be a sharp rival of Sprague) first began work on his electric cars, installing the dynamo that he used for a motor on the front platform "where it is at all times under the watchful eye of the driver". In Cleveland two ex patent examiners, named Bentley and Knight, gave birth to a street car that used coiled springs as drive belts. Years later Bentley remembered wryly that "These springs would break with a loud report about once an hour, and, until passengers got used to it, there was a serious commotion each time it occurred."

In Kansas City there was John C. Henry, a farmer who had lost everything in a grasshopper plague and who determinedly attempted to recoup by inventing electric street cars. Henry had no idea of how to control the speed of his motors and so he had ingenious if despairing recourse to a clutch and four speed transmission. And there was Professor Sidney Short's eerie "series system", an arrangement in which the cars were to be wired together like the lights on a Christmas tree, and which then used great ingenuity in circumventing this circuits drawbacks, which included the fact that only rarely did all the cars on a line wish to start and stop in unison. Electrical and mechanical naiveties like these were from the beginning conspicuously absent from Sprague's creations. It has been said of him that he was a man for whom machinery wanted to work. He succeeded not solely because he brought brilliant insights to circuit design, nor even that, unlike his competitors, he was rigorously trained in, and facile with, mathematical tools. An important factor in Sprague's success, it is now apparent, was that he had an instinct for elegant simplicity in design and for arrangements of mechanism that could be persuaded to work without endless finagling.

There is a matter of taste in engineering. From Sprague's point of view, something like Short's series circuit was plainly defective because it was based on needless complication. And of course Henry's innocent gearshift speed control was hardly worth considering for a moment; years before, back at the Torpedo Station in Newport, under Moses Farmer's indulgent eye, Sprague had built a little machine that, through series-parallel switching of its circuits, was easily controllable in torque and speed. Moreover, the lethally high voltages that had been toyed with, and the exposed current-carrying rails that Siemens, Edison, Field, and Daft used, were both unthinkable to Sprague because they would obviously be unacceptable to the public, at least on street railways. (This was a viewpoint that Daft swung around to after the horse was electrocuted; it was one of his anxieties on the Baltimore line that some drunken citizen might tumble across the bare rails and expire.) As for the belt drives tried by Edison, Van Depoele, and Bentley-Knight, these were mechanically ridiculous. "We'll have no belts", Sprague told Ed Johnson in his high and rather commanding voice. "Belts may be all right on lathes, but they have no place on a railroad! We'll use a gear drive."

By early 1885 the first machinery began to take shape. Sprague mounted two 12 1/2 horsepower motors on a conventional four-wheeled railway truck that he had borrowed from the Manhattan Elevated Railroad. As he had promised, the motors were geared to the wheels; no belts, chains, or friction drives were in sight. Inventors before Sprague, needless to say, had been well aware of the simplicity, reliability, and advantages of gears, but they had been stopped by an apparently insoluble problem: if a comparatively delicate motor were mounted where it could be directly geared to the unsprung wheels, it would soon be shaken to pieces as it pounded along. Whereas if it were supported on the spring-cushioned truck itself, and then geared to the unsprung wheels, jolts and jounces would smash the gears destructively in and out of mesh.

Sprague solved this problem with brilliant ingenuity. He called it his "wheelbarrow" mounting: one side of the motor was carried on the wheel axle and could pivot freely about it, and the other was spring-suspended from the truck frame. This meant that the motor was comparatively protected from the pounding of rough track, but it could move only in the precise arc that preserved the correct gear mesh. This idea, which in 1885 was of an engineering sophistication that made earlier drives seem like cave drawings, was to be universally adopted on electric railroads. It is still in use all over the world.

THE BIRTH OF ELECTRIC TRACTION

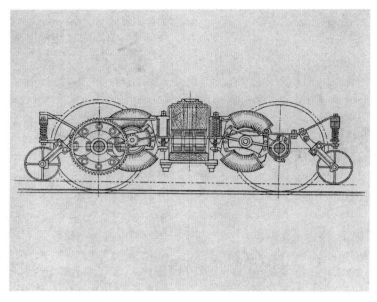

Sprague Railway Motor Truck Schematic
(courtesy of John L. Sprague)

It was not trolley cars but elevated lines that Sprague aimed for at first. The "els" were then drawn by small steam locomotives, and they seemed to him a highly promising place to begin. The lines were already in existence and generally profitable. The inaccessibility of the track to pedestrians and animals meant that a bare third rail could be used to complete the circuit. And electrification of an el would be a fine way to dramatize the possibilities of electric transportation, for the existing steam engines were widely objected to because of their noise and dirt. They were generally unloved for their habits of depositing a regular sootfall along their routes, varied by frequent showers of hot cinders drifting down from above.

To try out his first motorized rail truck, Sprague persuaded Johnson to lease a short experimental track that Edison and Field had been using some time before. This was a private stretch of rails at the Durant Sugar Refinery on East 24th Street in New York City, a stretch about 200 feet long laid in a canyon-like alley between two towering warehouses. The shortness was a severe drawback, but it wasn't costly to lease, and was fitted with both steam power and several battered dynamos left behind after the earlier experiments. Here, until late in 1886, Sprague worked unceasingly to perfect his ideas.

The first labors at the Durant track had to go to patching up the track and the current supply, and the second effort went to assemble something to run on it. This proved to be a railway flatcar with a dummy truck under one end and the motor truck under the other. Iron bars were stacked on the flat car to simulate the load of a regular elevated car body and passengers. Up and down the 200 feet of track in the alley the flatcar rolled while Sprague checked out variations in motor design, circuitry, and controllers. Current was picked up by two flanged bronze wheels that were pressed by springs against a central third rail. Mechanical brakes could be cranked on to keep the loaded car from crashing into the barriers at each end of the track. But both Sprague and his chief assistant of the period, a derby-hatted master mechanic named John Crawford, fell into the joyously dramatic habit of slamming the flat car's controller into reverse, and sliding to a stop in a shower of sparks. Burned-out motor were a nuisance until they were wired with what was then called a "safety catch", a short length of soft leaden wire that served as a fuse into the main circuit beside the controller.

After months of long effort, when the flat car was able to run up and down the alley track with quiet precision, Ed Johnson was allowed to bring moneyed and influential visitors around to see the new marvel. He brought several groups of executives of the Manhattan Elevated Railroad around for demonstration rides, and both Johnson and Sprague felt that they had gone away impressed. Finally, Johnson managed to produce the most important visitor of all, Jay Gould, a financier and multimillionaire who controlled a number of American railroads, including Manhattan Elevated. A short, dapper, bearded man of considerable presence, Gould silently watched the flatcar perform. Then Sprague and Johnson persuaded him to climb aboard and take up a position beside the controller, to see how easily the exciting new electric motors could be managed. What happened next was pure disaster. "Keenly alive to the importance of our visitor", Sprague said years later when the incident still rankled, "I suddenly reversed the motors and the instant excess rush of current blew the safety catch into a small volcano." This would have been bad enough, though still an essentially trivial mishap. What made it horrifying was that

V: THE FIRST SPRAGUE COMPANY

the silent, hard-eyed, and enormously important Mr. Gould suddenly panicked, and had to be grabbed to keep him from jumping off the still-moving car. It was a moment of collective embarrassment. Gould departed immediately, paying no attention to Sprague's hasty explanations that the wire that had exploded so alarmingly was really a safety device, the electrical equivalent of a safety valve. Even worse, especially from Johnson's viewpoint, he never returned. It later became evident that it was the memory of this momentary panic in the presence of others that stayed most distressingly alive in Jay Gould's mind. In any event, the directors of the Manhattan Elevated, who up to this point had been noticeably acquiescent to the idea of electrification, became immediately cooler.

The public attention from these Durant Sugar Refinery trials did earn a few nibbles of interest elsewhere. A Mr. Chinnock, superintendent of Edison's Pearl Street Central Station (which was still the biggest powerhouse in the world), seemed particularly interested in what was going on. Sprague divined that Chinnock, like so many Edison men of the time, was becoming restless at his own prospects for making a fortune for himself in those great growing days of electricity. Chinnock hinted that he represented a syndicate of Edison employees. Would Sprague be interested in selling one-sixth interest in his company for the sum of, say, $30,000?

It was a tempting offer. Writing twenty years later, in Century Magazine, Sprague remembered it this way:

"...his arguments were sound, being to the effect that if success came the remaining five-sixths interest would probably bring me riches; but if failure should be the outcome, $30,000 was not to be despised. Although I probably did not have money enough to pay my board for a month, I declined the offer, much to his surprise, expressed by the retort: 'Well, you're a .... fool!' Measured by every common sense view, I was. But the story has a sequel.

"At the end of April 1886, while away getting a much-needed rest, I received a telegram from Johnson, who was, if anything, strenuous, stating that he had promised Cyrus W. Field that four days later he would show a car in operation on the Elevated Railroad. It seemed an impossibility, but I hastened back and we got together car body, truck, and motors, and finished a controller, in spite of a strike, making our connections by candlelight.

"At one o'clock on the appointed day, an impressive crowd of railroad and banking interests had gathered. As we did not get current for testing until after their arrival, initial failure seemed assured, and I was fighting mad at the predicament in which I found myself. But I had to make an attempt; and finally, after trying first one machine and then the other with no response, in sheer desperation I threw both motors into circuit, moved the regulator, and the car responded perfectly. For two hours every feat which could be tried with the machines was performed without a hitch. With something of relief I finally saw the car deserted, and exhausted by the exciting experiences through which I had passed, I sat pondering over the run, when Chinnock came to me again, apparently much impressed with what he had seen, and this time offered $25,000 for a one twelfth interest. I cared little at the time, but he was persistent and finally got it; a few weeks later another twelfth went to someone else for $26,250...."

Now, finally, things began to move. Sales of the standard electric motors were climbing steeply, and Sprague and Johnson decided that the time had come to have a factory of their own. They leased a New York building, setting it aside for special developmental work, for standard motors were still to be made by the Edison Works. Though the officers of the elevated lines were still chilly, feelers began to come in from street railway lines in many parts of the country. On Johnson's advice, the authorized capital stock of the Sprague Electric Railway & Motor Company was increased ten-fold to $1,000,000.

It seemed to Sprague, that winter of 1886-7, that the stage was all set for something to happen. The perception was accurate, for the next few months were to be exhausting and rewarding beyond anything he could rationally have dreamed of.

VI: ON TO RICHMOND

> *"And it would have been a good step hence, even had not Richmond, a city whose Hellenic character was not confined to its architecture, but would have been recognized in its gradients by a Greek mountain goat, had been grouped about streets so steep it was painful to think of Poe toiling up them."*
>
> ——*Malcolm Lowry*

The capital of Virginia seemed, in 1887, an unlikely place for a pioneering technical development. As the seat of the Confederate government, Richmond had been fought for fiercely in no fewer than fifteen pitched battles and twenty-five lesser engagements; the Reconstruction years that followed had been scarcely less bitter. Restored as the state capital, Richmond was soon the scene of ominous racial stirrings, "black and tan" conventions, and exceedingly acrimonious political struggles. Hordes of carpetbaggers trooped into town. One governor, tossed out of office in 1886, had achieved the dubious distinction of conducting the most corrupt and gerrymandering administration in the state's long history. Still, the war had been over for more than two decades, and time was healing its scars. Richmond was resuming its position as one of the proudest cities of the South. Its capital building was architecturally renowned, based as it was on Jefferson's celebrated copy of the Roman temple at Nimes. Its twelve acres of grounds occupied the center and highest point of the hilly city; and inside the building, in a setting appropriate for a temple, was the famous Houdon statue of Washington, the foremost member of the Virginia Pantheon.

In the pleasant spring days of 1887 word got around that the very newest and most advanced form of transportation was soon to be introduced in Richmond: an electric street railway. Nor was this to be just another of the shaky little experimental lines that had been tried out in other parts of the country. This was to be a line that would course the mainstream of the city down from the best residential area to the center, where it would double-track to ring the Capitol itself, and then around and down steep slopes. It was, rumor had it, later certified by the Richmond Dispatch, to be by far the longest and most remarkable electric railroad in the entire world.

What lay behind these stories was a fascinating example of what would, years later, come to be called venture capitalism. A few months earlier a scouting foray had been made upon the city by a group of New York investors. Their syndicate, headed by an enterprising financier and promoter named Maurice B. Flynn, had been searching for a favorable factory site. But Flynn soon spotted what seemed to be a more profitable idea: Richmond had only one street railway, a rather sleepy horse- and mule-car line. Elsewhere in the country, the syndicate was well aware, cities of comparable size could support six or more horse-car lines, often in a way that made them valuable properties.

Working fast, Flynn formed the Union Passenger Railway of Richmond (UPR), obtained a franchise for an ambitious twelve-mile line, and called in some experienced street-railway men to build and operate it. Only then did the Yankee investors discover that Richmond's one-line condition wasn't solely a product of Southern lassitude. Sound technical reasons, such as the steepness and number of grades, the unpaved, mucky clay streets, and the large number of sharp turns meant that the route prescribed in the new franchise would be a "horse killer." Teams would have to be doubled on many sections, operating costs would be painful, and dreams of high profits vanished.

But Flynn was not easily discouraged. He remembered the New York newspaper stories about Sprague's experimental demonstrations on the elevated. He promptly summoned this slim and restless twenty-nine year-old. Had he ever considered electrifying a street car instead of an elevated train? Certainly, the

Sprague Company was at this very moment working on plans to modify two horse cars for a trial line in St. Joseph, Missouri. They would run on a stretch of track fully a mile long.

The response might have irritated Flynn, but it seems to have amused him. (A friend described Sprague at this period as "impatient, ceaselessly energetic; his voice is high-pitched, and carries a touch of dominance.") The financier drily explained that he was not contemplating anything of the scale of two horse cars in St. Joe. Nor even anything as tentative as the little experimental lines running elsewhere in the nation. Mr. Sprague should understand that what was being discussed here was a complete, freshly built, city-wide transportation system. It would have many curves, and some grades as steep as eight percent. It would not be profitable with animals. It would require as many as forty electric cars. Reliable and economical transportation would be expected from the beginning. Did Mr. Sprague, whose recent demonstrations on the Elevated had earned such technical praise, believe that such a system would be feasible? It certainly was. Would Mr. Sprague's firm like to consider taking the contract for electrical equipment? It most emphatically would!

Early in May, 1887, the Sprague Electric Railway and Motor Company signed a formal contract with the Union Passenger Railway Company of Richmond. Both parties signed in a flurry of congratulation and high purpose. Within months, in the travail of creating the world's first large trolley car system, each group was threatened with bankruptcy and fervently wishing the contract had never been thought of.

On the face of it, Sprague conceded later, the contract was hardly a prudent one for an undercapitalized and inexperienced firm. It required Sprague to bear all risk of failure, and it bound him to early and successful completion of his work. It specified that he was to electrify forty cars with two motors apiece, and fit out each car with all necessary control and lighting equipment. He was also to design and build a complete overhead wire current supply for twelve miles of track, and the complete electrical equipment in a 375-horsepower generating plant. At least thirty of the forty cars should be capable of running at the same time and of negotiating 8-percent grades. The work would have to be completed within ninety days. Then, after the line had been in successful operation for sixty days, Sprague would be paid $110,000.

When the contract was signed, Sprague had nothing on hand for the job beyond a few preliminary blueprints. No equipment left over from the el trials or planned for St. Joe would be useful on a task of this magnitude. He was uneasily aware that he had undertaken to build more electric cars than there then were in the entire world and that his, unlike the others, would really have to work. Although the ninety-day deadline would not begin ticking until the contractor, who was to lay the track, was far enough along to permit electrical work to begin, Sprague plunged at once into organizing his campaign.

The first step was to turn over all responsibility for the little St. Joe job to the foreman there, Dave Mason. The second was to staff the Richmond operation, since it would obviously be too big for one engineer alone, even though aided by mechanics and construction men. Sprague hired two young assistant engineers, both of them, by no coincidence, freshly graduated from government academies. Ensign S. Dana Greene, late of Annapolis (and son of the executive officer aboard the *Monitor* in 1862), would act as his deputy in Richmond. Lieut. Oscar T. Crosby, not long from West Point, would hold the fort at the New York office and at the Edison Machine Works, where most of the equipment would be built and tested. Neither young man had had much practical experience in electrical work; but they were both bright young engineers with the brisk, heads-up manner that their employer, himself only a few years older, greatly admired. In retrospect Sprague felt that he had been very lucky to find Crosby and Greene. "When difficulties multiplied," he noted, "they both showed pluck, enthusiasm, and endurance."

During May and most of June Sprague worked feverishly at the thousand and one decisions that had to be made. Hundreds of blueprints were drawn and redrawn for motors, gearing, controllers, and car circuits. Test and delivery schedules for the electrical equipment were worked out as though for a major

VI: ON TO RICHMOND

military operation. One particularly worrisome job was calculating and designing the trolley wire and feeder system; nothing like a twelve-mile electrification had ever been tried before, and an error that either under- or over-designed the wiring would be disastrous, either operationally or financially. It was also necessary to work with Ed Johnson to find ways of paying for this costly venture, with no money coming in until long after the work was complete.

It was a time of furious concentration. And because Sprague worked sixteen-hour days seven days a week, it was a time when the clouds that were to darken his marriage first began to appear. Mary was not, in her own terms, a jealous or demanding wife. The difficulty was simpler and yet more insoluble. Electricity rather bored her, and street railways didn't really seem very interesting either. And she deeply missed the gaiety, dances, and parties of life before her marriage.

As for Sprague himself, perhaps the most vivid description of him at the time was penned by the same friend who had said that "his voice was high-pitched, and carries a touch of dominance." The sketch went on:

> "He seems to be full of wire springs that constantly coil and uncoil inside of him. His eyes are bright and full of motion. His face is alive with insistency and driving force. It is the face of a fighter who is unable to recognize defeat. His sentences end with a click, like the snapping of a switch. He roams, light footed,

about the room and appears to be literally magnetized."

Even setting aside the springs and clicks perceived by this autistic observer, there is little question that, in those early summer weeks of 1887, Sprague was working at or beyond the limits of his powers. "Beyond" is perhaps the better word, because one night Mary found that his feverishness was far from figurative. Disregarding his protests, she summoned the doctor. "Typhoid fever," the physician pronounced. "A well-developed case. At best he'll need absolute rest in bed for a month or six weeks. Then, with luck, we can look forward to a cautious convalescence for, say, another six weeks."

Sprague passed his thirtieth birthday flat on his back, sicker than he had ever been in his life. Always one who preferred understatement, he nevertheless referred to this as a "critical illness." Mary and the doctor kept him in bed until late summer. Then a train trip out West was prescribed, nominally to help him regain his strength and actually to prevent him from plunging back into work at once. Mary, who had discovered that she was pregnant, did not go along.

Sprague came back through Missouri, stopping at St. Joseph just long enough to confer with Mason and to watch while his foreman put on a demonstration with one of the little converted horse cars. It showered sparks and did not seem to behave very well. But there was no time to check it. It was now September and

Sprague had been absent from the chance of his lifetime for nine crucially important weeks.

In Richmond Greene anxiously took Sprague around on an inspection tour. The contractor for the track had completed his work and departed. Sprague wrote later:

> "I got my first disappointed sight of the road in the fall. I shall never forget my feelings when, after inspecting the improvised car sheds at one end of the line, I reached the foot of the steepest hill on my return, and faced a grade varying from 4 to 10 percent and about a mile long. The condition of the track was simply execrable; it was built for profit, not permanence. The flat 27 pound tram rail of antiquated shape was poorly jointed, unevenly laid, and insecurely tied; the foundation was red clay. The main curves were sharp, some with a 27 foot radius; they had only one guard rail and spread easily. The car-house was an open lot on which were two roughly covered sheds."

Richmond Grade (courtesy of John L. Sprague)

But the track was finished; the grades and curves were conditions and not theories; and the calendar was ticking away. With Sprague in charge the work of electrification began to gather speed. Thirty-foot poles were set along every 125 feet of track. Then wire was strung and it was soon apparent that, on curves and turns, burying the poles five feet in the red clay was not enough. The tension of the wire overhead, tugging against the clay gumbo, soon tilted any of the poles to rakish angles. A number of them had to be removed and reset in a special stone and concrete foundation.

Work was also rushed on the new brick powerhouse, so handsome and modern that it became a favorite subject of local feature reporters. Wrote a man from the *Richmond Dispatch*:

VI: ON TO RICHMOND

> "It is in the heart of the city, 300 yards from the depots of the three railroads (coal can be obtained almost at its door). Inside it is so neat in appearance and finish one can scarcely realize he is in an engine room. Each engine drives two dynamos of 40,000 watts each, specially wound for 500 volts normal pressure. Water is supplied by steam pumps drawing from a city main or from a well in the yard."

As the first few cars neared readiness in the car shops and the first sections of "overhead" were wired, a trickle of visiting electrical and street- railway engineers arrived in town to look this ambitious venture over. (The trickle was to become a steady stream in future months.) To their knowing eyes it was evident that this self-assured young man was departing radically from all prior electric car practices. Unlike Van Depoele, he'd banished electric motors from the platforms, in order to gain space, eliminated belts and chains, and made his cars double-ended, so that they would not have to be turned around at each end of the track. Unlike Daft, Field, and Edison, he'd done away with the voltage across the two rails and his power was supplied by a single overhead wire, with the rails and the ground acting only as a return. This was fine in that it protected horses, dogs, and drunks from shocks and possible electrocution, assuming that it could be made to work. Unlike Professor Short and many arc-light experts, he was using a basic "multiple arc"/parallel circuit, one that hoisted many electrical eyebrows, and that the Professor, among others, prophesied was doomed to failure. Finally, he was proposing to run on a hilly, curvy, muddy, and unprecedentedly long track even though more experienced men in the field had learned by the hardest kind of experience that electric cars worked best (indeed, only) on short, straight, ideal lengths of track.

Most of this Sprague could serenely ignore. His design was based, after all, on his own best engineering judgment, and in this he had faith. As for the conditions of operation, it was obvious that electric traction would have an economic value only when it could cope with everyday conditions. Sprague knew instinctively what a trolley-car annalist defined almost seventy years later: "It is one thing to devise a mechanism which will behave itself in a sheltered world where its inventor can shower it with loving attentions, and quite another to build something that can survive in the everyday world of mud, rain, bankers, and abuse."

But two private anxieties did eat at Sprague. Were his circulations for the distribution system accurate? There was no way to be sure until thirty or more cars were drawing from the line at the same time, and that wouldn't occur, at the best, for weeks yet. The second anxiety was more immediate. Would the cars, when loaded, actually be able to climb those ten percent grades?

One night in November he shared his worries with Greene and Ed Johnson, who'd come down from New

VI: ON TO RICHMOND

York to see how matters were progressing. One of the first cars to be completed had just been tried out on the lesser slopes along the bottom of the mile-long hill. Despite its two seven-and-a-half horsepower motors and its single-stage gearing, it had not done very well. In fact, Greene told the gathering, he had found it necessary to station four or five husky men on the back platform, with instructions to "play the mule", to jump off and push hard whenever the car threatened to stall. Even so, the motors had become very hot and had eventually broken down from "crosses" in their armatures. Of course the voltage wasn't up to 450 yet. Things might be better if everything was working properly.

For once, Sprague wasn't strongly optimistic. He was convinced that the motors would have been able to handle the eight percent grades they had been designed for. But those ten percent stretches were going to be murderous, considering that the motors were going to be very hot to begin with. It might be necessary to refit them to put in an extra stage of gearing. Greene frowned. But how could this be done? There simply wasn't room for more gears. Where could they possibly put a jackshaft?

Sprague went on to unfold his deeper worry. What if the limitation, on the steepest grades, was not motor power at all, but wheel-to-rail adhesion? Suppose the wheels simply spun on wet, muddy rails along those steepest grades? As he unfolded this dismal possibility, Sprague and Greene stared at each other, and Ed Johnson turned his head between them.

Of course, Sprague went on, they might be able to invent something. Sand on the rails, or cogs and a rack, or some funicular arrangement, though that would obviously make problems. The best idea might be to borrow a leaf from those cable car people. So he took pencil and paper and began to sketch out his idea. They might dig a long vault under the tracks on the steep part of the hill. They'd put a powerful electric motor here, and rig it to draw an endless electric cable up the hill beneath the surface. Cars would hook onto the cable at the bottom. Greene, fascinated, watched the idea unfold.

But Ed Johnson was anything but fascinated. He was, instead, horrified at the facile way in which these bright young engineers could invent ingenious new ways in which to spend money. He stood up and made his first contribution to the conference: "Guess the first thing is to find out if a car can get up the grade by itself." So at nine that November night in 1887, the conference adjourned to a working trolley car to try it out on the worst hill. Sprague described it this way:

> "If we succeeded in climbing the hill I knew what would probably happen to the motors; but it was vital to learn if a self-propelled car could be made to go up that grade at all. We went steadily up that and another hill, around several curves, and finally reached the highest

point of the line in the heart of the city. I knew that the motors must be pretty hot.

"An enthusiastic crowd soon gathered (a theater nearby had just let out) and in the delay I was in hopes that the motors would cool down sufficiently to permit us to continue the journey. No sooner, however, had we started than I felt a peculiar bucking movement, and knew that we were disabled. The trouble was due to a crossed short circuited armature, then a little known difficulty. Unwilling to admit serious trouble, I told Greene, in a tone that could be overheard, that there was some slight trouble in the circuits and would he go for the instruments so that we could locate it. Then, turning out the lights, I lay down on a seat to wait, while the crowd gradually dispersed. After waiting a long time for Greene's return with those 'instruments,' and inwardly praying that he would be late, he came in sight with four of them, big powerful mules, the most effective aids which could be found in Richmond under the circumstances."

The discovery that the hills could be surmounted by wheels alone was cheering. But adding an extra stage of gearing to the motors to keep them from burning out cheered neither Greene, who did not see how it could be done, nor Johnson, who knew morosely that— whatever happened— it would cost time and money. Sprague went back to New York to work on the problem, and soon he had it: a highly ingenious double reduction gear in which the extra shaft, to save space and preserve the wheelbarrow mounting, passed right through the motor, though not in a vital spot. (One fascinating aspect of Sprague's gifts was that, quite separate from his electrical genius, he could also toss off under pressure a solution to a thorny mechanical problem that could well have stumped most machine designers. This was a faculty that, in conjunction with his skills and training, permitted him to run rings around such competitors, gifted amateurs as they were, as Daft and Van Depoele.) Working fast, Sprague arranged for Browne & Sharp to manufacture the special gears and shafts needed, and for Crosby to fit them to the motors still to be built and to modify the existing ones. Then, after a flying visit home — Mary hadn't felt up to making the trip to Virginia—Sprague hastened back to Richmond.

Troubles there continued to unfold as the first of the modified cars went jerkily out on their trial runs. (At first Sprague and Greene scheduled their trial runs at night, to minimize public embarrassment, but under increasing time pressure this reticence soon vanished.) One incessant difficulty was with the track. The rails spread and twisted with such abandon that a day without at least one derailment was a rare event. Sprague assigned a working crew full time to the job of rebuilding the track at each of the places, initially almost everywhere that derailments occurred. Soon it was found necessary to send out each trial car equipped to cope with the derailment it would probably encounter, a sturdy pole lashed to the side to help lever the car back on the rails, and a ladder for climbing up to help reestablish contact with the wire overhead. (This was before the trailing, wheeled trolley pole with its retriever rope had been devised.) The sight of the strange horseless cars lurching and sparking along with what seemed to be battering rams and scaling ladders lashed to their sides like a mediaeval assault party amused the citizens of Richmond. Sprague himself found nothing remotely funny about the picture, at least until enough years had passed to soften the memory.

By early December it had become obvious that Sprague didn't have a prayer of a chance of meeting the ninety-day deadline, mutually agreed on as falling at the end of the year. This meant that he and Ed Johnson would have to negotiate with the Union Passenger Railway for an extension. And while Superintendent Burt, the UPR's representative in Richmond, wasn't an unreasonable man to deal with, both Sprague and Johnson feared that an extension could not be cheaply purchased.

Their fears proved well grounded. No one kept a record of the negotiations, but judging by some thin-lipped references later, it was not amiable. Flynn noted that he was legally able simply to cancel the contract for nonperformance. The UPR had serious troubles of its own, including failure to meet franchise obligations and a heavy capital investment that, with no income coming in, threatened the company with bankruptcy. Sprague, alluding to difficulties arising from inferior track and grades steeper than specified, asked for sixty days extra. After much tugging and hauling, an understanding was reached that must have been mutually unsatisfactory. Sprague could have thirty days extension, not sixty, before he would have to begin carrying revenue passengers. In return for this concession, his final payment would be reduced from $110,000 to $90,000, of which only half would now be in cash, the remainder being in UPR bonds.

It must have seemed to Sprague, in December, 1887, that the low point of the Richmond venture had surely been reached. But this was a mistake, for the next few months were to be worse.

VII: A LURID GREEN GLARE

One deceptive aspect of technical pioneering is that— afterward—the solution looks so very much easier than it was. "Well, of course," one is tempted to say, "that was obviously the way that it should have been done. How can they not have seen it immediately?"

Consider for a moment the trolley, an upward-pressing, backward-leaning metal pole with a grooved wheel at its end and rope to pull it down or swing it around. To several generations of Americans this familiar contrivance can hardly have appeared very challenging. It must have seemed the simple and obvious way to lead electricity from a fixed overhead wire to the moving car beneath. And yet, on the level of contrivance though not of electrical theory, few details of electric street cars gave inventors more persistent trouble before 1888.

Partly the difficulty arose from the fact that the problem was trickier than it looks. Heavy currents had to pass; the wire above—as a matter of practicality—couldn't be counted on to be precisely over the centerline of the tracks; a whole family of non-interfering supports, connectors, and insulators had to be perfected; the cars beneath would inevitably lurch and rock; and "wyes" (forks) in the overhead had to be developed and placed in precise relationship to switches in the track below.

Sprague was fertile in inventing trolley mechanisms that promised to meet the requirements. His first try was a telescoping vertical pole, sprouting from the exact center of rotation of the car. It worked fairly well on straight track, though it came adrift when the car lurched, and it wouldn't track reliably through wyes. He designed another, and another, and another. Finally, thirty-nine different arrangements were built and tested, with varying degrees of dissatisfaction. Then Eugene Pommer, a young draftsman, shyly sketched out for Sprague his idea: a trailing pole, pivoted in two planes at its anchorage, and counterweighted to press upward. They quickly rigged one for trial and found with delight that it outperformed all the others. And Sprague, who never indulged in the prima donna poses of many electrical pioneers, rarely missed a chance to point out that it was quiet, shy Eugene Pommer who had helped lick that problem.

But in January 1888, the problems were so many that one fewer was hardly noticed. There were—early in the trials—the first rumbles of some wholly unexpected community-relations difficulties. A few eccentric and perhaps litigation-prone people along the route complained of receiving debilitating and indeed injurious shocks whenever a car rolled past. More disturbingly, subscribers to Richmond's telephone service, which was then using the ground as one conductor in its circuitry, complained vigorously. They reported that their delightfully modern but expensive instruments became worthless whenever a street car passed through the neighborhood, and transmitted only a hideous "hissing and frying noise." Again, a few iron water pipes buried in the ground not far from the powerhouse burst long before their natural time and, when dug up, were found to be eaten away with a suspicious new form of corrosion. (The ground return part of the trolley circuit was connected not only to the rails but also, with Sprague thoroughness, to the city water and gas pipes.) Again, one off-season thunderstorm had produced such alarming pyrotechnics along the twelve miles of electrified track—including blackened controllers and motors as well as burned-out car lights—as to foreshadow what would plainly be a major problem when the system operated in thunderstorm months.

If indeed it did. If indeed the UPR did not coldly cancel the contract on the grounds of nonperformance. Sprague was beset by a continuing difficulty that made all the others pale into relative triviality. The electric motors, his beloved, beautifully-calculated, ingeniously-designed motors simply did not work very well. They overheated, their costly new gears jammed, and they endlessly fell prey to "crosses" and grounds. Their troubles were technical, incessant, and thorny. And when, by patient and unremitting experiment, it proved possible to correct a particular fault, the very correction seemed likely to generate a new fault elsewhere.

All through January the basic problem was to get enough cars running to begin passenger service. Superintendent Burt, under pressure from Flynn and worried about the franchise and the total absence of revenue, pressed Sprague daily with alternating entreaties and threats to begin carrying passengers. Sprague wanted to delay as long as he possibly could (working furiously, meanwhile, to improve the equipment) because he knew that the step would be irreversible. Once the cars began carrying fare-paying passengers they would either have to keep running, or invite certain cancellation if service was suspended. Sprague, who seemed unwilling to admit even the possibility of failure, felt that it was better to undergo the pressures and recriminations that delay involved than to start operations with only a handful of undependable cars.

But at the beginning of February, when the month's dearly-bought extension had expired; he could resist no longer. The powerhouse and the overhead wires had been brought to fair shape. The track had been repaired to the extent that derailments were only a probability, not a certainty. And ten cars, the estimated minimum

VII: A LURID GREEN GLARE

for commercial service, had been fitted with the latest design improvements, and might be hoped to run for a time. Sprague described the dismal opening day this way:

> "As a preliminary to regular operation, we spent a day carrying loads of children without any serious trouble, and about the 2nd of February, 1888, in a drizzling rain, we opened the line for regular service.
>
> "The day was one of disappointment; we carried crowds of people, but car after car would suddenly stop in the street and refuse to move under any conditions, for the new gears had a freak of locking. The men got under the cars, took off the disgruntled gears, and continued if possible on the other motor, or bodily hauled the car off the track so that another could go by.
>
> "My first impression was that it was a mechanical fault, that the gears were not properly cut or that the castings had been distorted. But an Irish mechanic, Pat O'Shaughnessy, who had been with me for years, and who had a most happy mechanical judgment, insisted that it was for lack of proper oiling, and after a while had the cars running again."

The Richmond newspapers of the time, flushed with pride and wonder, gave their readers an optimistic (or perhaps charitable) interpretation of the new line. Everything went off smoothly in the first week, one paper announced. A number of horses had been frightened by the sight of cars moving along without visible source of power, but no serious runaways had resulted. Some annoyance had been caused by malicious lads who placed rocks on the rails. Readers who had not actually ridden the cars yet were informed that the fare was five cents, that cars were spaced about ten or twelve minutes apart, and that a trip from one end of the line to the other took about an hour. Two officials rode each car, a driver and a conductor, the latter being the captain of the car. Lady passengers wishing to have the car stopped for them need only raise one finger. A gong would be rung at cross streets to eliminate the possibility of collision. And at night the cars were brilliantly illuminated, not with kerosene lamps, but with incandescent electric bulbs.

During February and March almost everyone connected with the line worked to the edge of nervous and physical exhaustion. As often happens in such circumstances, a kind of weary camaraderie bound them together. Though Sprague was at the time a boss with a rawhide tongue, Pat O'Shaughnessy always remembered the little triumph he had achieved with one piece of impertinence. Sprague had brusquely told him to go to hell, and Pat cracked back that he didn't want to visit Sprague's home when he wasn't there. It wasn't much of a joke but everybody was tired enough to howl, and the gag became legendary on the line.

VII: A LURID GREEN GLARE

This same collective spirit brought a cheerful outcome to one day that had begun badly. Sprague woke to see from his hotel window that freezing rain during the night had coated the trolley wires with a glistening shield of ice. The line seemed absolutely shut down. Outside, where Sprague kept a small work car named Snowflake on a siding, he discovered to his surprise that there was current on the line, and that Snowflake's trolley pole jounced just vigorously enough to make intermittent contact and move the little car downhill. He set off on a voyage of exploration, morosely convinced that for that day at least they'd haul no passengers. But around the first turn, he came on a sight to gladden the eye. Climbing up the steep grade came a procession of cars, laden with passengers pleased to be riding rather than afoot that icy morning. Perched on the roof of the leading car, busily thwacking the ice from the wire with an upended broom, was the intrepid Pat O'Shaughnessy. "We resumed operations that day," Sprague noted, "With a light heart."

It was desirable, of course, to display a bright and shining countenance to the public, and to newspapermen in particular. On February 5, 1888, the New York World printed an article that was a monument to Sprague's and Johnson's ability to radiate optimism:

> "This road has now been in successful operation for some time past, and is a daily demonstration that all possible obstacles in street car

transportation have been successfully overcome by the system of the Sprague Electric Railway and Motor Company.

"The results have been extraordinary. During the past fortnight in the trial trips, closed 16-foot cars, carrying picked loads of 55 to 60 passengers, and having a total weight of 15,000 pounds, were operated on a 10-percent grade, often with a slippery and slimy rail, and on 27-foot curves, without the use of sand or extra help.

"These same grades and curves were ascended also without sand after one of the worst sleet storms which had visited this section for years. No severer test could have been made, and the power and tractive effort developed have exceeded the most sanguine expectations."

But behind the radiated cheerfulness was an almost frightening array of trouble. The list was a long one: a bitter technical and now legal battle with the phone company; continuing derailments, far more than could be laid to rock depositing juveniles; a distracting tendency for the car to go one way and the trolley pole another at turnouts; and incessant failures of insulation in wet weather. (Insulation was still primitive in the Eighties, and its frequent breakdown meant that everyone who worked on the controllers or who crawled beneath a car to check the motors was exposed to savage jolts of stray current.) And beyond all these difficulties, moreover, there loomed the disquieting question as to whether the motors could ever be made to run reliably.

Some problems did respond to attack. There was no technical way to remedy telephone interference other than to take the position, in court, that "the phone company did not own the earth." Lawyers for Sprague and UPR carried the day, and the telephone circuits were fitted with wire rather than ground returns. (Telephone engineers conceded, after tempers subsided, that this not only eliminated interference but gave superior service than before.) The only cure for derailments was to rebuild the defective track, and while this was slow and costly, it did promise eventual success.

Meantime, Sprague and Greene drew on their naval training to fit out cars with what they christened "kedges." Derailments were now occurring chiefly on sharp curves, where the cars were apt to plunge on straight ahead, leaving the rails completely and embedding their wheels in the clay. Re-railing them by levers, block-and- tackle, and muscle was slow and exhausting. The "kedges", jumper wires that, hooked to the overhead and clamped to a rail, restored power to the beached car, speeded up the task. As also did the good nature of the travelling public, for able-bodied male passengers and any bystanders were encouraged to lend a hand at the re-railing, and usually did so in an amiable mood.

Experience and time helped with some troubles. The stray currents that caused such disquieting shocks near the controllers and motors gradually disappeared with improvements in insulation and design. The electrolysis that created such havoc on buried pipes was found to come when the return current found a better path through the pipes than through the rails. The remedy, again slow and costly, was to improve the electrical bonding at the rail joints, and to lay a few special ground return wires. The ominous lightning problem was simply tabled until later in the spring, though Sprague did find time to sketch out designs for the device that would later be known as a lightning arrestor. And the exasperatingly willful way that the trolley pole had of following the wrong fork overhead was tamed by redesign and relocation of every overhead wye on the system.

But nothing seemed to help with the motors. Often in the evening rush hour, a loaded car could be seen climbing a hill with a lurid green glare sputtering and flashing from the motors beneath. Sprague would wince at the sight, because such destructive sparking meant at least $100 in repair costs. Worse, it meant loss of the car from service until replacement parts could be fitted. Crosby in New York and Sprague in Richmond set up an expensive and distressing two-way traffic, with burned-out or short-circuited motor parts travelling North by express to be rebuilt, and repaired ones flowing back as quickly as possible. Even when there was a backlog of spares, and it wasn't until April that the real danger of not having enough working cars to give service passed, the comparatively simple matter of replacement was nightmarish. This was because the motors had been modified so many times that many parts were no longer really interchangeable. Endless hours of shimming, machining, and cobbling were needed to piece together replacements for the motors that destroyed themselves so readily. After one week-long stretch of frantic and almost continuous labor to keep even a handful of cars running, Sprague dropped his normally serene manner to tell his associate, "Greene, this is hell!"

Technically, most trouble centered on the commutator, the spinning drum of bare copper segments against which the brushes pressed. In street car service, exposed to dirt and moisture, making incessant starts and stops under heavy loads, and with a reversal of direction at each end of the line, the commutators gave trouble never seen on stationary motors. Often a brand-new motor would start to fail after just one or two trips, and if its burnt, blistered, pitted commutator wasn't cleaned and smoothed at once, it would expire from a fatal short circuit.

Sprague tackled the problem with characteristic energy and intelligence and, for weeks on end, with seemingly little progress. He noticed that on certain motors fitted with two commutators, one of them gave far more trouble than the other. This seemed an exciting clue, though it soon dead-ended. He modified the motor circuits so that the arcing damage was divided equally between the two commutators. But after careful trial he concluded that distributed damage was really no gain over concentrated damage, and he scrapped the two-commutator motors. Next, after minute study of the blistered, pitted commutators that the mechanics were daily pulling from the motors, he began extensive tests of new designs and materials. Certain bronze and brass alloys seemed to work just a little bit better than the traditional copper bars. "Somewhat hurriedly," he later admitted, he ordered every motor on the system changed over. When this was done, at great cost in time, effort, and money, the new commutators seemed a little better by an almost imperceptible amount.

Next he attacked the problem from the brushes, the fixed conductors that rubbed against the spinning commutator. These were then made of metal, usually brass or a silicon bronze, and they too gave endless trouble. One problem was mechanical: they often worked fairly well for one direction of travel, but when the motors were reversed at the end of the line, they often "stubbed their toes" on the commutator, splitting or straddling the segments and promptly burning out the motor. An ingenious tilt-over brush holder stopped that vicious habit. But the brushes wore very fast, and their ends, sheared off by the rough commutators, sent a shower of glittering chips over the line so that "the track soon looked like a golden path." The few cars running were using about $9 worth of brass every day, and the motor men were under orders to inspect and replace the brushes every half trip. Sprague experimented with scores of different shapes, mountings, and materials for brushes. Here too certain combinations seemed, at best, very slightly less bad than others.

Van DePoele Dayton, OH 1888 (courtesy of John L. Sprague)

It was during this distracting time that Sprague was offered, through an intermediary, a chance to buy out Van Depoele, his most energetic competitor. He rejected the offer "partly because of confidence in my own work and lack of appreciation of Van Depoele's." This undoubtedly seemed wise under the circumstances, but it may nevertheless have been a mistake. For one thing, Van Depoele also was capable of electrical intuitions; he suggested the use of carbon brushes, and this material worked very well indeed. For another thing, a future patent decision would disallow Sprague's basic trolley patent application as of the date when he had filed it at London, attending the exposition for the Navy, thus giving slight primacy to Van Depoele. And a third reason was that Van Depoele's little firm shortly fell into the hands of the Thomson-Houston Co., of Lynn, Massachusetts, a lively outfit that was soon to jump into the trolley-making business and compete vigorously with Sprague. But these developments were of course veiled when Sprague made his decision.

Toward the end of March, at a time when the greatest bulk of technical difficulties were piling in on Sprague, and when so much money had been spent that the Richmond venture seemed an unalloyed disaster, Sprague got a telegram from New York. This city was just digging out from under the Great Blizzard of 1888, but the wire was not about the weather; it reported that Mary's and his baby was imminent. He hurried back, and a son, to be christened Frank d'Esmonde Sprague, was born on March 29, 1888.

At some time during April, so subtly that neither Sprague nor Greene were ever sure just when it happened, operation of the street cars began imperceptibly to grow easier. Many of the earlier troubles continued in some degree. But the rain of nightmarish difficulties gave way to a lighter sprinkle of still obstinate but lesser problems.

The sum of Sprague's changes on the motors reduced the sparking problem to manageable proportions. Then the change from metallic to carbon brushes, able to withstand the high temperature of arcing, helped a great deal. Experience-taught procedures on design and lubrication, and on the need of shielding the motors from the worst of the grit and mud, began to lengthen out the period in which a motor would run docilely and reliably. UPR Superintendent Burt noted from his records that, once they began to run right, electric motors on street car service displayed a delightful willingness to operate at very low cost. Projecting his figures, Burt foresaw that trolleys promised far lower costs per mile than either horse cars or cable railways.

While this must have pleased Sprague, what was more immediately exciting was the daily report on the number of cars available for duty. Both he and Greene were proud of the fact that, from the day commercial service opened, not a car on the UPR had ever been pulled by a horse or mule. But it had been a near thing in February and March, when the number of cars available had fluctuated around ten, and had occasionally sunk to a dismaying nine or eight. During April, the daily figure moved up to fifteen and then twenty. On May 4 it hit thirty, the theoretical normal for the line, and climbed, on one exciting day later that month, to a point when every one of the forty cars on the UPR could have been run if needed.

Sprague was also both elated and relieved when, with thirty cars running at once, his theoretical calculations about the size of the powerhouse and distribution system checked out with precision. When thirty cars were out on the line, with their lights on, the boilers, engines, and dynamos all showed readings that averaged almost exactly seventy-five percent of their normal capacities, and the trolley voltage everywhere held steady and high.

Not that everything turned to milk and honey overnight. The final legal skirmish with the telephone company did not end until May. Derailments continued to tie up traffic periodically. Trolley pole mountings were redesigned three times in an effort to reduce off-the-trolley delays. The first sharp thunderstorms of the spring brought all the expected troubles and then some, for the twelve miles of overhead wire were regularly struck by lightning. Sprague hastened the installation of lightning arrestors, devices that offered lightening preferred passages, as it were, to ground, luring it away from damaging passages through motors and lamps.

But until enough arrestors were installed, lightning strikes often produced terrifying blue flashovers by the controllers on the platforms at each end of the cars. Sprague noted that, in the case of a nearby strike, all the lamps in a car would be likely to burn out in the daytime, but not at night. So orders were posted for motor-men to turn lights on during a storm, on the idea (sound, as it worked out) that the more paths to ground that a high-voltage surge had, the less harm it might do. Motor-men, discovering that the fireworks by the controllers were more likely to be showy than dangerous, grew in time to be offhand about them.

VII: A LURID GREEN GLARE

In late spring of 1888—the exact date is unrecorded except that it was before May 15, when UPR formally accepted the Electrification in a letter of fulsome praise from Flynn and his group—something happened that was to enter the Richmond legend like Pat O'Shaughnessy and his broom. It was also crucial for Sprague's future career.

The event began with the arrival in town of an awesome personage named Henry M. Whitney, president and board chairman of the West End Railway of Boston. He was a financier who, years before, had gotten into the business almost by accident. He had purchased one little line passing his home on the conceit that it would be pleasant to ride to work on his own horse cars. Whitney had become fascinated with the financial possibilities of street railways. By buying up isolated lines and linking them together, in time he assembled the biggest and most profitable horse car system in the United States. Some 8,000 horses labored for Mr. Whitney, drawing more than 1,700 cars over 212 miles of track in and around metropolitan Boston.

But as the years rolled past it became obvious that the great days of the "animal railway" were numbered. Costs were high and intractable. In the 1870s, a terrifying epidemic called the "Great Epizootic" had emphasized the vulnerability of the lines to unpredictable disease. And the continuing reports, in the pages of the Street Railway Journal, of new developments in steam cars, electric cars, and cable cars, clearly foreshadowed the future. So Henry M. Whitney, accompanied by a pride of West End directors and by General Manager Longsteeet, set out to inspect the future.

In New York and Chicago the party had examined a number of cable car systems, alarmingly expensive to build but still very efficient. In Allegany City, Pennsylvania, they had surveyed a tiny electric system being nursed along by Messrs Bentley and Knight. This line, capable of only irregular service, was obviously unpromising. Longstreet, a convinced cable man, had almost persuaded Whitney to take the plunge. In fact, he admitted, he had already optioned the land that would be needed for the cable-drawing engine houses. But Whitney—as a kind of last step before committing his millions to the construction of a cable system in Boston— insisted that the party visit Richmond, where this young Sprague fellow was said to be doing clever things with electricity.

The visitation began promisingly. Ed Johnson hurried down from New York; as titular president of Sprague Electric Railway, he was the nearest approach to Whitney's opposite number, and he was also notably deft at dealing with the great ones. After the party had had a full-dress inspection tour of the system, and after Superintendent Burt's impressive cost projections were examined, Whitney was clearly impressed.

Then Mr. Longstreet, the West End's general manager and a blunt and forceful man with years of street railway experience, put his oar in. Hadn't young Mr. Sprague said that each electrified section of track was engineered "for a distributed load of four cars at once"? Didn't anyone realize that metropolitan street cars would inevitably encounter blockages? Or that far more than four cars would pile up? Wasn't this fact alone decisive for cable cars, drawn by immensely powerful steam engines in the powerhouse? Whatever assurances to the contrary might be given, didn't it stand to reason that, after a blockage, an attempt to start up a long line of trolley cars would almost certainly burn out the dynamos?

This resonantly stated pessimism stopped Whitney. The group broke up inconclusively for the day. Johnson feared that Longstreet's cable bias could well be a fatal snag. Sprague excused himself from the group, having "privately resolved to stage a demonstration of somewhat dramatic character." That night at the powerhouse, as service came to an end for the day, he and the engineer on duty set to work. They reset the main and feeder circuit breakers so they wouldn't open on overloads, and raised the voltage from its normal voltage of 450 to 500. They built up a top head of steam in each boiler. At one end of the line they assembled an array of twenty-two trolley cars, parked, almost touching, in a line more than a block long. After briefing the twenty-two motor men to stand ready to start up at the wave of a lantern, and ordering the powerhouse crew to "hang on no matter what", Sprague hurried off to Whitney's hotel. By then it was midnight and he had to wait while the sleepy visitors dressed.

At the scene, Sprague explained coolly that the cars were banked on a stretch designed to feed electricity to only four well-spaced cars. Then he waved the lantern. There must have been tension beneath the coolness; afterward he said that he hadn't any idea what would happen. Then the twenty-two lighted cars started up, each one drawing away as soon as its motorman had a few feet of headroom. To Sprague's eye the electrical draw was clearly severe, for the lamps in the cars dimmed down to a faint orange glow. In the powerhouse at the same time the voltmeter needles sagged from 500 to a bare 200 volts, and the steam engines labored and knocked alarmingly. But each of the twenty-two cars got away, and was soon bustling off into the darkness.

The stunt was a great success. The pessimistic Mr. Longstreet was silenced; the highly important Mr. Whitney was impressed all over again; and Sprague, at thirty-one, was fairly launched on earning the first of several personal fortunes that the next decades were to bring him.

In a short-term sense, the Richmond contract had proved to be a financial catastrophe. Counting material and labor costs, Sprague later estimated he had spent almost $160,000 to earn $90,000, and half of that was in UPR bonds. Only the continued and increasing prosperity of the motor business kept him from being bankrupted by his success, and for a time it seemed a near thing if even the motor business could pull him through.

But the loss was only temporary, for the lucrative new contracts that poured in afterward more than made up the losses. Even the shrewd but flinty Mr. Flynn, who had made life so difficult only a few months before, took a long look at the operating figures on the UPR and then ordered the electrification of forty more cars. In July, Flynn bought control of the only other street railway in Richmond, the elderly horse and mule car line that held a valuable franchise and announced plans to electrify that too.

Sprague himself, who never thought of himself as a shrewd businessman, helped out by a step that no public relations adviser could have bettered. He read a paper to the American Institute of Electrical Engineers at Columbia University in New York City that was blandly titled: "The Solution of Municipal Rapid Transit". Although written for and applauded by his engineering audience, the paper could hardly have been more precisely aimed at street car executives. It began with cost figures that showed that trolleys were not only faster and more efficient than horse cars, but markedly cheaper to run. It went on to demolish some of the supposed drawbacks and dangers to electric traction then circulating (with, it must be assumed, the enthusiastic approval of cable- car interests):

> "The riding of an electric car is far easier than that of any cable or horse car, starting and stopping more easily, and being in a large measure free from lurching and oscillation. There is no dust such as arises from the heels of horses.

"It has been said that an extended system cannot be operated by electricity, that lines may break down, that a large number of cars cannot be operated simultaneously, especially when bunched up, that wires burn out, that brushes burn up.

"True, these things have happened, and in case of defective workmanship or carelessness they may happen again. Although electricity is a force of unknown nature, and we know it by its effects, it is folly to hold that whatever faults in machinery may exist or accidents occur, they do not come within a very narrow and limited category; and powerful and mysterious as it is, and answering an impulse with the rapidity of lightning, it is at the same time the most tractable and law-abiding agent with which we have to deal.

"There is not a freak of which it is capable which we cannot guard against. It has not an attribute of which we cannot make positive use. It has no power of damage which cannot be controlled."

As it turned out, the success of the Richmond road could hardly have been more ideally timed. All over the country, in large cities and small, dissatisfaction with slow, smelly, crowded horse cars had been building up for a decade. Now, quite suddenly, it was possible to imagine, right here in one's own community, riding those fast, clean new electrics, so advanced and scientific in their strange new motors. The lines could run right out to, or beyond, the settled edges of town, behavior likely to perk the ears of any forward looking, real-estate-minded investor. They could actually cost less and make more than those highly profitable horse car lines; and, best of all, they could be installed right here and now, in this, the fastest growing and most progressive city in the entire state.

By early 1890, less than two years after the worst days at Richmond, more than two hundred trolley lines were running or building in the United States. More than half of them were either built by the Sprague Electric and Railway Company, or under its license.

VIII: THE METALLIC TASTE OF SUCCESS

> *"Thomson-Houston sales agents are allowed ample cash to pay the expenses of visiting city councilmen and other prospects—— they can charter trains, give people a good time, and show them around town, unlike our agents."*
>
> *— Confidential report to Sprague 1889*

For a year and a half after the Richmond venture had turned into a triumph, Sprague was caught up in the excitements of roaring commercial success. He was thirty-one years old, famous in the select world of electricity, and widely sought out for everything from consulting opinions to commencement addresses. (He noted, in a letter genially refusing an invitation for a biographical sketch before the august National Electric Light Association, that "my excessive modesty will not permit me to make known all my good points, and my pride will prevent me from giving away all my bad ones".) A contemporary describes him at this time as "thin and wiry, with blond hair and mustache, and a prominent Adam's apple that bobbed up and down inside his high starched collar. For the first time in his life he felt comfortably prosperous on his salary of $6,000, plus dividends from his stock. His salary was only half that drawn by Ed Johnson, but then it was Ed who had put up the money to begin with (the stock was fairly well spread around by now), and besides, Ed seemed to enjoy money more.

The offices of the Sprague Electric Railway and Motor Company (SERM) were on 16 & 18 Broad Street in New York City, and the factory— mainly for warehousing, inspection, and some assembly—was on West 30th Street. The company had grown spectacularly from the shaky little enterprise hatched in a Brockton rooming house five years before. A payroll from 1889 survives; it carries eighty-one names, and if the firm had done any considerable manufacturing itself, rather than farming it out to Edison Machine Works, it would have necessarily been three times bigger. The payroll makes fascinating reading today. Aside from President Johnson's $12,000 and Sprague's $6,000, there was $6,000 for general counsel John S. Wise, $3, 600 each for Greene and Crosby, tapering down to $416 to $312 a year for Miss Dickson and Miss Ritchie in Filing. Apart from the thriving and steadily growing business in motors for stationary uses, there was a skyrocketing business in electrifying street cars. It had grown overnight:

1887..........$29,970 (excluding $93,000 for Richmond)
1888...... $364,901
1889.... $1,512,308

Not that there weren't several banks of low-lying clouds on the horizon. One was the close, convenient, but never wholly satisfactory relationship with the Edison Machine Works in Schenectady. (It had originally been in New York City, but had been moved out abruptly in 1886, after its employees had shown an interest in unionizing.) Sprague did not like having manufacturing outside his supervision, and there were continuing disputes over whether windings and insulation were up to specifications. Temperamentally, too, the arrangement was not ideal; Sprague's and Edison's personalities were no more congenial than they had been five years before. There seem to have been several clashes on technical matters, including the direct-current versus alternating-current debate then agitating American electricians. Edison was deeply committed to direct current, in part because of a fierce rivalry with George Westinghouse, who had a strong position in alternating-current patents; and Sprague had had the temerity to write Edison several memos pointing out that there were many theoretical advantages to alternating current. His points were undoubtedly sound, but the wisdom in sending them to a man who was emotionally involved in a contrary position might perhaps have been questioned. Sprague was not ordinarily tactless, however, and he may have relished the chance to point out to Edison the weakness of his position.

Another crosscurrent developed at about the same time between Edison and Ed Johnson. The latter had steadily grown away from his earlier status as Edison's chief business executive, although he was still an officer of several Edison firms. The coolness developed to a point where Johnson, on request, sold back all his Edison stock for cash, and resigned his offices. Minor but waspish recriminations followed on both sides: Johnson saying that Edison was forsaking those who had worked loyally for him in the early days, and Edison remarking that the Sprague-Johnson enterprise "was a galling thorn among all the boys, and would break up the old association".

Throughout 1888 and the early part of 1889, though, this particular cloud remained only a distant thunderhead. For one thing, each business had grown rather to depend on the other. To build their own manufacturing facilities would have cost Sprague and Johnson a great deal of money, and would have forced them to dilute their own holdings further. And the Edison Machine Works, itself the most consistently profitable of all the Edison firms, discovered that Sprague orders, amounting to $75,000 to $100,000 a month, had climbed to be the most important in the plant.

VIII: THE METALLIC TASTE OF SUCCESS

Another factor that stabilized the situation, at least temporarily, was the stock interrelationship between the two firms. Not only had Johnson been, up to the time of rupture, a substantial minority holder of Edison stock, but Edison and his backer, Henry Villard, were both owners of substantial blocks of Sprague stock. (As, indeed, was J. Pierpont Morgan, who casually bought stock in promising little electric companies as a way of making money.) In the spring of 1889, needing capital for expansion, Johnson and Sprague had sold Edison and Villard twenty percent of the firm's common stock, previously unissued, and all of the preferred. It must be assumed that Villard was glad to take a step that would help the Edison Machine Works keep its biggest single customer. So with all of these combining factors at work, the situation rocked along. Some of Sprague's private correspondence in 1889 reflects worry that his prospering little firm might be taken over by Edison interests, a development that seemed to him to be about as desirable as being swallowed by a killer whale.

The other cloud on the horizon during that busy time was bigger, but somehow not so much ominous as exhilarating. This was the slam-bang competition for trolley contracts that was put up by the Thomson-Houston Company of Lynn, Massachusetts. The firm had been founded nine years before by a pair of inventor-professors, Elihu Thomson and Edwin J. Houston, to manufacture arc lights. The two professors shortly gave over the management of their firm to a singular man from Maine, Charles Coffin. A one-time shoe salesman, Coffin was tough, smart, tireless, and intensely competitive. He believed passionately in expansion. He bought the large but rather sleepy Brush Arc Light Company and soon dominated that industry. He obtained some slightly flawed patent rights and soon gave Edison brisk competition in the incandescent lighting business. He foresaw the economies of alternating current and, armed with some valuable Elihu Thompson patents on transformers and alternators, gave George Westinghouse a run for his money on alternating current. He saw that existing "middle-aged" patents (such as Edison's basic incandescent ones, due to expire in 1894) were chiefly of value for litigation; the really valuable ones were the young and strategic patents. So he hired a mathematical physicist named Charles Steinmetz and ordered him to build an impregnable patent fortress around high-voltage alternating current. Coffin snapped up Van Depoele's trolley business when Sprague turned it down (its principal asset was the trolley patent that was to be held prior to Sprague's) and began to compete vigorously for the profitable new business of electrifying the world's street cars.

VIII: THE METALLIC TASTE OF SUCCESS

*Renovated Bronx NYC trolley
(courtesy Branford Trolley Museum)*

Thomson-Houston, under Coffin's shrewd and driving leadership, was a rough competitor. Edison and Westinghouse, as well as Sprague, all felt pressure in ways that ranged from patent combat to energetic salesmanship and the skillful management of capital. Edison, for instance, often found himself short of cash for a reason that seemed inherent in the business: in setting up a new local lighting company, it generally was necessary to take back bonds of the new utility as part payment for the equipment. In time this absorbed a considerable proportion of Edison's capital; and while he found bankers, like Pierpont Morgan, willing enough to advance money when he was in a strong position and didn't need it, he learned that it was painful and costly to go to bankers when he did need it. But Thomson-Houston under Coffin felt no such pinch. His astute backers, mainly Boston financiers like Henry Lee Higginson and T. Jefferson Coolidge, encouraged T-H to accept bonds as partial payment if necessary to help sell the equipment. But instead of letting the money stay tied up, they transferred the bonds to a subsidiary, sold debentures secured by the bonds to the public, and promptly got the cash back.

Sprague felt T-H competition in both technical and sales areas. As a firm with influential connections in Boston, T-H promptly pried away from Sprague the lion's share of Whitney's West End electrification. And as soon as both Sprague and T-H equipment began operating simultaneously on different parts of that system, T-H sales agents fanned out over the country with infuriating stories of how well T-H equipment was behaving, and how unreliable and expensive the Sprague cars were. Sprague and Johnson were stung to counterattack. Industrial espionage was quite as much a part of business in the 1880s as today, and in Sprague's confidential files are a number of yellowing G-2 reports on what "The Enemy" was up to. At the onset the reports mainly discussed design; later they branched out into sales tactics and maintenance records. Here are excerpts from a confidential memo to Sprague, dated August 19, 1889, turned in by J. H. Bickford, a $120-a-month Sprague inspector:

VIII: THE METALLIC TASTE OF SUCCESS

Gentlemen:

"I have succeeded in getting the information on the T-H motor you were so anxious to obtain, namely, the method of insulating the armature...(six pages of description and analysis follow, concluding): The pinion and gear are thus held in place in a very effective way. I think we would do well to use a similar method on our # 6 motor.

"I should have been pleased to give you a more minute description of the motor but cannot, owing to the fact that a very careful watch is kept on it by the T.H. man."

Very truly,
J.H. Bickford

But modest little intelligence reports like this couldn't compare with a coup that was pulled off for Sprague later that year by an employee named W. A. Stadelman. By accompanying a friend who was a city councilman from Philadelphia, and by posing as prospective buyers of many trolley cars, Stadelman and his friend toured the T-H plant in Lynn and received the full sales treatment. This daring penetration brought much technical and tactical information that must have delighted Sprague. The following is condensed from a report thousands of words long:

"They give prospects the grand tour of the factory; the chief object seems to be to paralyze people with the sights they show them. Besides street-railway equipment, there's arc lighting, incandescents, transformers, and electric welding apparatus.

"They show off their pole-boring machine, and contrast it with shoddy methods used at E.M.W. They employ nothing but men, and pay them day wages, not piece work.

"They stress the field winding, saying there's no fear of the inductive effects supposed to rupture the insulation in ours. Nonsense: we found they have had ever so much trouble with the fields, and on the Allston road burned out 17 field coils in three weeks. The T-H machine is heavier; they claim Sprague is too light.

"Their pinion is superior, made of layers of steel and rawhide. They say that the Sprague road in Atlantic City has had great trouble with fiber pinions. We think they may have got that from agent Harrington."

It is possible to imagine the wires getting hot at this point as Sprague and Johnson prepare to sizzle poor loose-talking Mr. Harrington. But the report is only half done. After many more tidbits were acquired at Lynn, Stadelman and his city councilman, still in disguise, so to speak, went on to Schenectady to observe the Edison Machine Works building Sprague

VIII: THE METALLIC TASTE OF SUCCESS

equipment. Evidently this wasn't solely to make the deception in Lynn more plausible; there is also the suggestion that the Philadelphia councilman was actually shopping for trolleys, if in a way that accommodated a friend:

> "In Schenectady we were surprised to see boys and girls at work winding armatures. We found out for certain that they were paid piece work. We saw some very sloppy winding being done.
>
> "In conclusion, we thought that the construction was better, with superior machine work and superior finish. But the winding was not as good, nor the pole pieces and pinions. E.M.W. is not as well equipped as T.H., nor as large."

Stadelman concluded his report by noting that he was surprised that the Edison Machine Works wasn't working at night since there seemed to be so much work on hand. It doesn't seem to have occurred to him that it was less practical to use children on the night shift.

Not that vigorous competition from Thomson-Houston cast a serious pall over the Sprague offices on Broad Street. There was in fact so much business in hand that the chronic problems were to get enough production and to expand the staff of trolley-wise employees. Big electrification contracts were under way all over the map from New Orleans to Pittsburgh, Cleveland to Omaha. Queries, and even orders, began to flow in from all over the world. A Sprague system was installed in Halle Germany, by some agents doing business under the name of Allgemeine Deutsche Elektrizitaets-Gesellschaft (later known as AEG). From Melbourne, Australia, and several South American cities came tenders for bids on Sprague systems.

The first electric cars to run in Italy were Sprague-powered, running on a hilly track between Florence and Fiesole. The grades were worrisome, and Sprague wrote to the car-body manufacturer:

> "This truck will require an especially heavy wheel of extra width that I think Brill can supply. These trucks have got to operate on a very crooked road in which for three miles there is a grade to 7 1/2. There must be absolute reliability in the brakes."

Sprague may have thought of these words when, late in 1889, the first large-scale trolley accident in history took place on this road. A car running downhill got away from its motorman, careened wildly for a short distance, shedding passengers, and then crashed. Reports reaching the United States told of at least three people killed outright, with more than twenty others "wounded". An official investigation laid the blame on an over-exuberant motorman. Before service was allowed to resume, Sprague's agents were ordered to install a special master switch at each end of each car. The notion appears to have been that the conductor, who was not only captain of the crew and presumably also a more sober and cautious personality, could thereby take charge whenever speed became immoderate. The agents cheerfully installed the switches, not pointing out that a conductor could achieve the same effect simply by reaching out and pulling down the trolley cord.

During the summer of 1889 Sprague discovered that he was tired and resolved to go abroad for a rest. Characteristically, he decided to attend (indeed, to exhibit at) the Paris Exposition and to visit various electrical installations about the continent. This time his wife accompanied him, though d'Esmonde, aged sixteen months and his name not yet anglicized to Desmond, remained at home. Buried in Sprague's papers today is a copy of a very long letter, almost a journal, that he wrote about the trip. It gives a vivid picture of the young inventor touring Europe in search of new electrical developments.

At the Paris Exposition, he writes, "there is a poor display of American machinery in general, but a creditable display of electrical matters. But Germany is more advanced than we." Sprague's compulsive modesty seems to have kept him from recording that his own exhibit, his newest trolley car truck, won a coveted gold medal in Paris! In Berlin he meets with AEG executives and negotiates an agreement between AEG and Sprague Electric. They will share research;

they will quote each other shop prices for goods each manufactures for the other; and they will not compete in each other's territory. But Sprague is momentarily disquieted when the shrewd Germans insist that the agreement will have to remain provisional until the disquieting rumors of absorption of Sprague by Edison become clarified.

In Germany he's impressed and delighted with a huge new Siemens dynamo, technically very sophisticated, and he concludes that American powerhouses will follow the German path of using compound and even triple-expansion steam engines for maximum efficiency. (In 1889, a practical engineer like Sprague would almost certainly have dismissed the non-condensing steam turbines of the day as interesting but ridiculously inefficient.) He tries to find a working alternating current system to study, but can't locate one; he does collect German technical opinion to the effect that alternating current will have its headaches.

• In Vevey, Switzerland, he happily discovers a street-car system that had just opened the year before:

> "It was the time of the great wine fete in August, when all the country people around and about headed to Vevey. It is a charming little spot, crowded with these people. All night long the peasant classes tramped up and down the streets, no room for them even to sleep, and all day long they rode on the line of cars. There are five miles of single track, 10 cars, a dozen

VIII: THE METALLIC TASTE OF SUCCESS

turnouts. Current is collected from two split tubes overhead, looking like small hoses, and is picked up by "skates" riding on top.

"Every time they got to the end of the line a man would have to climb up on top, and unhook and rehook his cables to be ready to start back again. All this was a very pleasant sight to me. I have been called a Jonah. I think I am sometimes.

"Later we, my wife and I, went out on top of this car and went skating along four or five miles. The machine ran rather well. When they attempted to climb a grade they would slow up toward the top, and I could feel that armature almost sizzling. I would say to myself, I pity that machine."

At one point on the ride there was a blockage with four or five cars banked up and a good deal of French expostulation from motormen and conductors. Sprague spotted the cause of the trouble as a short in the overhead line, but he didn't feel his French was up to pointing it out.

"Those four cars hung there for about an hour. I managed to get off and walked down to their central station. I boldly enquired for the electrician as I knew he was not there. I left my wife sitting on a stone fence, and went in, thinking I might get inside this motor building by the use of a little bad French. I was treated very courteously and shown the cars and their inner workings. They had a motor which is very much of the general plan of our standard machine. But it had bad faults. It is carried under the car frame very rigidly. The line ran remarkably well. It was to me a very forcible demonstration of the utility of electrical propulsion under very adverse conditions. I came to the conclusion that we are way ahead in this country. I got back about 1:00 in the morning but was very satisfied."

The long letter/journal continues with detailed descriptions of other lines, including an early Siemens road in Frankfurt and the Sprague installation in Florence. (Sprague's reader was never explicitly told that Mary was not left sitting on the stone fence in Vevey!) The letter was evidently finished after his return from abroad, for it winds up: "I came back here somewhat freshened bodily and with new vigor of mind." As though in proof, he concludes with an optimistic summary of how matters look for his company:

"We found our present machines (about 1,000 in operation) were developing certain minor defects, but in no way radical. We are not only going to bring out new features but we are simply longing for the opportunity to

VIII: THE METALLIC TASTE OF SUCCESS

take a 50 or 60 car road and beat any record our adversaries have made on coal consumption.

"We will produce a system in which every car which is slowing down or on a down grade shall become a moving generator supplying power to other cars. It will save 30 to 40% on the coal bill.

"When a motor starts in the near future it is going to start with the armature free, progressively increasing in effort until it can move the car.

"I care not what T-H Co., or our friends the Short Electric Railway Co., whether called short on account of a short-lived career or short experience, say or do. We have that in our organization which will produce the very best piece of apparatus."

Back on Sprague's desk in the Broad Street office in the autumn of 1889, the correspondence lay thick, and the disquieting rumors lay thicker. For a few weeks Sprague buried himself in immediate problems. A memo to Ed Johnson advises immediate action on bidding for a line outside Paris "else T-H get in." He turns down a request for a speech. He studies and approves a design change coming in from Cleveland, where motor gears have been coming loose. He deals skeptically with an inventor who claims he has a low-cost method for refining Aluminum. (And then, despite the skepticism, buys a part interest in the process.) He responds acidly to an agent who complains that Sprague motors seem to burn out often; will he be so kind as to file detailed, specific reports in the future, not just general and unjustified criticism? He gives a bristling response to a threat of legal action from Thomson-Houston on the trolley patent; he'd most assuredly like to take it to court. Several times he distractedly replies to a Boston lawyer and friend named Gooch; no, he can't come to Boston just now, even though it may mean, as Gooch warns, that he may lose the valuable contact for the forthcoming Boston-to-Lowell car line.

The reason why Sprague had become distrait can be read, inferentially, in three papers in his confidential file. The first, dated 15 November 1889, was a sheaf of calculations on where the control of his company actually lay. It began with a little tabulation on common and preferred stock, and was superficially comforting. Of the 1,000,000 shares of common and 400,000 shares of preferred outstanding, some 620,000 shares of common are held by what Sprague has initially thought of as "his" side: Johnson, Sprague, Wise, and Drexel, Morgan & Company. Edison and Villard hold only 200,000 shares of the common and all the preferred. The 180,000 shares of common that are scattered are, he estimates, equally divided.

But then, in Sprague's thin sharp hand, the memo goes on to list what would happen if his assumptions should prove wrong. Two little syllogisms unfold alarming possibilities:

VIII: THE METALLIC TASTE OF SUCCESS

"If D M & Co. stay in, less than 100,000 will keep control out of Edison, even if they hold their stock. If D M & Co. stay out, 200,000 would be required.

"If a break is made with Edison on a condition of handing back their 520,000 (leaving out Mr. V's personal holdings), 400,000 would be required."

So if Pierpont Morgan did not choose to side with Sprague, the need for a very large sum of money was obvious. At this point the memo changed character. Its hurrying figures became a summary of present business and future prospects. For page after page Sprague listed glowing possibilities for expansion and profit. The sheets were the exact kind of aide-memoire that would be composed by a distracted inventor/engineer who was planning to hasten out to solicit some financier. Nothing is known about who he approached, whether Morgan or Villard or someone else.

The second of the three telltale papers in Sprague's file was dated three days later. It was a feverish memo to Ed Johnson, asking about the way an independent accountant would value the $100,000 per month bills from the Edison Machine Works. Sprague is convinced that— making a fair adjustment for profit and for the capital involved—he is overpaying E.M.W. by fully $10,000 per month. It is the kind of memo that could have been hastily written in preparation for negotiations with Edison and Villard.

The third letter, written a week later, went to Gooch, the man who had been importuning Sprague to come to Boston. It was a dignified, carefully phrased account of defeat, almost disaster:

"I had hoped to be able to step in and make a counter proposition, backed by plenty of capital, to offset the propositions made by the Edison Company. But the powers on the other side, Drexel, Morgan & Co., together with the uncertain element on which it is important to count, have forced me practically to the necessity of accepting their proposition. Johnson, Drexel, Morgan & Co., and Wise, on the part of his friends, recommend the acceptance of the proposition. And I, being then of course in a decided minority, made up my mind that the best thing to do was to accept as gracefully as possible.

"The propositions made are in some ways advantageous, but in view of the undoubted value of our works and the great source of profit it has been to their manufacturing organization, they might have afforded to be somewhat more liberal in their propositions. But as the matter stands, I will come out with actual capital enough to be independent of their wishes and desires, and if I live, will make them pay me a goodly sum before I am a year older.

VIII: THE METALLIC TASTE OF SUCCESS

"I should like to see the company get the Lowell contract, of course, but my solicitude is somewhat tempered by existing circumstances."

It is difficult to tell, more than seventy years later, what the loss of his thriving little firm meant to Sprague. He seems to have had no resentment toward Ed Johnson; they were to be friends and partners in new ventures for a decade to come. With Edison the situation was different, and an angry blow-up was to happen in a few months, that may well have been rooted in the tensions and pressures of 1889. Still, Sprague started out by accepting appointment as a consultant to, and director of, the new firm of Edison-General Electric, hardly the actions of a man who felt wronged in the absorption of his concern. It is also difficult to estimate how much money the take-over meant to Sprague personally since the details on his personal holdings are missing from his files. But considering both his stock holdings and certain patent royalties from AEG overseas (because they dealt with alternating current, the patents were scorned at the time by Edison), it seems probable that he emerged with EGE securities worth at least $100,000. In terms of the times, this could well have seemed an exciting personal fortune to a young man of modest tastes.

Another calming and even reassuring aspect of the take-over was undoubtedly explained to Sprague by Johnson. This was that the absorption of their company was only a trivial part of a far larger financial maneuver that was taking place simultaneously: the reorganization of a number of disheveled and inefficient Edison companies into what was to become the nucleus of General Electric. More than that, it was an intricate struggle for advantage and money between Henry Villard, now back on top as a financier and well-armed with European capital, and Pierpont Morgan, already world famous as a banker with an eerie skill at gaining control of profitable firms and even industries. With titans like this, Johnson must have explained, something like their little trolley-car company would only be a shingle on the wave.

Several soothing statements were mailed out for shareholder and public consumption. A letter to Sprague stockholders, signed jointly by Johnson and Sprague, contained this emollient and unlikely paragraph:

> "We thus find Mr. Sprague naturally and happily supplementing Mr. Edison in the work of perfecting the latter's original labors and this fact has rendered it not unfitting that the work of both should be carried forward under practically the same auspices."

And the Edison General Electric annual report for 1889 devoted much space to proudly detailing the new acquisition:

> "In the year 1888 the Sprague Company actively entered the field of the commercial

VIII: THE METALLIC TASTE OF SUCCESS

application of electricity to the operation of street railways, in which it has been so successful that, out of the 200 electric street railways now in operation and in the course of construction in the United States, the Sprague Company has equipped at least one half, and over 90 percent are operated on the general plan originally laid down by this Company as the pioneer in this field of electrical work, and based on its patents."

The next seven months were among the most irksome of Sprague's life. A decisive and tireless thirty-three-year-old (his detractors might have said cocksure), accustomed to managing his own firm with a strong hand, he found himself immersed in the large, loosely organized, and seemingly muscle-bound world of Edison General Electric. Here almost nothing happened fast, and when something did happen more often than not it seemed wrongheaded.

On the face of it he had little to complain of: $12,000 a year, first option on any personal inventions, a free hand as director and consultant. He settled on two main duties: a supervisory responsibility for his old company, and a continuing search for new little businesses or patents that EGE might profitably buy. From the beginning both duties proved exasperating. An impressionistic picture of his mood can be captured by leafing through his correspondence: "I see little but delays and incompetence, laziness and stupidity." "AEG is a smart firm but they are Teutonic and hairsplitting. Here it is January 20 and the contracts still haven't been signed." "Col. Frismuth (the aluminum-process inventor) must be put in his place. All his claims are inconsistent. And I've sunk $5,000!" From an inventor named Pratt, whose electric elevator Sprague hopes to bring to EGE: "Say the word and I'll come with satchel, grips, and drawings to open up the elevator campaign."

One aggravation is that for months on end Sprague must confer incessantly with lawyers. There was Wise, who was general counsel for the old firm, and Dyer & Seeley who were now its counsel, and Major Eaton, general counsel for the whole company. With these gentlemen and their associates and clerks, Sprague must discuss an endless list of patent suits and contract issues. There is drawn-out litigation with Bentley and Knight, ultimately settled in Sprague's favor; a host of suits over Thomson-Houston lines, some of them stand-offs and others favoring T-H; and a complicated set of negotiations with German firms, mainly AEG, over payments and royalties that Sprague is to receive personally. After interminable legal rites, this is settled as a lump payment of $25,000 plus future royalties. Sammy Insull, whom Sprague has learned to tolerate, and who is abroad on business that February, obligingly picks up for Sprague an AEG draft for the $2,000. But the royalties are held back (some of Sprague's patents are clouded by the T-H litigation) and lawyers must be resorted to again.

VIII: THE METALLIC TASTE OF SUCCESS

Technical problems are exasperating as well. The motors coming from the Schenectady factory are often non-uniform, which means that one of each pair tends to wear out prematurely. The refrain "carelessness at the factory" turns up in letter after letter. Coil windings should be changed; the commutator needs redesign! And yet Kreusi, the plant manager, is dead set against any change that will interfere with easy manufacture. Sometimes Sprague gets a chance to inspect T-H equipment and the experience is inflaming: "inferior and imitative design, but quality is so much better".

Hearing tales of an improved motor, Sprague quickly hunts down its builder. His quarry proves to be an eccentric Teuton, Rudolf Eickemeyer, who has built and is operating a small street car system in Yonkers, N. Y. At first the quest is unpromising; power from the motor gets to the wheels by a complicated and irrational system of connecting rods that give the cars an unfortunate duck-like waddle. But the motors are delightful, efficient and full of clever details. For long weeks Sprague tries to persuade EGE to hire Eickemeyer and his patents, but no action is taken.

By April 26, Sprague decides he can take it no more. (It is not, as it happens, the final blow-up though it must have seemed so at the time.) He dictates a long, sharp memo to the board of directors with an itemized list of frustrations.

The first indictment, startling to modern eyes, casually refers to a secret agreement on prices and guarantees that exists between Edison General Electric and Thomson-Houston, its archrival. (Although the first version of the Sherman antitrust law was enacted later in 1890, its intent and spirit were not to seep into the business community for, at the least, decades.) It was not the agreement that vexed Sprague (it was, he notes, "entered into for mutual benefits in good faith"), but the irritating fact that EGE was torpidly allowing T-H to violate it. He cited with vexation the situation in Newark, where T-H, despite a high bid, was about to get a fat contract "which we want and want badly" and all because T-H made a secret guarantee. "I unhesitatingly assert," Sprague fulminates, "that T-H *is* not acting in good faith!"

He moves on to a second galling topic: the sluggish and indifferent eye that EGE is directing toward forthcoming rivalry from Westinghouse. "They will soon actively enter the railway field, and if we sit with our hands tied, we will soon see such a blow given our railway interests as the Edison illuminating business has received from the inroads of the AC system, my advice concerning which, some two or three years ago, having been quietly shelved."

The threat from Westinghouse, he concedes, will not materialize at once. So far it is a "blueprint campaign", for Mr. Westinghouse has not a single railway motor, and has quarreled with Mr. Tesla, who invented the a-c motor. What they are planning I cannot say, although I have taken steps to know what goes on."

VIII: THE METALLIC TASTE OF SUCCESS

Finally he recites his exasperations about Eickemeyer. In the face of forthcoming improvements to be made by their competitors, he has been urging the need to secure these patents. "I have reason to believe that no less than three other parties have been making strenuous efforts to secure them. I have temporarily blocked them but feel I cannot hold the position long." He feels strongly enough about it to invest in Eickemeyer himself if the company will not. As indeed he and Johnson plan to invest in a battery company and the Pratt electric elevator if the company continues to be indifferent to them.

The full reaction to this angry manifesto is unrecorded. One result is that Sprague does get a go-ahead to sign up Eickemeyer, which he promptly does. One other result can be conjectured: Edison, who is no longer the chief business officer of EGE but still highly influential in all its technical decisions, can hardly take kindly to Sprague's abrasive mention of the blunder of underestimating alternating current. Matters rock along for some weeks until, early in June, the final blow-up occurs. Sprague's formal letter of resignation is bitter:

> "A twentieth only of the street cars in the U.S. have been electrified; suburban and heavy train work is as yet undeveloped; the mining industry is almost untouched; and yet this organization, with its army of employees, its great facilities, its strong financial connections, and the prestige attaching to pioneer and successful

work, is apparently content to allow these larger problems to be solved by others.

"I have achieved something of a reputation, and my name is inseparably connected with railway work. I am too young in years, too jealous of professional reputation, too well trained by education, experience, and natural taste, and too capable of earnest work, to become a nonentity and to stand still while others advance to the front as active workers in electrical science."

For weeks after this resignation had been turned in, someone (possibly Villard) attempted to patch up matters. In the classic fate of peacemakers, he earned only a stinging left hook. In Sprague's papers there is a faded, barely legible draft of passionate letter of protest sent to the president and board of directors of EGE:

> "Working for the company has become intolerable. He finds most favor who is most abusive of all things Sprague. He meets with coolest reception who does him smallest reverence. The Edison fetish must be upheld. No Edison motor turns a wheel on any railway.
>
> "The Eickemeyer armature is forced upon the reluctant acceptance of the Edison company, and straightaway the railway world is notified that Mr. Edison has made a great improvement

VIII: THE METALLIC TASTE OF SUCCESS

in armature winding, the 'Edison-Eickemeyer armature'.

> "One thing is evident: my future connection with your company is neither desired nor desirable. I am in sympathy with neither its policy nor its personnel.

What brought about the final quarrel between Sprague and Edison? Sprague was notably laconic in subsequent references; Edison never detailed his side of it. But there was a sharp personal dispute early in June of 1890. It seems to have broken out over an Edison proposal to scrap the overhead trolley completely, perhaps on the grounds that T-H lawyers were brandishing the Van Depoele patents dangerously, and replace it with a pet idea of Edison's own. This was to feed current through the running rails, one positive and one negative. Problems of electrocuting pedestrians and horses, Edison seems to have theorized, would be avoided by using extremely low voltages, maybe 25 volts or so.

The proposal must have startled and infuriated Sprague. One can imagine him raising his high voice to ridicule a notion that had been proven impractical a decade before, that indeed betrayed an abysmal ignorance of basic principles of electric traction. It seems likely that at this point the dispute became angry and personal. For years after, Sprague's few references were thin-lipped: "the company had for a time attempted to introduce a retrograde idea that adversely affected its business."

There are evidences, however, of the depths of bitterness created. Sprague once noted acidly that most of his trained staff, experienced street car engineers, soon departed to work for progressive companies. But the most telling and hurtful rejoinder was Edison's, probably suggested by the sentence in Sprague's resignation about how "my name is inseparably connected with railway work". Edison ordered that the word "Sprague" should not appear on any equipment built by Edison G.E., and that it should be removed from all existing equipment that came back for repair or modification. This hurt Sprague in his pride, and like all blows to this area, was doubly galling because of the necessity of not admitting it.

An ironic twist to this angry episode, at least as far as Edison was concerned, came two years later. In the interval Edison General Electric had done only moderately well (the early 1890s were a time of depression), and although the books were in the black, the company had a large debt and a poor earnings ratio. Thomson-Houston, though a smaller company, had in contrast been driving along powerfully, making more money on less business and perennially alarming its competitors. The patent situation, moreover, was growing intolerable; each company owned court-tested patents that the other needed badly. Prodded by Morgan, Villard (then president of Edison G.E.) paid a number of highly secret calls in Lynn during the fall of 1891 to negotiate a merger. They came to nothing; Coffin and his astute backers saw no overall advantage for

VIII: THE METALLIC TASTE OF SUCCESS

themselves. Whereupon Morgan summoned Coffin. If he wasn't interested in selling out, would he instead be interested in buying EGE? He would indeed, and with Morgan acting as banker, the merger went through in the spring of 1892. It was from the newspapers that Edison learned that his name would be dropped by the new concern. It would simply be known as "The General Electric Company." Those who knew him well said that Edison took it hard. Years later his secretary wrote:

"Something had died in Edison's heart. His pride had been wounded. He had a deep- seated enduring pride in his name. And this name had been violated, torn from the title of the great industry created by his genius."

IX: THE VERTICAL RAILWAY

> *"Two years ago this company was doing its little work in a loft. Its present shop site was a cow pasture. Its work was looked upon as an experiment. Today it has a large number of the best office buildings yet projected under contract.*
>
> —*From a prospectus of the Sprague Electric Elevator Company*

What does an exceptionally energetic man do when he abruptly leaves the work that he has been vigorously pursuing all his adult career? Though Sprague now had the means for a relaxed and leisurely life, this was for him not possible at 32, and quite at variance with temperament and habit. (It always would be; even in his seventies he showed only a limited capacity for leisure.)

Does he, perhaps, toy with the idea of working for what had recently been a rival firm? Although Sprague could unquestionably have gone to either Thomson-Houston or Westinghouse, he did not consider it for a moment. Partly this was because he was much in the habit of thinking of them as "The Enemy"; and partly it was because he would then have had to work against his own designs and patents. Another factor was his realization that the great pioneering days were over for street cars, that from now on emphasis would be on product-improving, penny-paring development of a sort that held little charm for him. Nor did he have, from the earliest days with Edison at Menlo Park, any taste for working for others, in directions specified for him. Sprague's independence, though sometimes prickly, was not so much rooted in conceit as in a cool and realistic estimate of how he worked best. He'd discovered that he had an almost uncontrollably antagonistic attitude toward any challenger. Working for others demanded too much time and energy in fighting for his own ideas. Working as his own master, the same energy could be more profitably channeled to attacking technical obstacles.

Obviously the first thing to do was to seek out new fields in electricity. His mind turned toward military and naval weapons (Sprague never forgot that he was a trained naval officer), and he ordered several samples of a dynamite gun that the Navy was then dallying with. He also began to study the applications of electricity to training and elevating big naval guns. But in only a few days he realized he had to take a vacation to simmer down after the exasperations of the last eight months. On July 23 he sailed on the *Teutonic* for a summer's rest abroad.

On his return in the fall Sprague plunged energetically into three major enterprises. The first was to join with his friends Louis Duncan and Cary T. Hutchinson in forming a group of consulting engineers; they'd see if they could interest any mainline railroads in electrification, plainly a coming thing in electricity. A second activity was to proselytize, in repeated speeches and technical papers, for an idea that was buzzing in his bonnet: that New York City imperatively needed a four-track underground railway (this was before the word "subway" had won wide currency). The third enterprise was to join with Ed Johnson and Charles Pratt in forming a company to make and install electric elevators. They would rent a factory, Sprague announced, work the bugs out of the design that Pratt had patented but never managed to get running right, and they would build themselves a brand-new and profitable industry, and work hard, make a lot of money, and have a whale of a time. It turned out to be a completely accurate prediction.

To inventive minds, an elevator is a natural concept, and it is not surprising that various types of elevators were repeatedly invented during the first half of the 19th Century. Beginning as materials hoists in factories, they had achieved considerable mechanical sophistication by midcentury. Before the Civil War, a factory mechanic named Otis had invented an effective safety catch that automatically kept a car from crashing if its supporting cables went slack.

From the mid-nineteenth century on, passenger elevators began to appear in hotels and public buildings, most often worked by steam or hydraulic power. Because the elevator has always had a lure for original minds, there were also some wonderfully odd ones. In several, the passenger car was in effect a nut that travelled a giant vertical iron screw. And in one breathtakingly risky type, actually used in the 1870s, there was no other power than gravity. The car was simply over- or under-balanced by a counterweight that was, in effect, a giant bucket of water. Its operator merely manipulated remote valves until the load was unbalanced, released his brakes, and took off. The car was capable of dazzling speeds, virtually those of a free fall. In practice the operator had to be not only highly skillful but also fairly lucky.

The steam elevator came to its fullest development by the 1870s. In the basement, by the boilers, was the hoisting machine, a big iron drum geared to a two-cylinder steam engine. Cables ran from the car to sheaves at the top of the shaft and thence down to the basement where they wound up on the drum. A second set of cables supported a counterweight that was as heavy as the car and its average load; these cables also ran to the same drum, winding on in the opposite direction.

In practice, steam elevators proved to be moderately satisfactory but exceedingly expensive. At least one fireman/engineer had to be on duty in the basement at all times. Worse, the technology of the period did not permit the cable to be wound on top of itself on the drum, which meant that, to store enough cable for even a moderate rise, the drum had to be awkwardly large. A second drawback showed up in occasional fatal accidents. If anything went wrong with the controls during a rise, the car could be drawn violently up against the overhead sheaves. This could destroy a safety mechanism mounted on top of the car, rip the cable attachments out, and leave the car free to plummet to the basement.

Hydraulic elevators, developing along with steam ones, survived longer and achieved greater success. In their simplest form, of course, they resembled the greasing lifts in some gasoline stations today: a car directly supported by a piston. This worked fairly well, though it obviously required an excavation that extended as far below the basement as the maximum rise extended above. (Collapsible pistons were occasionally invented but won little favor.)

Direct piston hydraulic elevators did display a few eccentricities. One was that, on an abrupt stop after a fast rise, the car could over travel a foot or two and then drop back on the water column with a jolt solid enough to show the whites of its passengers' eyes. Another was that, in some early installations, the abrupt changes in water pressure when several cars ran in unison could make all the toilets in the building overflow. A third was that chronically leaky valves would endow elevators with a whimsical tendency to wander away up or down the shaft if left unattended.

By the late 1880s, nevertheless, the hydraulic elevator had been brought to a state of considerable efficiency. On high rises, the direct piston could not be used since it would have had to run too deep, and there would have been conflict between rigidity and excessive weight for the long piston. So designers went to a shorter piston, lying on its side in the basement. It moved the car indirectly; as the piston advanced or retracted, it drew or slackened cables that ran to the car. By rigging cables in a multiplying combination, as in a block and tackle, a comparatively small movement of the piston would effect a large movement of the car. In big installations, and where city water pressure was unreliable, it was the custom to fit special steam pumps and pressure tanks. Hydraulic elevators showed several advantages over steam ones: they were a little quieter, a little faster, and a little less expensive. By eliminating the big wind-on drum, they could manage higher rises. And because solid stops could be fitted to restrict the piston's travel, they were protected against those smash-into-the-sheaves accidents.

It was on this scene of complication, cost, and master mechanic engineering that Sprague and Pratt appeared in 1891. Actually, it wasn't an entirely new application for electricity. As early as 1880, the ordinarily practical and lucid Werner Siemens had built a demonstration electric elevator that rivaled the water bucket cars in conceptual lunacy. Under his car and carried along with it, Siemens mounted a primitive electric motor. It drove a worm gear that engaged a stationary rack on the side of the shaft. When all went well, the entire contraption, motor and all, clawed its way up the shaft, rather like a monkey shinning up a palm tree.

From the earliest trolley years, Sprague had been aware that a few of his stationary motors were being used to power primitive elevators. The very first was fitted to a freight elevator built in the Pemberton Mills at Lawrence, Massachusetts in 1884. A constant speed 10-horsepower Sprague motor ran continuously in one direction. Control was obtained by the belts-and-countershaft method then widely used for factory machines, the system that millwrights of the day called the use of "fast and loose" pulleys. (Students of the history of idiom will be interested to know that the first adjective didn't mean "rapid" but a pulley fixed to its shaft.) In the Pemberton Mills elevator the operator tugged on a control rope that shifted the motor-driven belt from a loose pulley to either of two fast ones that lifted or lowered the platform. Belt slippage was sufficient to soften acceleration. Although the rig was primitive, it was a practical, everyday electric elevator, the first in history. And it has a special appeal for technical historians: it was the first "regenerative" application ever recorded, one in which, with an unbalanced load, electricity was actually pumped back into the mains. The effect was trivial, though it doubtless had an appeal to the Yankee mill owner mind.

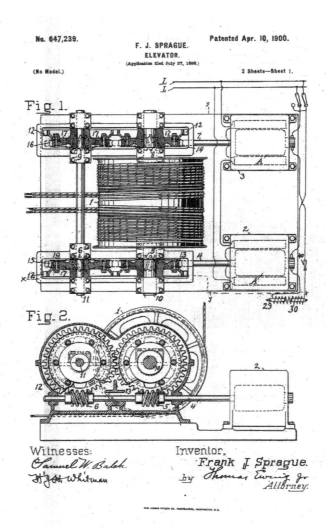

*Sprague Screw-type Electric Elevator Patent
(courtesy John L. Sprague)*

IX: THE VERTICAL RAILWAY

In 1889, when he was scouting for possible new fields for EGE, Sprague first met Charles R. Pratt, the man who was to be his partner in the elevator business. A graduate of M.I.T., Pratt was a mechanical engineer. He had been the assistant superintendent of a Boston sugar refinery and later an engineer for the Whittier and Otis elevator companies. Sprague had been intrigued by a patent that Pratt had just received for an elevator that would combine the best features of electrical and hydraulic operation. Pratt had made a demonstration installation in the Tremont House in Boston where, because he had little knowledge of electric motors, the machine failed to work well and was promptly taken out. As soon as EGE indicated that it wanted no part of this venture, Sprague introduced Pratt to Ed Johnson. By December 1891, the three men drew up an official agreement, although the Sprague Electric Elevator Company (SEEC) was not formed until the following year. Sprague and Johnson would provide initial capital, while Sprague would work on the electrical side and Pratt the mechanical side of developing the new machine. Pratt would get a temporary salary of $50 per week until the new firm got on its feet; and the Whittier Machine Company, the elevator firm that had been employing Pratt, would be mollified by being offered New England rights for selling the new machines. Both Sprague and Pratt seem to have been under the impression that the other had a rather prickly pride, so it was formally agreed that their product would be known commercially as "Sprague-Pratt Elevators".

Their plan was to develop and manufacture two different kinds of electric elevators. One would be for low-rise, moderate speed installations. It would be in essence an electrified version of the old steam elevator, with a reversible, speed-controllable motor driving a big iron hoisting drum. This would be suitable for everything from large dumb waiters to small passenger cars in moderate sized buildings.

The other kind, intended to give high-speed service in taller buildings, would be built around Pratt's patent. This was an eerie idea in the best elevator tradition: a kind of non-hydraulic hydraulic machine. In place of a big piston on its side in the basement, there was to be a large horizontal steel shaft there, threaded like a huge screw and gear driven by a powerful electric motor. On this screw was a big nut, or crosshead, that moved along the screw as it turned. Cable sheaves were attached to the crosshead, and cables were rigged in a multiplying fashion so that comparatively small travel by the crosshead delivered much larger movement by the car in the adjoining shaft.

The idea, though plagued by bugs in early versions, was not quite as eccentric as it seems to modern eyes. It was the first machine that could outperform the hydraulics in speed and height of rise, and that was cheaper to install and run. For twelve or fourteen years it remained the best "first class" elevator in the world. Then, some years after Sprague Electric Elevator Company was sold to Otis, the modern traction drive machine appeared to render obsolete all prior systems.

IX: THE VERTICAL RAILWAY

But this was to come later. First it was necessary for the hopeful little company to get a foothold in a business dominated by the lordly and well-established hydraulic companies. The first machine built was an experimental one installed in a shop that Sprague had leased on Twenty-Third Street in New York City. It gave a little trouble initially, but soon was running right, or seemed to be. So a contract was speedily signed to fit a similar machine in the Grand Hotel in New York. The contract wasn't a particularly big one, but the partners felt that it would be sure to draw valuable publicity.

But by the fall of 1891, when the Grand Hotel elevator first began running, it proved to be a dismal headache. The first trouble was the discovery that the slightly jerky control system that was perfectly satisfactory on trolley cars wasn't the least suitable for elevators. In a trolley nobody minded the gentle lurches when the motorman "notched up" his controller. But people standing apprehensively in a newfangled electric lift did not like vertical jouncing one bit. And anxiety aside, this jouncing did put an extra strain on the cables and sheaves.

To smooth out the starts, Sprague went to much more elaborate resistance grids in the controller. This eliminated the roughness. But then the new grids began burning out after very short life. The controller itself, a complicated mechanism in the basement operated by pilot motors, began acting up, its contacts burning and pitting frequently.

The troubles seemed to be those that would respond to patient analysis, though, and Sprague allowed the hotel to use the elevator to carry passengers. After only a few days of operation, a terrifying accident occurred at 11 a.m., 5 October 1891. The car was ascending normally that morning with six people aboard. When the operator tried to stop at an upper floor it abruptly changed direction and dropped, at twice normal speed, to crash against the basement bumpers.

As luck would have it, the machinery was being inspected, at that very moment, by a team of technical men. They were representatives of a large New York architectural firm that Sprague hoped would recommend the new elevator to its clients.

But, as matters turned out, the accident did more good than harm. No one in the car was injured. Careful investigation, in which the visiting inspectors were tactfully encouraged to participate, showed that the accident had resulted from a defect in the pilot motor that ran the reversing lever on the controller. It had slammed the big motor from full speed in one direction to full speed in the other. The shock had disarranged the safeties, sending the car to the basement. (One inspector's report explained that the incident proved the inherent safety of the new design: even when the controls went completely berserk, it didn't kill people.) In three days redesigned controls and safeties were installed and tested, and the elevator was back in service.

What gave Sprague and Pratt more worry was the way in which grids and contacts kept burning out; if

IX: THE VERTICAL RAILWAY

they couldn't make the machine run without a crew of electricians and spare parts in the basement, they had no chance to compete with the hydraulics. Weeks of day-and-night work by the whole crew (which was now straw-bossed by Pat O'Shaughnessy from the Richmond days) were spent in trying for reliability. Sprague worked himself almost to exhaustion, stopping for only a few hours rest in the daytime. He was painfully aware that the publicity they were counting on was a two-edged affair; if they didn't get reliability soon, and officially turn the elevator over to the hotel, they risked an awkwardly public failure.

A new controller was hastily built with much heavier contacts. A number of different grids were tried out and found wanting. Then on a hunch, Sprague suggested to Pratt (who had had foundry experience) that he might make up some experimental grids out of cast iron. Pratt demurred mildly since it was— in 1891—a highly unlikely idea, but then he assented and made up several sets. To the jubilation of the whole crew they worked fine and lasted indefinitely. (Cast-iron grids, in fact, soon came into almost universal use.) Within a month the elevator was officially turned over to the Grand Hotel and the partners went looking for new worlds to conquer.

All during the busy, slam-bang period of his career, Sprague troubled very little about what was the prudent thing to do. Musing about it later he denied that he had ever been rash; it was just that in any conflict between prudence and self-confidence, prudence always lost. Plainly the next thing to do was to seek out a modestly profitable contract for a slightly larger installation. Instead, with appalling self-confidence, Sprague mounted a campaign for the biggest and most exacting high-speed elevator installation in New York City. This was in the new Postal Telegraph Building about to go up on Broadway. It was to have two express and four local elevators, running at brisk speeds over a rise of fourteen stories. The Sprague-Pratt tender for this job brought hoots of derision from the hydraulic elevator interests. About the kindest comment from the competition was that "success is far beyond the possibility of electric mechanics." But when it came down to the time of decision, Sprague pulled out a trump card. After all, he argued, electricity had made the telegraph possible. Surely electricity should receive preference in running the elevators in so impressive a building that had been created by the telegraph.

The argument carried the day and Sprague Electric Elevator Company won the big contract. For stringency and one-sidedness, however, it was far worse than even the Richmond trolley contract five years before. It stipulated that the elevators were to equal or better first-class hydraulic ones in speed, capacity, safety, and ease of control. It further specified that they were to take less space and need less maintenance than hydraulics. Finally, they were to show operating costs no more than half the cost of equivalent hydraulics. Sprague blithely signed this contract on 8 October 1892, complete with a barbed penalty clause as its stinger: if his machines were not satisfactory in every respect, his company would tear them out and replace them with the best hydraulic machines, at no cost to the building's owners.

As installation got under way, difficulties began to pile up in customary fashion. Some arose from the fact that nothing like these elevators had ever been built before. (The single one in the Grand Hotel was far smaller and slower.) This meant that scores of parts had to be designed, built, tried out, redesigned, and tried out once more. A second set of difficulties, particularly worrisome in view of the economical operation that had been promised, arose from the large amount of parasitic friction inherent in the screw and travelling nut design. Sprague and Pratt went to the use of antifriction steel balls within the nut, and these gave endless trouble. One of the earliest memories of Sprague's son, Desmond, was being taken to see his father's work in the basement of the Postal Telegraph Building. His infant eye was delighted by the bright shiny balls that often dropped out of the machinery. But the five-year-old was alert enough to notice that nobody else was happy whenever the balls came tumbling down.

All during these months Sprague was tireless, inspired, and inventive. Sometimes it seemed as if he was almost eager for new difficulties to turn up so that he could attack them. It was a key to his personality that he was exhilarated by trouble and energized by hard work. For long stretches he went home only to catch a little sleep (his marriage had by this time deteriorated to a state of casual and abstracted civility on the few occasions when he and Mary met). Those on the crew who had been with Sprague in Richmond found themselves caught up in the same mood as in the old days. It was the mood established by a fearsomely energetic and hard-working boss, sharp-tongued and not to be crossed, who somehow managed to win loyalty rather than antagonism, and to inspire his crew to share his single minded concentration.

A natural byproduct of this mood was a kind of wild elation when matters went well. It was a time for celebration when some problem was licked or some part of the job completed. For the rest of his life Sprague remembered with a shiver one evening when this elation had nearly killed them all. They had just finished rigging the cables of the first express elevator. Its motor and controller were hooked up. The car ran up and down the shaft with exhilarating precision. On impulse Sprague ran the car down to the basement and called for the whole crew to join him. Everybody but one man climbed aboard, and then the car shot upward at a dizzy 400 feet a minute. Then, trying to stop, Sprague worked the control lever. Nothing happened; the contacts had apparently welded themselves together. Furiously working the handle, Sprague realized that they were facing disaster since the automatic limit switches and car safeties hadn't yet been installed. "There flashed a vision", he said later, "of heading into the overhead sheaves at 400 feet a minute, the snapping of the cables, and then a four-second, fourteen-story free drop, with a tangled mass of humanity and metal the object of a coroner's inspection".

But when the car had shot a few feet above the top floor, it suddenly and miraculously stopped. The one man left behind in the basement had chanced to be watching the hoisting mechanism. When he saw it run to the full limits of its travel, he suddenly, on an impulse he didn't fully understand, snatched open the master switch. It was an impulse that saved a dozen lives.

Sprague, needless to say, responded with characteristic rigor. Never, he formally enunciated, was either he or anyone else in the company ever to be allowed to ride a car until its full complement of safety circuits had been installed and tested. And that was an order.

The other memorable event during the building of the Postal Telegraph elevators was of a totally different sort, so inconspicuous as to be unremarked at the time. All six machines were in running condition and almost ready to turn over to the building as finished. Sprague was making final tests on the cars, and each of them went through its paces in docile and mannerly fashion. Looking back years later, Sprague decided that it must have been a Sunday, for there was no one else there to help him.

How, he wondered, would the cars behave if they all chanced to start up at once? Would the sudden demand for current open up a circuit breaker? There seemed no convenient way to check; he obviously couldn't ride in six cars at once. It dawned on him that it wouldn't be hard to rig a temporary circuit; he could wire a centralized control for the pilot motors, the little ones that moved the contacts in the big controllers. In less than an hour he had it hooked up. When he threw a switch in the basement, all six elevators started upward simultaneously. And as he had rather suspected would be the case, no circuit breaker opened. For a few minutes he amused himself by running the empty elevators in unison. Then they began getting out of step with each other, due to minor differences in motors and hoists, and he dismantled the hook-up. For several years the incident slipped from his memory; there was no reason to remember it.

By now the wayward and stubborn behavior of the Postal Telegraph elevators had disappeared. They worked beautifully. The building's architects inspected and approved them and the building committee for Postal Telegraph, after checking maintenance and operating costs, made final contract payments. Sprague received a letter from the architects that was almost ideal for testimonial use:

> "In recommending to the building committee of the Postal Telegraph Company that they would be perfectly safe in adopting the Sprague-Pratt electric elevator in preference to any other system, we expressed our opinion that these machines marked a radical departure in elevator practice, and that they would eventually prove as great an advance over the

hydraulic elevator as the hydraulic did over the steam elevator.

"In economy of space occupied, speed, ease of motion, safety, and cost of running, the building committee, as well as ourselves, are decidedly of the opinion that the results have far exceeded our expectations."

As testimonials went, Sprague could hardly have wanted better, especially in the way it casually relegated hydraulics to the past. The only trouble was that there were no prospects to show this shining praise to. The severe business depression of the Mid-1890s was in full swing, and no one could be found to engage the services of the proud little company.

The 1890s were diffuse, restless years for Sprague. Before then he had concentrated almost like a burning glass on one preoccupation at a time. In these years (as will be unfolded in the following chapter) he simultaneously juggled a number of enterprises at once. Electric elevators did not seem a major technical challenge after the Postal Telegraph installation. For months at a stretch he would pay little attention to the shop. Then, unexpectedly, an idea would pop into his mind. He would let everything else slide, spending immoderate hours at the drawing board and in the machine shop, work out and patent some new development and then move restlessly on to some other enterprise.

Many features of modern elevators were first worked out by Sprague in this curiously discontinuous fashion. Aside from the cast-iron grids and pilot motor control system, there was the self-centering operator's control that stopped the car if released (and that became known, to no one's delight, as the "dead-man's control"). Another invention was an automatic floor alignment system. And another was the first entirely automatic self-service elevator, complete with a set of door interlocks, automatic leveling, and a rudimentary electric "brain" to make decisions about the sequence of operations. About the only element in the modern elevator, in fact, that Sprague didn't invent was the traction drive now generally used; and it can be inferred that this was less because he was unaware of the defects in the screw-and-nut drive than the fact that its patents were Pratt's chief contribution to the business.

Certainly one factor in the restlessness of those years for Sprague was his growing recognition that his marriage was on the rocks. Despite periodic efforts on both sides, it was past smoothing over. Mary was sociable and gregarious; people were important to her. She wanted a life where she could entertain and be entertained, not one where her husband, abstracted and unpredictable, would wholly forget to show up for, say, a long-planned dinner party. And Sprague's position was that it was irrational to expect him to drop some excitingly difficult and important technical problem just to sit around and make small-talk with stupefying dull people.

In 1895 they faced up to the long-postponed decision, and Mary got a divorce. It was a curiously amiable one, or at least became amiable as soon as the decision was taken. There was no pulling and hauling over Desmond; he was ready for boarding school anyhow, and his vacations were informally divided. For decades Mary continued to depend on Sprague for counsel in the management of her affairs. Years later, when both of them had remarried and Mary went to Germany to live, she and her husband gave Sprague power of attorney to manage their American securities and property. The amiability proved far more durable than the marriage had. During the first World War, when Mary and her husband were barred from reentering the country (technically they were enemy aliens), Sprague hastened to Washington to persuade State Department officials to let him serve as sponsor for their readmission. Since he was at the time an eminent member of President Wilson's Navy Board, the travelers were promptly readmitted.

The lean and shaky years for the little elevator company lasted through 1894. Twice in the worst of the Depression, Sprague had to dip into his own pocket to keep the company from bankruptcy; and the stock that he received in repayment, though then largely worthless, was in a few years to add substantially to his personal fortune. For when business picked up for the company, it picked up fast. Total billings for 1894 amounted to only $10,000. But for the first six months of 1895 they rose to $325,000, and continued to climb thereafter at a steep rate.

Prosperity brought its troubles too. Sprague found himself involved deeply in the daily exasperations of business management. Pratt had even less taste or qualification for management than Sprague had, and Ed Johnson, who was in prosperous and relaxed semi-retirement, was unwilling to concern himself with daily operations. So it fell to Sprague to float new stock issues, to seek out and renew bank loans, to fret over expenses and payroll, and to make the endless decisions required by sudden expansion. The company had outgrown its Twenty-third Street loft, and in 1894 moved the manufacturing work to Watsessing, New Jersey, a half hour from New York city. Here it underwent a series of expansions until it became a full-scale industrial operation, complete with smoking chimneys, eight hundred and fifty employees, and—when the wind was wrong—the source of a peculiar smell in nearby Bloomfield, New Jersey. (The odor came from a building where a patent insulation, a mixture of asphalt and other compounds, was brewed in large vats into which cables were dipped. Local comment had it that the "elevator plant sometimes smelled like spontaneous combustion in an old suit of painter's overalls.")

Although the elevator company occupied the largest part of the factory, it was also home for a fascinating array of other Sprague-Johnson enterprises. One was a profitable cable and insulation business, a principal supplier to powerhouses and substations in the country. It also made something new but promising: a flexible metal conduit having spirally wound armor around it. In another corner of the plant was a tidy little shop that manufactured special service motors and generators of a sort that couldn't be obtained from big companies like Westinghouse and General Electric. And in still another nook at Watsessing was a curious but profitable little company devoted to something that echoed the years at Annapolis: it made patented automatic watertight doors for shipboard use.

As his enterprises proliferated, Sprague began to experience the classic problems of an industrialist. One was cash-on-hand; he constantly found himself theoretically prospering but hard put to meet his bills and payroll. Another was labor trouble. The first serious strike, not directed at the company but at a building where elevators were being installed, had the effect of upsetting his carefully planned bank credit timetable. No sooner was this settled when a second strike was called, this one at the plant and that shut down operations for six weeks. He showed himself to be a firm but calm and unemotional negotiator, finally settling on almost precisely the terms he had originally offered. This fact, plus some odd coincidences in the timing of the strikes, led him to the perhaps faintly paranoid belief that "the strike was fomented by certain hydraulic elevator interests". And yet this was perhaps not a delusion of persecution, for the electric elevator business was growing to a size that created a rough struggle for survival between the two types of machines.

Still another crisis arose when the company treasurer decamped without warning to Europe, leaving behind an incoherent note of farewell on his desk. So far as could be determined, he had taken no assets with him, but the company books were discovered to be in such chaos as to raise the question whether they could ever be straightened out. Sprague persuaded his younger brother, Charley, then assistant treasurer of a North Adams firm and an experienced accountant, to quit his job and come help unravel the tangle. Charley, always highly responsive to his elder brother, arrived and plunged in. He later became treasurer and a director of the elevator company.

But even after Charley had the books restored to order, and later hired a high-priced accounting expert to install a new system of dazzling complexity, Sprague never felt really satisfied with the books. (His irritation with the conventions of accounting was perhaps a reflection of a subconscious annoyance with the entire business world.) No engineer or mathematician worth his salt, Sprague declaimed, should put up with what businessmen seemed to accept as a matter of course. Who could rationally be content with cost figures that were so murky and slippery that pricing a product had to be an intuitive decision? What on earth was the use of trial balances and statements that were weeks out of date by the time the accountants could be persuaded to release them? It grew to be almost a mathematical recreation with Sprague to invent improved accounting systems. In time Charley and his associates learned to listen civilly and do nothing whatever when Sprague would excitedly propose a revolutionary new accounting system.

IX: THE VERTICAL RAILWAY

The pleasures and excitements of being a large scale industrialist were largely lost on Sprague. One distraction was his feeling that new things were coming in the world of electricity that were far more absorbing to him than factory management. So in the fall of 1898, when an exceptionally attractive offer for the business came from the Otis Elevator Company, he accepted with only a little hesitation. In October 1898 the firm was sold for more than $1,000,000, plus royalty rights to two-thirds of all foreign business, plus rights to lease back the plant and equipment at a nominal rental for five more years.

Sprague accepted cheerfully, not just because everyone agreed that it was a liberal offer, but also because he was by then deeply involved in something far more exciting to him than the vertical railway had ever been.

X: AN IDEA IN SEARCH OF A RAILROAD

"As regards the system of train propulsion, as distinct from the locomotive system ordinarily employed for moving trains, I feel confident that the very radical departure Mr. Sprague has made will be found to be the true solution of electric-train propulsion."

—*sentence buried in a long technical report on a new Sprague patent*

Anyone assessing Sprague's career in June 1895 would have been struck by its strong Horatio Alger overtones. It might, in fact, have seemed almost improbably pat: the poor boy who had had to make his own way from early years, the serious but confident young inventor who had resolutely gambled against long odds and won, the brilliantly successful engineer who by his thirties had built two new industries and an impressive personal fortune.

And yet to a shrewd and informed observer in 1895 who probed beneath the surface, the career wouldn't have been all glitter. He had been forced out of a business he had founded and loved. A marriage had not survived a head-on collision with his career. His elevator company was drowning him in a sea of business cares for which he had little real aptitude. And most frustrating of all, he had gotten almost nowhere in establishing his cherished belief that electricity's greatest future lay in powering railroad trains. (To make the last matter doubly galling, there was a feeling in the air in 1895 that other people, not Sprague, would soon be the innovators in this field.)

Sprague's obsession with the possibilities of electricity on rails had been recurring for more than a dozen years. It dated from the time when, as a wide-eyed young ensign at the Crystal Palace Exhibition, he'd ridden the London underground and had a coughing spell when the locomotive's smoke had billowed in. It seemed to him now that the biggest opportunities for electricity lay in urban rapid transit, particularly as a way of getting rid of those obnoxious cinderspraying locomotives which ran on the elevated railroads. Beginning in 1890, right after his departure from Edison- GE, Sprague lay siege to the elevateds. He discovered that these lines had intensely conservative management, and Jay Gould—the man who had panicked in public on a Sprague test car—was deaf to anything Sprague proposed. Sometimes it seemed that the door was so firmly closed that a better avenue might be to tackle the great main-line railroads themselves. For seven years Sprague worked energetically to arouse interest in either field.

Partly he worked as a propagandist. In 1890, he delivered a paper advocating a four-track underground electric railway as the only logical solution to New York's choking congestion. (This was before the word "subway", or its concept, had won any currency.) In 1891 he tried another tack. He offered in the pages of the New York Post to install two electric trains, one locomotive-drawn and one with motors under the cars, on the Manhattan Elevated. He offered to build them at his own expense, and to electrify a test section of track, with no recompense at all unless the equipment did everything he predicted. A deafening silence from Gould and his directors greeted this offer.

A month later he delivered another rapid-transit paper at the Electric Club. In May 1891, he read another one to the American Institute of Electrical Engineers. Later that month he repeated and amplified his offer to electrify part of one elevated at his own risk. And the following year, in his inaugural address as president of the AIEE, came still another elaborate paper, this one optimistically titled "Coming Development of Electric Railways."

The total lack of response that his one-man campaign won from elevated managements didn't discourage Sprague. At least he kept returning to the fray, repeating in 1895 and 1896 his offer to electrify test sections of the elevateds.

His approaches to the main-line railroads were scarcely more successful. Twice, though, there had been flurries of excitement. At the close of 1891 he received a visit from, of all people, Henry Villard, the president of Edison-GE. But it was not in this capacity that the financier looked up Sprague. Far from it, since Villard was soon to join Sprague, Johnson, Insull, and indeed Edison himself in the large body of disgruntled graduates from Edison-GE. The merger with Thomson-Houston had just gone through; and Pierpont Morgan had "suggested" to Villard that Charles A. Coffin, T-H's hard-driving boss, would be his preference as chief executive officer of General Electric. (Coffin, incidentally, was to remain a grey eminence of GE until as late as 1922.) So Villard, who had not enjoyed his period as president of Edison-GE, was cheerfully returning to his earlier love, the Northern Pacific Railroad.

Villard was one of the most extraordinary men that Sprague had met. Born of a distinguished German family, he had at eighteen quarreled with his strict father, run away to America, taught himself English, law, and journalism, and became successively: a correspondent for German newspapers, a reporter and war correspondent in English, a personal friend of Lincoln's, and the star reporter for first James Gordon Bennett's *New York Herald* and then Horace Greeley's *New-York Tribune*. Perceptive and luminously intelligent, Villard succeeded at almost everything he put his hand to. In the

Seventies, after careers of distinction in social work and civil service reform, he turned to business and finance. Soon he gained control of several strategic steamship and railroad lines in Oregon. By the Eighties he was a wealthy and powerful financier, head of the Northern Pacific and a casual patron (to the tune of $40,000) of Edison's first electric locomotive at Menlo Park.

During the turmoil of the last year at Edison-GE, Villard had watched the development of the Sprague-Edison conflict and several times intervened to smooth matters over. Now, in this visit of December 1891, he wanted to renew his acquaintance with the young inventor who had resigned in such a flurry. He recalled hearing Mr. Sprague predict that electricity was *the* coming motive power for railroads. This was something that the Northern Pacific should know more about. Would he care to design and supervise the construction of an experimental locomotive to put his theories to the proof?

The question was like asking a cat if it would care for catnip. Sprague elatedly explained that it was for just such a chance as this that the consulting firm of Sprague, Duncan, & Hutchinson had been formed. A contract was quickly signed with the North American Company, a Villard subsidiary. On Sprague's drawing board there soon appeared plans for an electric locomotive of awesome proportions. It would weigh sixty tons, and its eight driving wheels would be powered by four huge gearless motors built concentrically about the axles. They would be capable of an unprecedented

1000 horsepower. (In 1892, when fifteen horsepower was felt to be lavish for a trolley car, this total was almost unthinkable.)

Sprague took the plans himself to Villard in Chicago, his sharpened pencil enthusiastically pointing out all the advanced features that this monster would have. But it was a gloomy visit; the old financier did not in his usual way respond to enthusiasm with enthusiasm. Things were not going well, he confided, with the Northern Pacific. The depression was deepening; earnings were off and money tight; electrification of even one division of the railroad would take unthinkable expenditure. It was not even certain that he could retain control of the railroad. Nevertheless, Villard went on quietly, he would stick by his word to Mr. Sprague: the marvelous locomotive would be built. But it should be clear in advance that, until the depression passed, nothing further could be expected.

Under these disheartening conditions, Sprague watched over the construction of the biggest electric locomotive in the world. (Still smarting over the past, he ordered the special motors from Westinghouse rather than from GE.) For the monster's trials a short stretch of track outside Chicago was temporarily electrified. After a few weeks of teething troubles and adjustment, the sixty-ton locomotive performed well, passing every test and displaying a fine ability to snatch up a string of loaded freights. But Villard's pessimistic warning was borne out, and the monster never had a chance to enter service. For months it lay idle on a siding. In

1893 Villard lost control of the railroad and was forced to retire. The new management was unsympathetic and the locomotive was soon dismantled, its parts sold for scrap. It was a bitter disappointment for Sprague.

But adversity, as so regularly happened with Sprague, proved to have its uses. Two years later he found he could draw heavily on this experience when he won a chance to help design the first mainline electrification in America. This was disappointingly short, just three miles, but it was still big-time railroading. The job was on a tunnel district of the Baltimore & Ohio, a stretch where the smoke-belching steam locomotives had proved unsatisfactory and even dangerous.

Sprague's locomotives went into service in 1895, bustling capably to and fro on their little three-mile trips. They were similar to but bigger than the Villard locomotive: ninety-six ton eight-wheelers each driven by four motors totaling 1,440 horsepower. They drew power from an overhead conductor via a pantograph. This time they used motors and control equipment built by General Electric; the old resentment had cooled against the company, since it was no longer a place where Edison's voice could be heard.

For all its technical success, this little electrification seemed to Sprague a thin embodiment of his dream for electric transportation. It wasn't for speed, smoothness, efficiency, and silence that the locomotives rolled through the tunnel district, but simply because they did not make clouds of smoke. Electricity, he knew, could be better than that.

It is necessary at this point to be slightly technical. Readers whose eyes glaze at the very thought are encouraged, nevertheless, to persevere bravely; it will all be over in a moment and won't hurt a bit. For the details are basic to an understanding of what would prove to be Sprague's greatest and most influential invention. The husky direct-current motors then in use on trolleys, elevators, and locomotives could not be turned off and on at the flick of a small switch. For one thing, it was often necessary to reverse them. Electrically this called for changing the relationship of connections inside. Practically, it was done by leading heavy wires out to a special switch that made one set of connections for forward running, and a different set for reversing. But directional control was the least of it; speed control brought far greater complications.

It is a deplorable trait of electric motors that—when starting under load, they are gluttons for current. If given all they'd take, they'd gulp too much and promptly burn themselves out. But it is a temporary habit, for once they are spinning briskly, this appetite for amperes falls off. A related difficulty arises from the fact that an ideal traction motor is expected to display different characteristics at different times. When starting it should be slow-turning but very powerful; once the vehicle has accelerated, it needs less torque but much more speed.

By the 1890s the problem was not theoretically difficult, though its solution was physically cumbersome. If a motor tried to draw too much current while starting, you simply added circuitry that fed it—at first—only what it could safely have, usually in a series of steps. One way to do this was to connect electrical resistances, or grids, to the controller, rigging it so that each notch of the speed control handle cut out part of the resistance, letting more current flow.

More sophisticated ways of doing the same thing were also in use. Motors were often built with several separate field windings on them, and the leads to them brought out to the controller. There they might be rigged in a special switching arrangement. This would connect them in series, strung together like older Christmas tree lights, for starting purposes; and then reconnect them in parallel, independently wired to the power supply for high-speed running. This gave both increased power at starting and higher speed at the other end. More complicated variations were often tried. On trolley cars, for example, the controller usually connected the field windings of two motors together in series at the start, later switching them to parallel for fast running.

All this was familiar and basic to Sprague. It was, in fact, one of the many areas in which he had pioneered. Back in 1880 at the Newport Torpedo Station, when Professor Farmer had given the young ensign the freedom of the shops to build any experimental machine he liked, it was a series-parallel dynamo that he chose first from the ideas in his notebook the first series-parallel machine in American technical history. In 1887, during the Richmond days Sprague had been granted basic patents on series-parallel motor control, patents acquired in the take-over by GE and now very lucrative.

The two basic methods of speed control were often ingeniously combined. When a motorman started a trolley, for instance, he moved the brass controller handle to the first notch. This connected the windings in series and fed current cut down by all steps of the resistance grid. Each of the next three (say) notches of the handle would eliminate part of the resistance. When it was all gone, the next notch would switch the windings from series to parallel and put the full resistance back in the circuit. Then the remaining notches would progressively drop resistances until the car was at full speed.

The system grew so familiar that the limitations it imposed were largely overlooked. Bulky grids and controllers were needed to govern the motors. Scores of heavy copper wires linked the parts of the system. On elevators the rig differed from that in trolleys. Partly this was because the grids had to be more elaborate to eliminate anxious-making jerkiness. And partly it was because it wasn't practical to put the controller in the elevator itself; too many heavy wires would have had to run too long a distance. So Sprague simply put the controller close to its big motor. Then he provided a little pilot motor on the controller, giving it the job of moving the controls in response to the position of the operator's handle in the elevator.

Any electrical engineer asked to link a string of trolleys or railroad cars so they could all be run from the front end would, in 1895, have thrown up his hands at the complete impracticality of the notion. Why, he'd need thousands of dollars' worth of heavy copper wire, and there'd be a rat's nest of cables at each coupling, and the voltage drop and losses in the system would be intolerable, and the motors certainly wouldn't run right in such a crazy hook-up.

Ironically, Sprague himself once gently scoffed at the idea. In 1890, a student at Cornell had written him: why wouldn't it be practical to run a train of cars, each with its own motors, from a single point? "The chief objection," Sprague wrote back, "is that trouble in one motor will interfere with the others. Connection would be exceedingly complicated, and the art has not progressed to a state that any trouble whatsoever will not interfere with everything."

If years later Sprague ever saw that carbon in his files, he must have smiled wryly. It was the worst opinion he was ever to deliver, and he would spend much energy and skill in proving it so.

In June of 1895, Sprague wasn't consciously thinking of motor control at all. It was a depressing year for him: the time of his divorce, the time when the elevator company faced endless problems of expansion, strikes, and insufficient capital. Worse, the campaign he had so energetically waged to interest the elevated railways in electricity was showing signs of succeeding at last, but without Sprague. Two years before, at the World's Fair, GE had made an impression with a showy elevated locomotive. Now in 1895 the first break came when the big Metropolitan Elevated in Chicago was electrified, using GE locomotives.

Sprague expected that he would at least be hired as a consultant on this or several other electrifications under study, but nothing developed. Jay Gould had died three years before, and there was probably little or no animus directed at Sprague by elevated managements. Perhaps it was just a question of the wisdom of inviting in a strong-minded zealot, a man whose plant could only manufacture passenger elevators. Why not deal directly with firms like GE or Westinghouse, who had plenty of engineers on tap?

After advocating railroad electrification so long, Sprague had curiously mixed feelings when it began to come. It was plainly a step forward. Soot and cinders would be eliminated. There'd be economies in having one or two big powerhouses in place of dozens of poorly tended little boilers up and down the tracks. And electric motors, unlike steam engines, used energy only when they were working.

But to his analytical mind, the substitution of one kind of locomotive for another didn't promise as much gain as it should. On the elevateds, steam locomotives were unsatisfactory for other reasons than dirtiness and cost. They simply weren't very powerful, being able to draw only three or four cars with distinctly sluggish acceleration. The trouble was that a more capable locomotive would be too heavy, too concentrated a load for the elevated structure. The problem wasn't any inherent limitation in the power of a steam cylinder or an electric motor; it was just that a locomotive's drawbar pull was a function of the weight it put on its drivers. Because a locomotive couldn't pull more unless it weighed more, and because the structure couldn't tolerate heavier engines, the chances that electrification could improve service seemed very slight.

Suddenly Sprague's mind flashed back to that time in the basement of the Postal Telegraph Building when he had wired six elevators together to test simultaneous operation. His next idea, perhaps the sharpest and most profitable of his life, was to do away with the heavy and inefficient locomotive completely. He would make each car in an elevated train self-propelled. Couplings between cars would no longer tow them, but would just tie the train together, correcting for minor differences in motor efficiency or load.

He wouldn't even try to string the intricate control circuitry for each motor along the train. Instead, each car would be a self-contained unit, complete with its own controller. Then he'd add a small, separate master control, just as in the elevators, with pilot motors to move each main controller in unison. It would be like having an automatic motorman in each car, compelled to copy slavishly what the real motorman did in front.

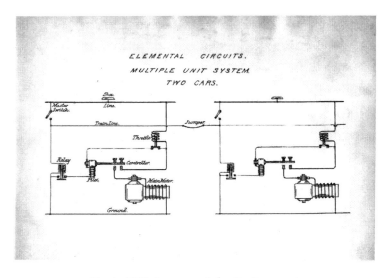

Basic MU (courtesy John L. Sprague)

Quickly Sprague roughed out the circuitry for his multiple-unit control system (the term was descriptive but not idiomatic, and subsequent generations of electrical engineers and railroad men have all called it "MU"). He dispatched a sheaf of caveats to the Patent Office. At Watsessing he hurriedly assembled a test rig, at first three and then five big elevator motors set up in a gallery of the main plant. Each had its own controller nearby; each pilot motor was linked to a central control station. Soon the rig was working promisingly, although occasionally one unit would perversely drop out of step with its brothers. (It didn't seem to be a serious problem, and theoretically it wasn't. But it took months of design and redesign and circuit modification to create a controller-of-controllers that invariably kept the big motors precisely in step. Sprague knew that it was not enough to create an arrangement that worked under ideal circumstances. He kept rebuilding and improving the circuits and switches to achieve maximum reliability in the harsher conditions of rail use, and to make a hook-up that wouldn't be disabled by failure of individual parts.)

The more Sprague pondered MU, the more exciting it seemed for elevated and subway trains. To begin with, there were all the basic advantages of electricity over steam. Then MU completely eliminated the heavy, structure-racking locomotive. Every single wheel on the entire train could be powered, which meant that the total weight of the train and its load was available for traction without wheel-spinning. Which meant, in turn, that the train would start up far faster than a locomotive-drawn one could possibly. Simple calculation showed that on frequent stop service, faster acceleration brought big gains in running time and in reduced headroom between trains.

There were also more subtle benefits. Speed would not vary with the size of the train, as it had up to now. In the rush hour, a ten-car train could pull out of a station just as briskly as a two-car one could. And there was a fine new flexibility in train make-up. No expensive turn-around loops or wye tracks were needed. As the rush hour approached, they'd just couple together the number of cars needed for each train, without regard to the direction they were pointed in or their sequence, and set off to provide really efficient mass transportation.

It seemed to Frank Sprague, that June of 1895, as if the MU concept was an uncommonly promising one. So indeed it proved to be in the years ahead. It greatly multiplied the passenger-carrying capacity of the elevated lines; it was the essential invention that made subways possible; and it became basic on the high-traffic passenger railroads. Every weekday for more than a century it has provided transportation for many millions of people. And it was to make Sprague a really wealthy man.

Before any of these things came to pass, Sprague had to fight battles, and take risks, scarcely less hair-raising than those in Richmond a decade before.

One year after his first MU idea, Sprague felt he was ready for a full-scale demonstration. The big motors in the north gallery of the Watsessing shops were hooked up with his best control system. They could start, run slowly or fast, stop, and reverse in exact unison at the command of the pilot controller. They never fell out of step now, and trouble at one spot rarely disabled the whole system. Several well-regarded experts had been invited to study the idea and file reports. (The verdicts were all favorable, although in the manner of expert reports, they were also cautious, obscure, and liberally fitted with escape hatches.)

With this armament in hand, and confident that the ghost of Jay Gould had been laid to rest, Sprague made a carefully planned approach to the officers of the Manhattan Railroad Company. This was no flamboyant newspaper challenge but a temperate, several times rewritten letter dated 6 June 1896. He respectfully requested permission to make a trial on the Ninth Avenue line in New York. It would involve an absolute minimum of disruption of regular steam service in daytime hours. His company would assume all costs, and it would be a real test. He would electrify enough double track and switches so as to permit the most searching test possible. Five cars would be electrically equipped with motors having the capacity to handle the cars at express speeds. Each of the cars would have a special new control that allowed operation from either end, or from the end of a train composed of from one to five cars.

His answer was a dismaying no.

This stony disinterest in something that could improve service and increase profits was baffling to Sprague. It seemed completely irrational. The response has been ingeniously explained by Harold C. Passer, writing in a series of corporate histories for the Harvard Business School. What Sprague was up against, Passer theorized, was the almost instinctive reluctance of the managers of an existing business to make radical changes in it. Although the concept of progress is appealing to most owners and managers, they also feel a strong resistance to change from a familiar and comfortable way of doing things. A going concern typically stops short of anything beyond relatively slight change. Big changes almost always come from new companies, or new managements of bankrupt ones. For these are men with no stake in maintaining the familiar.

As inventors after Sprague would observe, the famous line could often be rewritten to read: "Progress is our most important slogan."

XI: THE CANAL BANK AND THE ALLEY L; SUCCESS FOR MU; THE TRIUMPH OF MU

Then you came to Chicago, and the story was that you had no shop, no organization, no installers just a toothbrush and an idea. But ye gods, what an idea!

—B.E. Sunny

Certain patterns recurred curiously during the crises in Sprague's life. At Richmond he had committed himself to a stringent contract with few plans and no equipment and had been disabled by serious illness at the worst possible time. During and just after the exhausting fight to save his company from absorption in the fall of 1889, a severe attack of the grippe had put him in bed for weeks. During the critical Postal

Telegraph gamble his health had stood up under the strain, but again he willingly accepted tremendous pressure from a harshly one-sided contract as a means of demonstrating something he passionately believed in.

Early in 1897, these same patterns began slowly to form again. On 18 February, Sprague made still another earnest proposal to the Manhattan Railroad for a chance to demonstrate electrification at his own expense. It got no answer. He then resolved to shelve MU. The booming elevator business with its turmoil of expansion, strikes, and chronic need for short-term loans demanded his full attention. Checking on an elevator installation in New York's Waldorf-Astoria Hotel, Sprague absently stepped backward from a scaffold and fell to the basement, breaking both legs. He couldn't possibly be out of the casts, the doctors told him, in time for his scheduled sailing for London early in April. But this was to be no pleasure trip, and Sprague flatly refused to cancel it.

The trip seemed vital to him because it was a chance to win the contract for the biggest elevator installation in the world. This was for the Central London Railway, then boring a deep new tube line that ran from the Bank of England to *Shepard's Bush*. No less than forty-nine large high-rise elevators were to be built. Winning the contract would be a glorious feather in the cap of the Sprague Electric Elevator Company, and a conclusive defeat for the hydraulic machines. From his hospital bed Sprague mapped out details of his campaign for the contract. He'd arrive in London with full preliminary blueprints for the job. But he'd also bring along his fastest draftsman, just in case some unexpected modification came up. He'd also ship over a number of his fanciest elevator motors, controllers, and car safeties; and he'd bring along an expert installer from the Watsessing plant. Together they'd set up a demonstration in London that would pop the eyes of those Britishers. Shrewdly he foresaw that local representation might be a help, and he engaged Sir William Moir, then of the consulting firm of E. Parson & Sons, to provide guidance and counsel.

At the end of March, when Sprague was making his first trials at walking by crutch, a distraction arose. A letter arrived from Leslie Carter, president of the South Side Elevated Railway in Chicago. Mr. Carter had heard engineers speak well of Mr. Sprague's ability; how much would he charge to provide certain small consulting services?

Sprague had, he confessed later, never even heard of the South Side. He hastily made inquiries. It was a large elevated system, steam-powered, known in Chicago as the "Alley L". But it had been carelessly run, foundered under rising costs, and gone bankrupt. Carter was the new boss for the receivers. The gossip was that he was planning to electrify, using GE locomotive-cars drawing several trailers. (A locomotive-car was an engine with space for carrying some passengers; and it was a compromise that lessened, but didn't eliminate, the drawbacks of a locomotive.) If the rumor was right that

GE had the inside track on the job, there seemed little chance for MU. So Sprague tried to stall the engagement. "For immediate consultation I quoted a fee that would eliminate me, because I had to get to London."

But the distraction continued. An old friend dropped in to see Sprague: William J. Clark, now an engineering salesman for GE and head of the railway department. He confirmed that the South Side was preparing plans to electrify, very possibly with GE-powered locomotive-cars. But nothing was firm yet; Carter wouldn't award contracts for a week or two. Clark and his assistant, a bright young engineer named Frank Shepard, turned out to be very interested in the MU idea they'd heard about. It was true that GE wanted and expected to get the South Side business. And yet if they should not, how fine it would be if the job should fall to Sprague. Shepard had already pointed out, Clark added amiably, that MU would call for many more motors and controllers than locomotive-cars would, equipment that GE would be happy to subcontract for Sprague.

In the next two days another old friend named Fred Sargent made a flying trip from Chicago to see Sprague. He was presently a partner in the engineering firm of Sargent and Lundy, chief consultants to Carter for the Alley L's electrification. It was they who had talked up Sprague to Carter. Why on earth was their old friend unwilling to check their plans for the Alley L's new powerhouses? In particular, to pass on the unconventional new steam condensers they planned to try.

It was very simple, Sprague explained. He was sailing in a few days to try for the biggest elevator installation in the world. Maybe it would be possible after he returned. Besides, Sargent knew more about steam condensers than he ever had. But Sargent was persistent. Why not put off the sailing for just a little. It would only take a couple of days, a week at the outside. After all, they were very radical air-cooled condensers. He and Lundy would feel a lot easier if he'd check their prints and calculations. The word "radical" helped to hook Sprague. He postponed his sailing for a week, wiring Carter that he'd be pleased to be a temporary consultant at his standard fee.

A week later Sprague dictated his report: the new powerhouse condensers appeared to be satisfactory as designed. It was a week that changed Sprague's life, because during it Fred Sargent had discovered Sprague's MU work. He was so impressed that he wired his partner to come at once to New York, bringing along all existing prints on the forthcoming Alley L electrification.

Lundy, like Clark and Sergant, was another old friend of Sprague's. The tie was closer in his case, since he had worked for Sprague in the wild and exhausting months in Richmond a decade before. Not that a contract for something as important as the electrification of an elevated line would be decided simply on the basis of past friendship. All that friendship and professional respect meant was that unconventional proposals would be coolly evaluated and not rejected out of hand. Sargent and Lundy studied Sprague's patents and circuit drawings. They examined the elevator motor mock-up at the Watsessing factory, and made some projections of what MU might promise on the Alley L in terms of costs and schedule times.

Then they gave Sprague their verdict. If he made a formal tender to Carter for the whole South Side job, they would support it, because on paper MU plainly promised remarkable benefits. But Sprague should of course realize that nothing could be guaranteed. The decision was Carter's alone. And the competition would be rough. Besides GE two other manufacturers were competing for the job on a locomotive-car basis. And Sprague would certainly have to give up his London trip until the matter was decided.

Sprague, excited, distracted, and still hobbling on crutches, pondered his decision for a day. He simply had to go to London; the *Shepard's Bush* Elevator contract was too important not to be fought for with every resource he could bring to bear. And yet a chance, however remote, to install MU on a big-city elevated line was exhilarating just to think about. At any other time than now he would work very hard to make this Carter, a shrewd Scotsman according to Lundy, realize the folly of sticking to the locomotive idea.

Characteristically, Sprague resolved his dilemma with arithmetic. He studied the schedule for the *Shepard's Bush* bids. If he sent an advance party, cabled full instructions to Sir William, and resolved to be satisfied with arriving at the last possible minute, he could postpone his sailing until 29 April. This would give him precisely twenty-three days to unsell Carter and his South Side directors on their existing plans, and to swing them over to Sprague-installed MU control. It was not necessary to decide which of the two contracts was better; he would go after both. They were to be twenty-three of the most flurried days of Sprague's life, crammed with telegrams, attacks, defenses, counterattacks, a frantic trip to Chicago, and a fine cliff-hanging climax. In outline, the drive went this way.

On 7 April, writing formally as a consultant for the line, Sprague recommended to Carter that locomotives be abandoned in favor of self-propelled cars under MU control. He outlined at length the benefits to be expected in higher speeds, greater capacity, reduced costs, and improved earnings.

Waiting for this letter to arrive, Sprague discovered that a South Side director was passing through New York. He looked him up and worked him over hard. One result of this was to provide a giggle years later when emotions cooled. B. E. Sunny, the G.E. district manager in Chicago, recalled that he had dropped in on the South Side's general manager, a Mr. Hopkins, to pick up the signed contracts for the locomotives. But there was no contract, and Hopkins was annoyed at the directors. As he heard it—Hopkins said— one of the line's directors had been accosted in New York by some fellow with a military title. This fellow had just equipped a hotel with a dumb waiter that delivered cocktails to upper floors, and he wanted to use the same principles in electrifying the South Side Railroad. Both Hopkins and Sunny found this hilarious, a perfect example of the natural wrongheadedness of company directors. When several days later Sunny found out that the fellow with the military title was Lieut. Frank Sprague, the engineer who had perfected trolley cars and electric elevators, the hilarity disappeared at once for the GE man.

Meantime the Sprague proposal was stirring up controversy in the South Side offices. Sargent and Lundy came out strongly in favor of it. Representatives of other bidders mounted an attack. Did Mr. Carter realize that MU was just a theory, an idea that had never been tried out on rails? Or that locomotive cars were thoroughly tested, with thousands of miles of successful operation behind them? That this Sprague had no suitable plant or manufacturing facilities, and no crew of experienced equipment installers? And that at least one of the other bidders was prepared to increase his guaranteed schedule speeds for locomotive trains to 18 m.p.h. as opposed to Sprague's 15 m.p.h.?

Sprague bounced back fighting. He resigned as consultant and made a formal personal tender for the electrification of one hundred and twenty cars. He dismissed the higher speed promised by a competitor as technically unfeasible, pointing out that this promise had come from a "commercial agent" rather than from an engineer of world repute whom the company had employed as a technical consultant. He implied, but did not quite state, the haughty opinion that laymen who engaged professional advisers should logically abide by their advice in technical matters. As the issue turned increasingly to engineering, the traffic in long telegrams between New York and Chicago began to pile up. So Sprague leased a private wire and a pair of Western Union's fastest operators. Then he invited Carter and his engineers to go to a Chicago telegraph office for a conference by telegram. For one whole day the wire hummed with an abstruse discussion of whether MU would really work.

As time began to run out, Carter summoned Sprague to Chicago for a confrontation with the South Side's board. What guarantees could he offer, they asked bluntly, that his claims for this untried system were warranted. It was the kind of question that Sprague always fielded with great dignity. No guarantee, he replied, beyond that of his professional reputation, which would be very much at stake in this contract. Well, did he seriously propose to build railroad equipment in an elevator shop? Only in small part; he would flatly prophesy that within two weeks after his receipt of the contract, his present competitors would be scrambling for subcontracts to supply him with motors, primary controllers, and generators. The distinctive and most critical parts of MU he would manufacture himself. Carter and his directors thanked him; they would consider the matter further.

Back in New York, packing for the London trip, Sprague felt that the decision was touch-and-go. The real sticking point, he sensed, was that blasted 3 m.p.h.

that his competitor had promised. He worked all one night through, making comparative sets of acceleration curves for locomotives and MU cars. Looking at them by dawn, it seemed to him certain that they would demolish the claim. But now there wasn't time enough for him to go back to Chicago. He summoned a young assistant, L. W. McKay, and gave him the graphs and his orders: "Mac, you're Scotch and so's Carter. Take the fastest train you can to Chicago. Study these curves carefully on the way out. When you get there, kill that 18-mile claim."

In two days Sprague got the long-awaited wire from Carter: the South Side would give him the contract if he would post a $100,000 forfeit bond. And on the morning of the 29th, McKay arrived back to report the details of the proposed contract. (It would be drawn up in due course by South Side lawyers.) It would call for installing two hundred and forty motors in one hundred and twenty cars, and fitting them with control mechanisms, lights, heaters, brakes, and motormen's cabs. The South Side would ship a train of six cars to whatever location Sprague designated. Here he would provide an electrified test track at least a mile long, and would undertake to have a six-car train in operation by 15 July of that year. The contract could be cancelled by the South Side if its engineers were not satisfied with its performance. The remaining one hundred and fourteen cars would be equipped and tested in Chicago, with the same cancellation privilege. All electrification and testing on the South Side's tracks would have to be done without interruption of regular service by the steam trains. For completely satisfactory execution of all this, Sprague would receive $300,000.

Sprague wired Carter acceptance, adding that he would see to the bond as soon as he returned from London. He assembled his staff and told them to begin work at once on planning MU equipment; he'd send further instructions by cable and mail. And he gave McKay power of attorney to sign the contract when it arrived. (It isn't clear why he picked an inexperienced young engineer to approve a contract that the South Side lawyers would undoubtedly slant toward their own interests. Perhaps it was a foresighted idea that if any dispute arose, his action would seem that of complete good faith. Or perhaps Sprague had an unconscious need to pit himself against contracts of outrageous stringency.) And then on the afternoon of 29 April he stumped up the gangplank to the liner, still on those infuriating crutches. They'd been a busy but exciting twenty-three days.

It was on 24 June that Sprague strode down the gangplank to Manhattan once again. Although the casts and crutches had disappeared, the intervening eight weeks had been anything but a rest cure. In London he had encountered a monumental deliberation that, combined with engineering conservatism, speedily drained his never large reserves of patience. By his first week he discovered that since electric elevators were almost unknown in England, they were regarded with suspicion. In fact the British were unaccustomed to *any* elevators of the size called for in the *Shepard's Bush* plans. The nearest approach to them that Sprague could locate were several large but slow and wheezy hydraulics in Glasgow. Since they were being forced by circumstance into the necessity of pioneering, the authorities were wholly unresponsive to the slambang, discuss-and-decide pace that Sprague tried to establish.

He'd started out with a great head of steam built up on shipboard. He had set up his demonstration of motors and controllers in the basement of the Hotel Cecil, and when all was gleaming, invited officials from the Central London Railway to come and admire them. In due course one or two gentlemen came, said "Hmm," thanked him civilly, and disappeared. Then he had made a formal tender for the entire installation to the board chairman, Sir Richard Farrant, who had said "Hmm" too. After some delay it became evident that the man Sprague had to persuade was the general consulting engineer for the Tubes, Sir Benjamin Baker, who was sometimes accessible briefly, by appointment. A man of dignity and presence, Sir Benjamin was world-famous for his work on the cantilevered Firth of Forth Bridge and on the Aswan Dam in Egypt. He had a polite but profound skepticism, no experience whatever with electric lifts, and a highly developed facility for saying "Hmm."

The days stretched into weeks and May rolled past. Although a bit of an Anglophile ever since his happy months at the Crystal Palace Exhibition, Sprague yearned for the brisker pace of American business. He tried everything he could think of to hurry a decision. Since a skepticism about electric elevators seemed to be a sticking point, he offered to pay cable costs for any inquiry about how installations in America had worked out. The offer was not accepted. In early June Sprague reported to his office that he thought they had a fair chance of winning out over the hydraulics, but only after a British engineer had come to the U.S. to inspect electric installations.

Meantime the South Side contract was nagging at a part of his mind. He had no doubt of success, there seems no evidence that Sprague was ever seriously assailed by self-doubt, but the 15 July deadline for a running six-car MU train was getting uncomfortably close. He dispatched a steady flow of letters, drawings, cables, and admonitions to his office, but he had the frustrated feeling that things really weren't running there the way they should be. One ominous report reached him that the Watsessing plant might be shut down by another strike. There was one cheerful development. W. J. Clark, the friend who was manager of GE's railroad department, had followed him to England in an effort to get the subcontract for the two hundred and forty big traction motors and primary controllers. Clark got his order, and in return promised Sprague the use of the GE electrified test track at Schenectady. So that problem at least was solved.

In a final effort to close the elevator contract, Sprague made an appointment with Sir Benjamin to propose a new idea. He offered to begin work at once, without commitment. At least one elevator of the largest size would be installed as fast as possible. He would be quite willing to have his offer stand or fall, without recourse, on the results of tests made as soon as the machine was running. Sir Benjamin said "Hmm" several times, and then added that while this was really a most generous offer, it was not the way things should be done, was it, and one really must not let oneself be stampeded into premature decisions, must one? Sprague had the weary feeling that it was the Manhattan Railroad all over again, only politer.

By the second week in June his patience had entirely run out. He booked passage home and called on Sir Richard, the board chairman, to say goodbye. Quite casually Sir Richard inquired "Could you not manage to wait over one more steamer?" Sprague asked, "Does this mean the contract will be awarded to me?" The question was too blunt; the board chairman said only, with highly developed vagueness, that it just might, who knows, be worthwhile, or indeed perhaps not.

But several days later the weeks of carefully husbanded patience paid off. On 14 June, Sprague cabled home that he had just signed a $500,000 contract for forty-nine large elevators. (He added that it was a stringent contract, something that can have surprised no one in the company.) On the 16th he sailed for home, his elation dampened by news that the Watsessing plant had been closed down tight by a strike. It promised incalculable delays for his MU controllers.

According to the contract with the South Side that McKay had signed in his absence, Sprague had just twenty-one days from his arrival to get a six-car MU train running on the test track. Not just running, either; but behaving well enough to pass the scrutiny of skeptical engineers. It came to him that the preliminary work on MU two years before was actually not ideal groundwork, for it had dealt with elevator motors and controllers, not traction ones. Worse, it had simply been circuit development. What was needed now was a practical mechanism, in other words a working combination of bronze, steel, copper, and fiber that could infallibly make the twelve motors in a six-car train turn in precise unison.

The day he landed Sprague called a conference in his room in the Manhattan Hotel. He learned from his associates that matters looked gloomy. They were going to miss the deadline; the only question was by how much. Two or three weeks late seemed a fair estimate. In view of the strike, the South Side would probably be acquiescent. But actually the strike was only part of it; there had been delays everywhere. One serious one had been a change in the design of the master controllers. Sprague listened silently while E. R. Carichoff, one of his best designers on elevator controls, explained why he had decided to scrap the earlier design and begin anew. The tension in the room relaxed when Sprague approved the decision and the new design.

There were, he discovered, a few bits of good news. The South Side's six cars were waiting in

Schenectady. The motors and controllers had been manufactured and were waiting. And though Watsessing was shut down tight, a number of the new controllers (some not finished) had been removed first. It might be possible to make anything else needed in private machine shops. The problem now was simply to put everything together in Schenectady and make it work.

So began weeks of the most concentrated day-and-night labor in Sprague's life. It was Richmond all over again, and worse than the most arduous days with the first elevators. The locale was a car shed and adjoining shop near GE's test track in Schenectady. Weed-grown, but level and straight, the electrified track stretched along one bank of the old Erie Canal. (It was not until the feverish days were past that anyone reflected on the appropriateness of this as a site for the birth of a revolutionary new means of transportation.)

Working with Sprague as engineers was the best crew that he could assemble. There was Alex McIver and H. B. Steger, newly-hired to supervise the actual installation in Chicago; S. H. Libby, in charge of engineering liaison with GE and the South Side; and Charles E. Hyatt and E. R. Carichoff, expert designers of switchgear and controllers. The master mechanic on the job was Pat O'Shaughnessy, more grizzled than in the Richmond days, but still displaying the same "most happy mechanical judgment". Though a bear for work, Pat was still the one man in the crew who never blew up.

As before, Sprague's normally equable manner disappeared under the pressures of fatigue and tension. But as Pat amiably noted, the near presence of the Erie Canal made Sprague's temper easier to handle than before. In the earlier days his tongue had been the weapon to duck. Now whenever something malevolently broke or short-circuited, it was only necessary to stand out of the line of fire while Sprague, erupting with ocean-going language, wrenched out the defective part and heaved it into the canal, to disappear with a gratifying and calming ker-plunsh. If the malfunctioning part was too big to be ripped out, Sprague would settle for the controller handle. For a few seconds after the brass handle whizzed into the water, no one would say anything. Then Sprague would quietly say "Get another, boys," and Pat would produce another handle from the stock of spares in his toolbox.

The South Side engineers turned out not to be ogres after all. (In fact there is some evidence that Sprague infected them with the spirit of unrestricted collective labor, and they pitched in to help too.) On 16 July, the first successful demonstration of two-car MU control took place. By Sunday, 25 July, Sprague's fortieth birthday, all six cars were connected together for the first time and run smoothly up and down the track. Leslie Carter and other officials from the South Side were there, and to show them how simple and reliable MU was, Sprague turned over the controls to his ten-year old son Desmond (after the divorce from Mary, no further effort was made to spell the lad's name d'Esmonde). The following day Sprague sent word of his triumph to the American Institute of Electrical Engineers. The AIEE was meeting that year in the late Prof. Moses Farmer's home in Elliott, Maine, to celebrate the fiftieth anniversary of the old gentleman's first demonstration of a battery-powered car. Sprague sent off a long, proud telegram to Miss Sarah Farmer, the professor's daughter, regretting his absence but stating that his success on the anniversary was an "auspicious augury." He ended the wire with a boast in which a sidelong glance at the unmentioned Edison could perhaps be detected:

> "The advancement of the electric railway in the decade since the installation at Richmond is unparalleled, and no advance in the industrial world has had a more widespread and beneficial effect on the social and moral well-being of the community. In 1887 there were scarcely 100 miles of track; now there are nearly 14,000 miles. From 150 cars, the equipment has grown to over 35,000, propelled by 52,000 motors."

The test train was run in Schenectady with various experimental hookups until 6 August. It was pronounced a complete success; and the first part of the contract was marked fulfilled. But what neither the South Side officials nor anyone else outside the company ever saw was a record of those exhausting weeks that Sprague privately compiled a year later. His motive was not solely to make a historical record; it was to buttress his patent structure with an accounting of when and how each detail of the system came into being. Partly this was because he still smarted over the way in which the Van Depoele trolley patent had won out over his own. Partly it was because he realized that the MU patents, obviously extremely valuable, would inevitably be fought over in the courts, and he wanted to make them as airtight as possible.

The precise date of each conception and change makes little difference now; but the picture these records create of those weeks is fascinating today. Some of the reports unconsciously characterize their writers. Carichoff neatly and precisely ticked off each variation he designed for the master controllers. Libby remembered that he and Sprague hit on the idea for one detail by recalling a tricky linkage once noted on naval searchlights. Pat O'Shaughnessy, among specific dated details, remembered a giddy time on the afternoon of 27 July. He and Sprague, elated over the success of the train, resolved to try out the automatic electric couplers with the train on the run. (They both pretended it was a serious experiment, although the image is inescapable of pure juvenile high spirits.) Pat recalled how he and the boss, each at the controls of a three car train, had careened along at thirty m.p.h., gaily coupling and disconnecting on the run with a series of wonderful lurches and bangs.

But the most telling of all these vivid recollections came from H. B. Steger. He'd kept a diary for three weeks at Schenectady, until it drowned in fatigue, and was thus able to nail down details better than the others. Although his report was written in wooden engineering argot, Steger beautifully developed the truth of one ancient mechanical aphorism: if when the pressure is on, something can possibly go wrong, it will:

> "The MU controllers had been assembled in the SEEC shops, and due to the limited time much detail had been overlooked, which caused much unnecessary labor. Two main controllers were taken in hand and worked upon at the same time. After being tested and adjusted they were placed under two of the cars and bolted to the bottoms of same.
>
> "The platform switches (MU controllers) were then put in position, one for each platform, and wired to their relays. Then it was decided to change the position of the main controllers from under the cars and place them inside, under the side seats. It was then found necessary to move the hand switches in order to make room for the airbrake valve.
>
> "It was also found that the switches were too small to be wired conveniently, and the contacts were too close together. So orders were given for new ones, but the first ones were meantime put back in place and wired to the relays with difficulty. The next four days went to adjusting the controllers, changing the position of the

pilot switches, and arranging the other cars for controllers.

"On the afternoon of the 16th two cars were operated for about two hours, but had little troubles, most of which were caused by the springs that held the relay plungers. They were hard to adjust, and would not retain adjustment. The 17th was spent in running two cars and making adjustments, etc. On the 19th the relays were taken off the last two controllers and cut down to about half former size, rewired, and placed upside down on the sides of the cars under seats. Plungers were cut off and put in without springs, depending on gravity, which was more reliable than springs.

"On the 20th two more cars were taken to the tracks, one of which proved not complete when an attempt was made to run it. The car motors were improperly connected. We also had trouble with the reverser solenoids not pulling down strong enough to make good contact. The 21st and 22nd were spent in changing springs in the solenoids, making changes in wiring necessary. (From this time on I do not remember dates). Five cars were in operation within the next two or three days, but many changes in wiring had to be made to allow room for pipe and air-brake apparatus. Great annoyance was caused by the fact that the hand switches had no stops to prevent the reverser cylinder from being thrown when the car was running, the motors then taking heavy current. This was soon changed on all cars, of which five were running. Then one of them gave trouble on account of its motor brushes not making reliable contact with the commutator.

"Also one of the controllers grounded the line connection and burnt the wire in two. Then it was discovered that if the line was broken on any one of the controllers, it would then derange all of the rest. This was provided for. All went well until motor connections were removed from the controllers on the first two cars in order to relocate the controllers as on the other four. It was a rush job and mistakes were made. When the wiring was first put back, the motors in one car bucked each other, and the resistance was put in wrong in the other, and the next day was spent getting them in shape. Six cars were then running and tests were made for amperage and speed. During this test one motor became short-circuited due to badly made brush-holders and burned off the line wire. All holders were fixed and tests went on, and it was found that the motors would accelerate by jerks. More resistance was placed in the circuit, which partially prevented this trouble, but it was then found that the motors were capable of more speed than was necessary (38 m.p.h.), so different gears were ordered but not immediately available. Then the train of six cars was operated satisfactorily, needing only to have the automatic "throttle" adjusted, but a positive and reliable adjustment proved difficult. Workmen on air-brake equipment caused considerable trouble by moving and even cutting wires..."

Anyone who had ever been part of development work under pressure will know exactly what Steger was describing. The good part of it was that matters were never so tough again. Plenty went wrong in the twelve months before the Alley L was fully electrified, but they were mostly one- and two-day crises, soon remedied. Sprague and his crew moved on to Chicago in August. Each took over special parts of the job. McIver and Steger concentrated on the third rail and power supply, and Carichoff on the controllers. Pat O'Shaughnessy set up a production line at the Wells French Car Works, where the Alley L's cars arrived in batches of ten at a time to be electrified.

By November there were almost forty cars ready for use, but the powerhouses and third rails weren't scheduled to be finished until the following spring. The delay galled Sprague; he foresaw that they would undoubtedly have unexpected bugs in the cars when they tried them in service, and this enforced delay would be a perfect time to do any reworking needed. So he persuaded the Alley L to work out an accommodation with the Metropolitan Elevated in Chicago to permit the running of some electrified cars on their track. (The Met was the line that had converted to electric locomotives in 1895.)

Sprague's hunch was a sound one; there were indeed plenty of bugs. An embarrassing one turned up on the very first trial. Sprague took a five-car train out onto the Metropolitan's main track, and there the control system expired, blocking the track and threatening to snarl transportation on the Loop. Frenzied checking indicated that the trouble was an accidental ground in the "train line", the circuit that linked each master controller. But there was no possible way of hunting it down quickly. Sprague ordered every motor in the train disconnected but the two in the head car. This pair, groaning and smoking in protest, were enough to move the faux pas to the shelter of a siding.

The runs on the Met's tracks, continuing through November and December, proved highly useful. Those joyous automatic couplers, so much fun in Schenectady didn't work out and were replaced. A three-car school train, used to teach motormen to handle the new cars, revealed one peculiar quirk. If the current was cut off in the third rail when a car was moving briskly, the car simply coasted to a stop. But if the motorman carelessly left the control handle all "notched up"(didn't return it to the OFF position), a giant booby trap was constructed for the instant when the juice was restored. A huge current would be drawn, circuit breakers would crash open, and smoky excitements occur generally. Sprague rejected a theory that the remedy was to tell motormen never to do this; it was his opinion that people were even more fallible than machinery. So he and Carichoff brewed up a clever little device that did the remembering for a motorman: current couldn't be sent to the motors after an interruption until the handle was first spun back to OFF.

But as so often happens in technical pioneering, the fix created trouble elsewhere. When each car in a train rolled through a switch in the track, with its temporary break in the third rail, the simple-witted protective device thought this was a current interruption and went into wholly needless action. The remedy for this was to connect all the third-rail shoes in a train into a single circuit. It was something that turned out, one sleety day, to make up for the embarrassment of that stalled train on the first trial. Sprague found that, with all the shoes on his five-car train rubbing on the ice-glazed rail, he could pick up juice when the Met's locomotives couldn't. He had the pleasant satisfaction of first pushing the stalled trains onto sidings, and then providing service with his own equipment.

By April 1898, the Alley L was ready for the first use of electricity on its own tracks. After-hours testing had gone well, but the first day of passenger service was nightmarish, a final display of the malevolence of inanimate objects. Twenty electric cars were put into service, and seventeen of them promptly failed, one in flames. But a tense autopsy that night disclosed that the difficulty was more embarrassing than serious. The failures were all traceable to a batch of defective rheostats from GE that could be readily replaced.

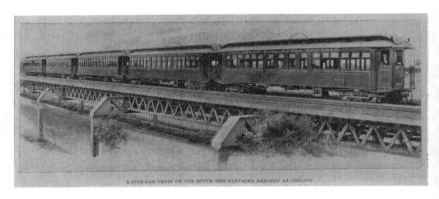

Five-car Alley L MU train (courtesy of Chapin Library, Williams College

It was the last bit of major trouble for MU. The new equipment began to run with a smooth reliability that surprised everyone. By August all one hundred and twenty cars were in operation, and the last steam locomotive was sold. Before the year was out Carter knew that the balance sheets were exciting; and at the year's end he reported to his directors that the effects of MU were astonishing. In November, net earnings of the line were $39,000, compared with $10,000 under steam the year before. In December, net earnings went to $45,000 from $14,000. His accountants reported that these delightful figures resulted, as Sprague had forecast, from interlocking circumstances. The cars were markedly cheaper to run and maintain, which lowered costs; and they were also both faster and more conveniently arranged for the traffic at the moment, which sharply increased revenue.

Word of anything that both decreases costs and increases revenue spreads through the business world at virtually the speed of light. One result was that the South Side's stock went from $32 to $105 a share. And another result was that for the third time in his life Sprague found himself caught up in a turbulent business success. This one promised to be the biggest and wildest yet.

XII: SWINGING ONTO NEW COURSES

After Sprague, it was clear that no elevated could continue to use steam. In both street and elevated railways, Sprague showed outstanding vision, stamina, technical ability, and courage.

—*Prof. Harold K. Passer*

Sometimes when surveying the slopes and highlands of men's careers, one has a sense of a natural divide, a line that separates two adjoining but different watersheds in a man's life. This was eminently true of Sprague. Between 1898 and 1902 his life swung onto new courses. Before, he had been almost ferociously single-minded, feeding on opposition, preoccupied almost obsessively with his battles for electric transportation. But after the success of MU, his personality and interests both gradually changed.

Still hardworking, inventive, and proud, he grew more relaxed and able to display a wry sense of humor. He acquired broader interests and developed a knack for purely social friendships. Although he fought and won a number of new battles, there was now less of a compulsion to attack the difficult solely because it was difficult.

Many reasons accounted for this gradual change. The success of MU was resounding. It brought him such fame, at least in the electrical and transportation worlds, as to lay at rest any lingering possibility that he could be thought of as simply an apprentice to the wizard. It also sharply increased his personal fortune so much so, in fact, as to make it difficult but not impossible to hold to his preferred New England guise of being merely "comfortable." And a second marriage took place in those change-of-course years that was clearly a response to, and perhaps partly a cause of, this personality change. His marriage was a success from the beginning, and brought him companionship, a new family, and a new range of friendships.

A final factor in Sprague's change may have been his increasing specialization in electricity. During his twenties, at a time when few people knew much about practical electricity, Sprague had had to concern himself with generation and distribution as well as with the application of power. But now, from his forties on, the electrical world had become very different. There was a large and growing body of practical knowledge. Alternating current was bringing radical changes in

XII: SWINGING ONTO NEW COURSES

generation and distribution. Working electrical engineers were becoming specialists. Quite instinctively Sprague took as his own the field of automatic control circuits. This had been the part of elevator work and MU had interested him the most. The possibilities were almost untouched. And it was ideally suited for an ingenious and unconventional mind.

First, though, there were to be some busy, contentious, and wildly exciting years, reminiscent of the time after Richmond a decade before. Reminiscent, but very different in outcome, because Sprague was not the sort of man who made the same mistakes twice. This time he prepared his positions in company control and in patents with extraordinary care.

By 1897, the position of the elevator company had become increasingly anomalous. After the MU success at Schenectady, Sprague had transferred the South Side contract, previously a personal one, to the company. And the company itself had sold its elevator business to Otis for $1,250,000, reserving the use of the plant for five years and retaining part of the foreign business. Clearly it was time to tidy up the corporate structure. In the late autumn of 1897 Sprague and Ed Johnson assembled committees representing chief stockholders of the elevator company and the insulation and conduit business, an unobtrusive but profitable operation. By early spring of the following year the intricate details were worked out: the two companies were merged into a new one, the Sprague Electric Company capitalized at $5,000,000.

SEC began life with a healthy but heterogeneous package of assets: a plant and machinery it could retain for almost five years; a large amount of cash and Otis stock; various thriving little businesses in conduit, insulation, and special generators; a profitable overseas elevator business; and the South Side MU contract. Most valuable of all its assets, at least potentially, were the MU rights.

Although Sprague had been quick to file caveats (a procedure, abolished in 1910, by which an inventor could file a statement of conception, to establish a date, prior to filing a formal patent application) at each stage in MU development, he and his patent lawyer, Thomas Ewing, had held back in filing a formal patent application until it was as completely airtight as human ingenuity could possibly make it. (Tom Ewing later confessed that he would wake at night during this period, fretting over new ideas of defining multiple unit control in more lawyer-proof terms.) Finally, on 30 April 1898, the application was filed at the Patent Office, studded with separate and laboriously-defined claims.

The contract that Sprague negotiated with SEC for its use of this patent was highly nourishing. It called for a payment of $50,000 in cash and $350,000 in stock, plus a royalty that (on a sliding scale of company profits) varied from 50 cents to $1 per horsepower of MU equipment installed.

A list of SEC's stockholders in 1899 shows that Sprague held slightly more than a quarter of all shares of common. Ed Johnson was the next largest holder, with a bit less. Henry Villard held an eighth. Pierpont Morgan, still buying into technically promising electric companies, held an innocuous five percent. Names out of Sprague's past dotted the list of small shareholders: Oscar Crosby, Dana Greene, John Kreusi, Sammy Insull. (Oddly, General P. G. T. Beauregard of New Orleans was a small stockholder.) But quite the most baffling holder of a handful of shares was Thomas A. Edison. There is no evidence either way, but one can imagine that they could have been an ironical gift from Sprague so that Edison would be certain to note the dividend rate. It is also quite possible that the shares were bought by Edison himself as an amiable gesture; the two men, on their infrequent meetings, had by now managed to achieve a kind of laconic public civility.

Toward his corporate, rather than personal, rivals Sprague had at the beginning of 1898 a wary guarded truce. GE had sold him the motors, primary controllers, and rheostats needed for the South Side job; and Westinghouse had been the subcontractor for powerhouse equipment. These two big companies, after savage battles earlier in the 1890s, had also established a precarious truce with each other; in 1896 they had made a confidential agreement dividing up business in controllers, trolley mechanisms, and brakes. Sprague had no personal animosity toward either company. He knew most of the engineers at both firms and had trained many of them himself. Dana Greene had risen to head GE's lighting division; Clark of GE had been a great help during the birth of MU; and Clark's bright young aide, Frank Shepard, was now Sprague's right hand man.

But this precarious peace blew up as soon as MU became an obvious commercial success. To both Coffin— the highly aggressive head of GE—and to George Westinghouse, MU was obviously going to be too lucrative to be ignored. The managers and owners of every elevated line in the country took vibrant note of the fact that just one year of MU had boosted the Chicago Alley L's net from almost zero to a glistening $350,000. To these men, MU proffered no dubious little benefit— such as not scattering soot, or of giving customers better service—instead, it offered something really important, which was doubling or quadrupling profits. So both GE and Westinghouse set up crash programs to bring out competitive MU systems.

Working day and night, Westinghouse soon came out with an eerie system that used compressed air to govern the movements of primary controllers in each car of a train. It amused Sprague, being both complicated and a little uncertain. He thought it was the kind of system any engineer should be delighted to compete against. GE's entry, however, was something else again. GE turned out an MU system that was all-electric, highly efficient, and outrageously close to Sprague's own. At the head of the program Coffin had put a smart, tough engineer named E.W. Rice, a man who years later became president of GE. From

Sprague's viewpoint, a disquieting aspect was that Rice had in 1895 received a patent on an idea that might seem to lawyers and judges as if it were a basic MU concept. Sprague knew very well that it wasn't, but he was chilled by a large and remorseless competitor that seemingly had not only appropriated his idea but also headed the program with the one man in the country best able to muddy the fact.

Probably, though, this kind of rough tactics did not come as a surprise. Tom Ewing had been much aware of Rice's patent when he had drawn up Sprague's application, and had devoted much thought and skill to writing around it. And everyone knew that Coffin had used a similar bare knuckles gambit with Edison years before. This had been when Coffin had been running Thomson-Houston, and had jumped into a slam-bang incandescent lamp battle with Edison. He had bought some prior patents that, although flawed, appeared strong enough to sustain years of litigation. Meantime, while the lawyers were performing their rites, the business was there to be fought over. Edison had finally won his infringement case, but it was a Pyrrhic victory, coming as it did just before the patents expired.

The battle between Sprague and Coffin turned out to be a fine ferocious combat, rough enough to send bystanders to cover with fingers in their ears. For all that Coffin was an experienced fighter, he made two major mistakes. The first, perhaps arising from the relative smallness of SEC, was in seriously underestimating his opponent. The second was in twice attempting to bluff Sprague with a sudden show of teeth. For two and a half years the dogfight went on, spilling over a dozen contracts and courtrooms.

The opening round was a feint on Coffin's part, evidently calculated to emphasize to Sprague his dependence on large suppliers. It came when each side was in a race to grab as much of the business as possible while the lawyers were readying their rites and writs. GE went out after the Manhattan Railway and won a contract. Sprague countered by capturing a competitive contract for the Brooklyn Elevated. Then came Coffin's feint: GE refused to fill a tiny $365 order for certain switches that Sprague needed in Brooklyn. Sprague's rejoinder was prompt: he cancelled a $40,000 order for GE motors to be used for London elevators. Expanding the motor-manufacturing line in Watsessing, he let it be known that he was saving $10,000 by making the motors himself. As he wrote in a related note to Lundy, "Thus endeth the first lesson. And we will teach them a few more."

At this stage the inter-company relationship was paradoxical. No one rocked the boat about the traction motors, controllers, generators, and rotary converters that Sprague was ordering from GE and Westinghouse for MU installations. Sprague knew that he really didn't have the facilities to make them economically. And neither of his big rivals really wished to pass up lucrative subcontracts on installation jobs that they had not won.

XII: SWINGING ONTO NEW COURSES

Then SEC, GE, and Westinghouse all staged major campaigns to install MU in Boston, the biggest remaining system in the country. Sprague made an extra effort, though he was pessimistic because of GE's excellent financial connections there. The competition turned out to be a dead heat; Boston Elevated announced that it would stage a comparative test of all MU equipment. The trials were run off in April 1900, and Sprague won both the test and the contract. Sprague was delighted and crowed by extensively quoting the president of the Boston Elevated,

"The Sprague system, more than any other, provided greater safeguards on the operation of the train, both in the protection of the apparatus and in taking care of the emergencies which arise in public service, by the use of various interlocked automatic safety devices..."

The setback in Boston was hard for the aggressive Mr. Coffin to take. GE bared its teeth a second time, and announced tersely that it would henceforth cease to supply motors and controllers to Sprague. (Nominal grounds were that SEC was infringing a GE motor control patent.) Sprague was ready with a counterpunch; he announced that he would purchase from Westinghouse such equipment as he did not manufacture himself. The thought that all the profitable subcontracted business would now go to GE's archrival seems to have inflamed Coffin still more, for motors were not included in the secret pact between the two companies, and had been a bone of contention for years. GE promptly filed suit against Sprague for infringement of its series-parallel motor control patents. And again Sprague was ready: he promptly filed suit against GE for infringement of his MU patents. This was an exhilarating time for Sprague, the biggest and most gorgeous scrap of his life. Looking past the immediate conflict, he saw that if he was going to wage indefinite battle with such titans as GE and, ultimately, Westinghouse, he would have to enlarge his company enormously. Much more capital would be needed, a bigger engineering staff, much more manufacturing. Even more important, he would need to be stronger on alternating current, with the patents and facilities needed to make big alternating-current generators, rotary converters, and transformers. For some months Sprague thought hard about building a third electrical super-company. He searched for a company to merge with that had the requisite experience and patents, and found it, the Stanley Electric Company, of Pittsfield, Massachusetts. It was not big enough to swallow SEC but it did have a thriving little business in alternating-current equipment. A Stanley had worked at Westinghouse alongside Tesla during the pioneering alternating-current days.) Preliminary negotiations for a merger were begun, and went well. And then, suddenly, Sprague broke off without explaining why. It may have been that he got a hint that Stanley's alternating-current patents might not stand up in court. Or it may have been that he had long second thoughts about the pleasures and frustrations of large-scale industrial enterprise.

XII: SWINGING ONTO NEW COURSES

Meantime the struggle with GE went on. From the beginning it had been a little dirty. During the months when both companies were scuffling for the Brooklyn contract, Sprague's New York office was broken into. At first nothing seemed to be missing; then it was discovered that Shepard's desk had been rifled and Lundy's engineering analysis of the Brooklyn job was gone. Sprague ran advertisements in the New York papers offering $1,000 for its return until a friend, who was on the Board of the Boston Elevated Company, tipped him off: Lundy's figures were being quoted by GE representatives. This checked out with past performance. Electrical men recalled the time, back in 1893, when GE and Westinghouse had been at each other's throats over the Niagara Falls power contract. A sheriff armed with a court order had uncovered a roll of stolen Westinghouse blueprints in GE's Lynn plant. Sprague, boiling mad, was pondering whether to go to court over the theft when, suddenly, the matter became academic: he won the contract.

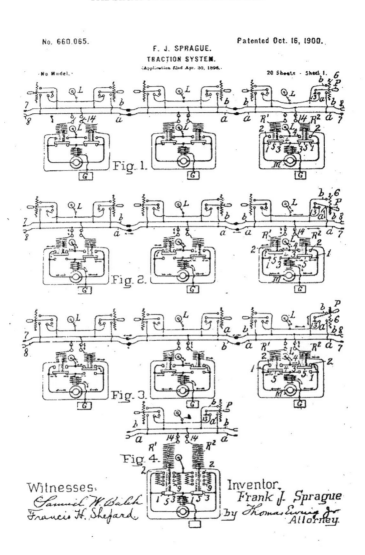

*Basic Sprague MU Patent 660,065
(courtesy John L. Sprague)*

XII: SWINGING ONTO NEW COURSES

Meantime the two Sprague-GE patent lawsuits were marching steadily through the courts. The suit against Sprague was an oddity: it accused him of infringing a patent originally issued to him. This was the patent on series-parallel motor control that dated back to Richmond. He had assigned it to the Sprague Electric Railway and Motor Company. When Edison-GE had taken over, the patent went along, as later it had when EGE merged with Thomson-Houston. Using the patent in psychological warfare, Coffin was contending that Sprague was employing a circuit that was no longer his own.

Sprague's countersuit, accusing GE of infringing his MU patent, was the heart of both actions. As the case developed, it became increasingly evident that Sprague's Schenectady details and Tom Ewing's sleepless nights had gone to good purpose. The MU patent was beautifully drawn, and buttressed by an impressive array of confirmation. Sprague's lawyers were able to cast serious doubt as to whether GE's MU could have arisen from the Rice patent alone. Early in the spring of 1902, the GE lawyers had the unpleasant duty of warning Coffin that he should be prepared for the loss of his suit against Sprague. Quite apart from emotion, this was alarming news to the head of GE, because two incalculable but large sums were at stake. One was the value of future MU installations, now broadening out to include subways and suburban railroads. The second was the risk of punitive damages assessed against MU installations that GE had already made, notably on the Manhattan Railroad.

Aggressive and tough as he was, Coffin was also coolly realistic and flexible. If he was about to lose a battle that he simply couldn't afford to lose, the only possible thing to do was to knuckle under and gain control of Sprague's MU patent on Sprague's own terms. Sometime early in 1902, operating through intermediaries, Coffin began negotiations to buy the Sprague Electric Company.

By May 1902, the deal was publicly announced. It was as complicated as two sets of alert corporation lawyers could make it, but in outline the terms ran this way: not counting patents and goodwill, SEC was appraised as having $2.7 million in assets and $1.1 million in liabilities, or a net worth of something more than $1.6 million. For this plus the patents, which were all that GE really wanted, GE would pay Sprague stockholders $3,350,000. It would also pay Sprague personally $75,000 in cash and $100,000 in bonds, and would retain him for fifteen years at $10,000 a year as an MU consultant. Finally, it would undertake to describe the system in the future as "Sprague General Electric Multiple-Unit Control."

Counting his SEC stock, Sprague thus received well over $1 million for his MU patent. (It had of course also been profitable to him in the four previous years.) But as an internal GE memo of the time put it, there was "no other way that we could get possession of a patent which was absolutely necessary to our business."

XII: SWINGING ONTO NEW COURSES

At the moment of triumph, Sprague couldn't help savoring the fact that his victory had been won over the biggest electrical company in the U.S., headed by a man with a reputation for being an exceedingly tough fighter. For all this, it proved to be a strangely impersonal struggle, with no lingering acrimony. Sprague soon managed a rapprochement with GE that remained in force for the rest of his life. The consultant contract was renewed in 1918, then signed for GE by, of all people, E. W. Rice.

But the sweetest morsel of triumph was reserved for 1932, at the time of Sprague's 75th birthday. He learned then that, years before, Coffin had described the MU patent as the most valuable that the company ever owned. Speaking to an internal audience at GE, Coffin had (Sprague learned) remarked that there was "about that fellow's work a definiteness and practicality which has never been equaled, even by the 'Wizard of Menlo Park.'"

But both Coffin and Edison were dead when word of this handsome compliment got back to Sprague. Which must have taken a little of the savor out of it.

To return to the new courses that Sprague's life took around the turn of the century, his second marriage was unquestionably an important factor. In the spring of 1899 he had been introduced by friends to Harriet C. Jones, twenty years his junior and just back from a grand tour abroad. She was the daughter of a retired Army captain and, like Sprague, Connecticut-bred. He liked her at once, delighted to find an attractive girl who did not think that electrical engineering was automatically boring. In turn he grew gradually willing to concede that such other worlds as music, literature, and architecture were not always intensely boring either. They were married on 11 October 1899, and Sprague found a measure of good-spirited companionship that he had never known before.

Harriet and Children, 1906, left to right: Robert, Althea, Julian (courtesy John L. Sprague)

XII: SWINGING ONTO NEW COURSES

A son, Robert, was born the following year; another son, Julian, was born in 1903; and a daughter, Althea, came along in 1906. But the new family didn't interfere with the new companionship. In 1902 they took a summer-long tour of Europe. In 1903 Sprague bought a gleaming new Winton automobile in which he and Harriet, in dusters and goggles, chugged happily and adventurously through the Berkshire hills. In 1905 there was another summer-long tour of Europe with the small children along. In 1906 Harriet persuaded her husband to buy a summer place in Sharon, Connecticut. As she had evidently foreseen, his initial reluctance to be tied down to a country home very speedily gave way to jets of enthusiasm.

For the first time in his life, Sprague found a nonprofessional outlet for his energies and imagination. The house, a handsome Colonial structure, was relocated and enlarged. Architects, carpenters, and landscape gardeners swarmed over the place. New flower and vegetable gardens, as well as tennis and croquet courts, appeared on the fourteen-acre estate. Seed catalogues and tomes on shrubs and trees overflowed Sprague's desk. Weekends in the country grew from the grudging Saturday afternoon and Sunday that had been Sprague's lifetime habit, and now often extending from Thursday to Tuesday. In New York his startled associates were often presented with boxes of fresh vegetables and lavish baskets of flowers; and William Cox, Sprague's gardener, once estimated, possibly with mixed feelings, that there were 10,000 peonies in bloom and more coming. Horticulturists and magazine photographers began making appointments to see the Sharon place. It grew in several years to be not just a show place but a source of endless pleasure and relaxation to a man whose whole prior life had been spent in uncommonly concentrated work.

During his forties and fifties, Sprague's personality flowered along with his gardens. His rather cool cockiness disappeared; he managed to avoid the pitfall so many successful men have of turning into a thorny and tedious autocrat. Instead, Sprague grew more relaxed, modest, and genial, with an easy new facility at dealing with people. Under Harriet's gentle guidance he acquired a new circle of friends. Harriet had been a friend of Mark Twain's daughter Clara, and through her Sprague met the old humorist. They gathered for dinner and talk on many summer evenings at Redding and Sharon. Mark Twain took a shine to the engineer who was twenty-two years his junior. (Perhaps he recognized an echo of the Connecticut Yankee, or perhaps the interest arose from Mark Twain's own dismal lack of success, years before, with his typesetting machine.) Albert Bigelow Paine described sitting on the screened porch in the summer dusk, listening to Mark Twain and sometimes William Dean Howells question Sprague about the strange worlds of engineering and mathematics and electricity. Often the talk would curve into amiable dispute, with Twain prodding Sprague about the sorry way the world seemed to be heading, and Sprague vigorously defending the times against the old gentleman's saturnine views.

Mark Twain was always grateful for one small service that Sprague provided. When Clara Clemens married Ossip Gabrilowitsch, a small but exasperating crisis arose at the private ceremony. No one had thought to hire a photographer to take any wedding pictures. So Sprague trotted out to his Winton, came back with a folding Kodak, and hastily snapped the only pictures made that day. (They turned out fine.)

In New York City, where the Sprague family lived most of the year in a house on West End Avenue, Sprague's life broadened out too. Going to a concert or gallery had long since ceased to be the chore it had been in days gone by, and the theater became a special enthusiasm for him. Sprague met and struck up a lifelong friendship with Oliver Herford, (the author among much other memorable light verse of the deathless limerick about the young lady wedged in the transom). Herford inevitably wrote some lines about his friend: "He made the world the priceless gifts/ of motors and electric lifts/ without which, it is safe to say/ the world would be downstairs today..."

One of the closest and most rewarding new friendships that came to Sprague was also one of the most unlikely. Beginning early in the century Brander Matthews, then professor of dramatic literature at Columbia, started holding Sunday evening "at homes" for playwrights, actors, poets, and critics living in or visiting New York. Matthews was already building an international reputation as a student of the theater and playwright, and invitations to join this weekly circle were highly prized. Sprague's introduction arose through his wife – Harriet was a close friend of Matthews' daughter Edith – but he and Matthews hit it off well from the start and Sprague was asked to be a regular member of the group. For several decades Sprague kept his Sunday evenings free in the winter to join the gatherings. Matthews was a few years older than Sprague, cultivated, charming, and with a rather fastidious taste. Sprague was quietly assured, with a new modesty and wry humor in manner, and a skill at explaining technology and engineering to a literary circle that professed never to understand such things.

The friendship lasted until both were old men. After Brander Matthews' wife died, Harriet Sprague took over the head of the table, and Sprague later acceded to a request to watch over Matthews' affairs in case of need. Clayton Hamilton, an editor and author who was a friend of both men, described the relationship in these words:

> "For more than half a century Brander Matthews had known every man of letters, every man of the theater, every artist who was worth knowing, in New York, in London, and in Paris. Yet when he was ultimately incapacitated, the one friend upon whom he relied absolutely to look after him was not an artist but an engineer, Frank Sprague."

XIII: THE HABIT OF A LIFETIME

"The man who blazed this trail in electric traction was as nervous and impatient as a compass, but human and friendly. He had such a critical eye he would break a conversation, march across the room, and straighten a picture; and he insisted that every new chimney at his country home be absolutely plumb."

—*James W. Holden*

It would be highly inaccurate to assume that, after the sale of his company to GE, Sprague spent the last three decades left to him in cultivated leisure and literary conversations. A man who appeared to derive energy from spending it, he found the hard work of persuading others to swallow fresh technical ideas a continuously zestful pleasure. These were to be decades in which he would fight still more battles, for electrification of main-line railroads, for higher operating voltages, for automatic train control circuits that would make accidents impossible, and for a variety of other developments such as improved naval weapons and radical new elevators. At least one of these—automatic train control—was to be as long and thorny a struggle as anything that had gone before. But in these new battles, Sprague now had two new advantages. One was that he had achieved, among engineers, a worldwide reputation as a man whose proposals should be taken very seriously indeed. The other was the fact that the march of technology was moving to catch up with Sprague; his ideas seemed steadily less radical to businessmen and bankers.

After the sale of his company in 1902, Sprague plunged almost immediately into the problems of mainline electrification. The ripest spot for it was in New York City, where both the New York Central and the New York, New Haven, and Hartford railroads funneled their traffic into four jammed tracks leading down Manhattan Island to Grand Central Station. It was a highly unsatisfactory situation, one that had been steadily worsening ever since Commodore Vanderbilt had begun the first Grand Central in 1869. By the turn of the century the tracks were clearly inadequate. The lack of sufficient car-cleaning, storage, and turnaround tracks at the station meant that trains had to be brought in, unloaded, backed out to a yard miles to the north for cleaning and storage, and then backed in again for loading with passengers, -a crazily cumbersome system that deeply cut into the capacity of the four choke-point tracks.

Worse, the last five miles in to the terminal were in the Park Avenue tunnel. Smoke and billowing steam clouds in close quarters were not just an annoyance, but a serious hazard. Despite rules for firemen and engineers, as well as speed limits that choked down traffic still more, the tunnel was widely recognized as risky. On 8 January 1902 a passenger train ran past red lights that were evidently obscured by smoke or steam and smashed into another with a large loss of life. After an investigation, the New York State Legislature ordered the railroads to electrify the tracks within five years. The law-makers brushed aside agonizing questions of feasibility and cost with a rather magic-wand assumption that they could be answered somehow, and indeed would have to be where the "health and safety of the public" was concerned.

The technical problems were immense, as Sprague shortly discovered. (He was appointed to the Central's Committee for Electrification, a group of august experts headed by the railroad's chief engineer, William J. Wilgus.)To begin with, there were basic, complicated, and interlocked decisions to be made: alternating or direct current; third rail or overhead wire; moderate or high voltage; electrify only to the tunnel's mouth (where there was no space for locomotive changes) or farther out; and if so, how far? It must be remembered that these decisions had to be taken at a time when there were almost no guiding experience patterns.

There were also the obstacles of staggering cost, to electrify, to build the huge new terminal needed, and to provide enough tracks to give good service with room for growth, and to do it at the spot where land costs were among the highest in the world. These requirements seemed costly beyond the resources of even a rich and prospering railroad.

Deliberations of the committee, which went on over months and years, were confidential. Wilgus was by agreement its sole public spokesman. But the character of its decisions, which echoed virtually all of Sprague's personal ideas, suggest that he was at least highly influential. It was decided to use moderate-voltage direct current. It would be supplied by a third rail, safer in close quarters than a high-voltage overhead alternating-current system. (As for the New Haven's maverick decision to try an 11,000-volt overhead alternating-current arrangement, this was of course its privilege, on its own tracks. But where it came into Grand Central on the New York Central's tracks, it would have to use the third-rail direct current that the Wilgus committee specified.) Elaborate calculations suggested that, for maximum efficiency, electrification should be extended thirty-five miles out on the main line and almost twenty-five miles on the Harlem branch. Sprague multiple-unit trains would be used to carry the swelling commuting traffic; they did not have to be turned around in the station, being double-ended.

As for the prohibitive costs, these were to be whittled down by a plan of great daring. Instead of buying more land, the Central would take advantage of the fact that electric traction, unlike steam, didn't have to be out in the open. They'd put everything deep underground, build a system of massive columns and beams, and roof over the entire 46-track, two-level train yard. Then it would be possible to lease out "air rights" for the seventy acres of highly valuable real estate thus created. The skyscraper office buildings and hotels built over the tracks would provide a rental income that would make the whole grandiose project feasible.

In 1907, the electric trains began to run (the Terminal itself wasn't finished for a few years). To draw the through trains there were little GE-built gearless locomotives. They too were rigged so that they could use MU control with two locomotives in tandem for heavy trains, and single ones for light loads. The system worked beautifully from the beginning, increasing track capacity by more than a third. Fifty- five years later, the system (and some of the original equipment) was still working fine, hauling scores of thousands of people in and out of the city every day.

Sprague and Wilgus worked closely together and made a smooth running team. Together they designed a third rail that ingeniously avoided the drawbacks of all previous ones. It was being found on the elevateds that conventional third rails were likely to become useless when coated with sleet and freezing rain. And though 600 volts of direct current was not proving nearly as lethal as 11,000-volt alternating current, the unprotected rail was still a serious hazard to track workers, train crews, and the youngsters or hoboes who scaled the fences. So Sprague and Wilgus (both insisting that it was a collective idea) designed and patented an upside-down rail. It was suspended from side brackets and completely protected on all but the underside by a close-fitting wooden sheath. Besides permitting regular operation in icy weather, the rail proved to be one of the safest electrically charged conductors ever made. After its appearance on the New York Central, other railroads began to show an interest. So the two men formed the Standard Third Rail Company, and licensed a number of additional installations.

Except where its tracks joined the Central's for the run into Manhattan, the New Haven Railroad made use of a different electrification system, drawing high-voltage alternating current from an overhead wire to power single-phase alternating current traction motors. Sharp technical controversy arose as to whether this Westinghouse system was more efficient than the GE direct-current system used by the Central. It turned out to be a singularly intricate question, and one capable of stirring up astonishing acrimony among engineers. Although Sprague lined up on the direct current side, at least for traction motors, he showed no strong emotional identification or bias. He cheerfully conceded that alternating current was obviously better for distributing power up to the trackside substations, and he suggested that a higher-voltage direct current than was then in use would probably be cheaper. At the same time he argued, and proved, that direct-current traction motors were far easier to control smoothly and efficiently than were their single-phase rivals.

Actually this was a recurrence, on main-line electrification, of the old "war of the currents" that had been stirring up electrical engineers ever since the 1880s. Decades before, as a youngster at Menlo Park, Sprague had given Edison several memoranda pointing out that alternating current would greatly widen the small service areas of Edison's first powerhouses. But by 1886 Edison had become violently opposed to alternating current in any form. He doggedly stuck to this opinion (which he later conceded to have been his biggest single technical mistake) for decades. Using his skill at creating newspaper publicity, Edison had waged a ferocious anti-alternating current campaign. He electrocuted a large number of dogs and cats using alternating current in public demonstration; he publicized the use of alternating current in the first capital-punishment electrocutions; and with the shrewdness of a born publicist, he worked hard to spread the use of the verb "to Westinghouse" as a slangy synonym for "to electrocute."

Although this early and unsuccessful campaign was fifteen years past when Sprague took up a similar battle, the differences in tactics between the two men were instructive. Sprague was too much an engineer to dig himself into a stubborn fortified position. (After all, technical developments might come along to change the then drawbacks to 11,000-volt alternating current traction.) All during his work as GE's principal consultant on railroad electrification, he argued that engineering decisions could only be based on comparative costs, comparative efficiency, comparative safety. During the first decade of the century, when Sprague did constant battle with Westinghouse, not only on the Central and New Haven electrifications but also on the Chicago, Milwaukee & St. Paul in the Midwest, and the Southern Pacific in the far west, he preferred to compete with figures rather than with emotions. The infighting was sometimes rough, as when Westinghouse subsidized anti-Sprague articles, or when both sides strove to publicize the other's accidents, but it never sunk to the ferocity of the war of the currents. For all his combativeness, Sprague never lost a measure of detachment. Writing in the Electric Railway Journal in 1916, at a time when virtually all main-line electrifications, with one or two exceptions, had turned to his own favorite high-tension direct current, Sprague was able to see much good in some alternating traction systems, notably the sophisticated polyphase ones that had begun to appear abroad.

His consultant work for GE and for several railroads on electrification led Sprague into something far more important than the recurrence of the old battle of the currents. Much of the controversy had turned on rail safety, and Sprague began to study official accident reports, not just on electrified lines, with increasing fascination. He noted that there were numerous

XIII: THE HABIT OF A LIFETIME

railroad accidents not caused by such ancient troublemakers as a broken rail, a split switch, or a dropped brake beam. Nor were they attributable to the signal system, for this, particularly in the block-signal system, had been brought to a high level of reliability. Instead, a disquietingly large number of accidents came simply from human failure. Typically, they arose from situations where, because of illness, inattention, carelessness, or incompetence, a motorman or engineer simply disregarded a red signal and plunged heedlessly into disaster.

The frequency of human failure accidents startled Sprague. He read with incredulity the testimony after an accident in New York City on the IRT elevated. The record of the motorman at fault in this case revealed that during his seventeen years of service he had been reprimanded or censured eighteen times, and had been suspended eleven times for offenses that ranged from minor collisions, running past junctions at high speeds, repeatedly overrunning red signals, and habitually peering out the side window of his cab.

"Do you consider this record indicates he was a safe man?" investigators asked an IRT official.

"Of course I have naturally got to say that it does. I do believe that it does...or at least it does not indicate that he was an unsafe man."

"Do you have other men in the employ of the company with similar records?"

"I suppose we have, yes sir."

Sprague was flabbergasted.

It came to Sprague that here preeminently was a field where his facility with automatic control circuitry was urgently needed. It was a field where his taste for technically thorny problems could find ample scope. One part of the solution was comparatively simple. This was to adapt for railroads the "dead man's control" that he had put on elevators years before, the device that, if a hand left the control, immediately cut off power and applied brakes. As applied to subways, elevateds, and electrified railroads, it could be a spring-loaded button fitted to the center of the controller handle. On steam locomotives, where the engineer's driving hand had to be free to move between the throttle and the Johnson bar, the "conscious and attentive" switch could be a spring-loaded pedal. In either case, if the man in charge of a train fell asleep, or fainted, or had a heart attack, his speeding train would immediately be braked to a stop.

This was only part of automatic control. More important was the problem of the inexplicable aberration, the disquieting situation where an engineer, although technically conscious and alert, simply went careening through a red signal to disaster, or raced by a slow signal with unabated speed. This was more difficult to cope with; matters of judgment and degree were involved, and it was obviously not desirable to take control away from an engineer except when the situation demanded it. Moreover, the problem of communication between fixed points along the track and a moving locomotive was not simple. Plainly it wouldn't be a clean design to invent some mechanical tripper along the track that could shut down a speeding train. There'd be a chance that track-walkers or hoboes might set it off or derange it, and besides any mechanical tripper would be dangerously vulnerable to snow and ice.

As Sprague visualized it, the need was for a foolproof, economically feasible electrical control system that would leave an engineer in full charge of his train unless he wholly disregarded a danger signal. Then, and only then, would the automatic circuit take over to bring the train to a safe stop. And even that might be too restrictive, for it was possible to imagine circumstances where an alert and competent engineer might wish to disregard a malfunctioning signal and proceed cautiously. So Sprague, who had come to believe that the essence of successful invention was to define objectives precisely, envisioned an ideal control system having these features:

1. It would stop a train at once if its engineer slumped unconscious over his controls.

2. It would also stop a train if the engineer raced by a red signal.

3. It would allow the engineer, if he deliberately punched an "acknowledge" button, to proceed slowly past a warning signal.

4. The entire system would be electrical, without mechanical trippers, protected against weather and tampering, reliable, not prohibitively costly or sensitive, and "compatible" with all the different kinds of equipment that rode the rails.

Designing and perfecting something to do all this preoccupied Sprague for years. In 1906, when work was just beginning, he formed his fourth company, this one called the Sprague Safety Control and Signal Corporation. After tests he concluded that the best pick-up connection between a rocking, speeding locomotive and a fixed track position would be an inductive electromagnetic link. Visitors to his laboratory during the period recall seeing him experiment with a pendulum having a coil attached to its lower end, arranged to swing at varying spacing past a fixed electromagnet beneath, with Sprague carefully recording the variation in the pulse of induced current caused by different spacing. Once he had the principles and basic circuitry worked out, Sprague returned to the GE test track near Schenectady, the same place on the bank of the Erie Canal where MU had been tried out years before, and set about making automatic train control a practical reality.

As always with pioneering, it didn't come easily. The job was essentially that of changing a tricky and sensitive mechanism that sometimes worked into a simplified and durable mechanism that always worked. Slowly he brought ATC, as it was soon termed, around to where it behaved to his liking. Once he invited an artist friend, Paul Dougherty, along to witness some tests, and his guest was awed by the way, when a train was purposely run through a red signal, it was gently caught and brought to a stop as though by an unseen hand. Later on, at the Sprague home, Dougherty heard someone describe the new principle as "like having someone in the cab to warn the engineer." He was struck by the prosaicness of this description. "On the contrary," Dougherty explained, "it is really like having God in the cab to warn the engineer."

Automatic train control, though perfected and patented before the war, and installed on many Class I railroads during the Twenties, was the least profitable of Sprague's major inventions. For one thing, it had a long and costly development period. After the Schenectady tests there was another set of trials, also at Sprague's expense, on the New York Central's main line near Yonkers, N. Y. And then in the Twenties, when the Interstate Commerce Commission ordered nineteen railroads to install this or an equivalent safety system, Sprague had to fight a long and costly patent-infringement action. He ultimately won his case, but by this time many of the country's railroads had come on hard times, and the chance of recouping his large investment had passed. But even though, in net, automatic train control depleted rather than added to Sprague's personal fortune, it remained one of his inventions of which he was most proud. And understandably so, for railroad men believe that surely hundreds and possibly thousands of lives have been saved by that unseen hand in the cab.

Sprague never forgot that he had been trained as an officer in the U.S. Navy. Back in the 1890s, he had made automatic watertight bulkhead doors for the Navy; had experimented with electric gun-turret drives; and had been fascinated by a compressed-air dynamite gun for patrol craft. As the Spanish-American War flared and he was up to his neck in the Alley L, he attempted to get into the fight. Some old carbons in his files tell the story. The first letter went to Theodore Roosevelt, then Assistant Secretary of the Navy, on 8 March 1898. Sprague recommended the formation of a "Volunteer Electrical Corps."

"...If the Department will give me command of a fast sea-going boat, which should be not less than 150 feet and, if possible, of 20 knots or more speed, I will, in addition to any armaments which the Department will supply, equip it with 5 or 6 pneumatic dynamite guns, 600 rounds of ammunition, and a picked volunteer crew ready for active service.

"I am led to make this suggestion having in view the limited rapid-fire armament the smaller boats carry, their inferiority as compared to a torpedo-boat destroyer, and the necessity of the most efficient patrol work for a fleet.

"The dynamite gun is built by the Sims Dudley Defense Co...I have not the remotest interest in the company. The gun's features include a 1 1/2 mile trajectory and a destructive power of 75 pounds of gunpowder.

"The Sprague Electric Company can, by working day and night, turn out 6 of these guns within 30 days, which it will do at my expense. Sims Dudley will supply the ammunition at its own expense..."

Shortly thereafter Sprague got a note from William W. Cook, the lawyer for the Sprague Electric Company. It was the first of a fine sardonic exchange. Cook wrote to Sprague:

"I understand that the martial strain of blood in your veins impels you not merely to take an ordinary part in the war now imminent, but to undertake a part in the service involving the greatest personal danger possible. May I suggest that it would seem the most elementary part of wisdom to see if you could straighten out your affairs with this company before you get yourself shot at?"

Sprague's reply, dated April 23, 1898, was written in the same vein:

"It is quite true that I have ambitions to go where I can recover my appreciation of the smell of sulphur, preparatory to my future state. But just now I am indulging in a little war on account of failures in apparatus arising from rheostats supplied us by GE which, instead of allowing our road here to go ahead in a normal and Christian-like way, have been causing me some trouble, not, let me impress upon you very forcibly, in any way dependent upon or affecting the many beauties of the MU system, which I have tried to instill into your legal mind.

"I had expected to be back by Monday, and I shall try not to be unduly delayed. Say, by the way, why don't you form a legal regiment? It ought to break down any barrier.

"Most respectfully,

"P.S.: You might be seasick."

From Washington there was no immediate response, possibly because Theodore Roosevelt had resigned to form his own Rough Riders regiment. In due course Sprague received a form letter of thanks and a suggestion that he might present himself for medical examination at his own convenience, following which, if satisfactory, some form of active duty might be considered. And then something happened that shattered this dream; at the Watsessing plant that May Sprague received an eye injury that all but blinded him. It wasn't until mid-June that he was able to read again, and by then Dewey's victory at Manila Bay had changed the entire complexion of the naval campaign.

XIII: THE HABIT OF A LIFETIME

Naval Advisory Board, Edison (standing 3rd from right) and Sprague (far right). (Courtesy of John L. Sprague)

By the time the first World War broke out in Europe Sprague was nearing his sixties, and he had no delusions that he could talk himself into active service. Then something else came along that seemed the next best thing. In 1915 the Secretary of the Navy, Josephus Daniels, announced that he would appoint a Naval Advisory Board of Inventors, a group of scientists and inventors whose minds, Daniels said, would be placed at the service of their country.

At the outset Daniels was apparently thinking mainly in terms of preparedness propaganda; he seems to have envisioned a small group of names like Edison, Sprague, and Wilbur Wright that could serve as a symbol. But Edison (who chaired the Board), firmly seconded by Sprague, rebelled at the idea of a figurehead function. Both men advised Daniels to approach each of the large engineering and scientific societies, asking them to nominate one or two preeminent men from each field. This was done, and late in 1915 an unexpectedly distinguished Naval Advisory Board convened for the first time. Its members, in addition to Sprague and Edison, included Baekeland, Maxim, Sperry, Cooper-Hewitt, and Whitney. Later additions included Compton, Millikan, and De Forest.

At first the Navy obviously didn't know what to do with its advisory board of brains. The young Assistant Secretary of the Navy, a civil young man named Franklin Roosevelt, was polite but rather vague; and the admirals in charge clearly regarded them with reserve and suspicion. Sprague was the only one of the group who was Annapolis-trained and therefore not automatically to be dismissed as an ignorant landlubber. And even he did not endear himself to the admirals for, after taking a month's cruise with the Atlantic Fleet at the start of 1916, he came back to make a public report that, in view of its sharpness and plain speaking, can hardly have won him friends at naval headquarters:

> "While we have some splendid individual ships, we have no well-balanced fleet. Instead of occupying second place among world powers, I doubt if we are better than fourth in actual fighting capacity.

"We have no cruisers on the British Lion or Tiger class...and no dreadnaughts with a speed greater than 22 knots. Our submarines, although they, as well as a large majority of fundamental new departures in marine architecture and naval progress, originated in the U.S., are unworthy of the name."

The Naval Board, though made up of civilians without legal standing and without welcome from the admirals in charge, began to function effectively toward the end of 1916. It forced the founding of the Naval Research Laboratory. (Edison, shocked to discover that the Navy had had no research organization worthy of the name, tried unsuccessfully to have the NRL located away from Washington and Annapolis, and bossed only by civilians.) The Board also organized itself, listed the main technical problems confronting the Navy, and divided itself into special committees to grapple with each of them.

Sprague found himself chairman of committees on electricity and shipbuilding, and member of other committees on submarines, ordnance, explosives, and special problems. As it turned out, Sprague worked very hard for the duration of the war on two chief problems, armor-piercing shells and improved depth charges. The former were of a new type (designed jointly by Sprague and by his son Desmond, then a young Cornell-trained engineer) that were devised to explode not on impact but only after maximum penetration. The improvements that Sprague made in depth charges were—because of the severity of the U-boat threat in 1917—more important in affecting the course of the war. Earlier depth charges issued by the Navy had proved to be both primitive and uncertain. Sprague increased the explosive charge and developed a new pressure-sensitive firing mechanism that could be counted on to detonate the charge at any preset depth. Desmond, whose attitude toward his father had a tinge of hero-worship, later wrote that "the old man daily risked his life in testing out depth charges and shells off Sandy Hook."

The praise didn't come solely from Sprague's son. Years later, after ruffled feathers in the Navy Department had had a chance to smooth down, a historian's assessment of the Naval Board wartime achievements could be made. What stood out from the perspective of history were three accomplishments: founding of the Naval Research Laboratory, the development of submarine detection methods by DeForest and Whitney, and the major improvement on depth charges done by Sprague.

XIII: THE HABIT OF A LIFETIME

Frank J. Sprague circa 1919 (Courtesy John L. Sprague)

The 1920s were a busy, restless, but not altogether satisfactory decade for Sprague. The problem was not age; though moving from his sixties to his seventies, he remained lively, hard-working, and endlessly curious in his intellectual interests. An engineer who worked with him during the period describes him this way:

> "I was struck by the quietness and modesty of the fellow. He surely knew that he was already being described as the 'father of electric traction.' And he'd already collected a sheaf of honorary degrees and medals by then. I'd heard some talk about his temper and tongue, but he never set off any rockets at our meetings. Although he rarely said much, when he did it was exactly to the point. It was the way he managed to lead the group."

One continuing drain on Sprague during the period was the long-drawn-out litigating and politicking that automatic train control demanded. It was a financial drain as well; and by the time the stock-market collapsed Sprague had to face the fact that, although not impoverished, he was no longer a rich man.

Another Depression-shadowed development was the fact that he was able to make only a technical but not a commercial success of an idea that came to him in 1927 when he was seventy. He had been musing about the economics of skyscraper size. One limitation on building height was the increasing amount of nonrevenue space that had to be given to elevator shafts. After a certain height the immense number of cubic feet that

XIII: THE HABIT OF A LIFETIME

were eaten up by these vertical railroads began to make height uneconomic.

Whereupon Sprague snapped his fingers. Why should an elevator shaft be a one-car railroad? The sensible answer would be to provide two separate elevators in one shaft. The upper one would be a local-express, running express from the lobby to a point part way up the building and then making local stops. The lower car, riding the same rails but with its own hoist mechanism, would make local stops on the lower floors. And as for collisions it wouldn't be hard to make them impossible, using a variant on the automatic train control principle.

Sprague worked out the details, got a series of patents, and built several working models to demonstrate the idea. Several large real-estate operators nibbled at the notion, sheering off after they learned that building-code officials felt that the concept was "unsafe on the face of it." This was an irritating delay, though seemingly no more than that. By the time that Sprague had brought the building-code officials around, the Great Depression was in full swing, and no new construction of a scale that could use the idea going up. The dual-elevator plan had to stay on the shelf until 1931 when Westinghouse, building new quarters in East Pittsburgh, obtained a license from Sprague to use his patents. So he had the pleasure of seeing at least one installation made of this unconventional but highly logical idea.

Another development of the twenties that pleased Sprague came when his son Bob launched out in the electrical (more properly, electronic) business for himself. Bob, Sprague's second son and the oldest by the second marriage, had been an early radio amateur as a youngster, and his bent for radio stayed with him after he grew up. An Annapolis graduate in 1919 (accelerated two years from the class of 1921, no small feat), he had been assigned in the mid-Twenties to work on the *U.S.S. Lexington*, the Navy's first originally-designed carrier, when she was building in Fore River, Massachusetts. Married and living in nearby Quincy, in his spare time Bob built a radio gadget that seemed to have commercial possibilities. It was an accessory tone control, a selector switch coupled to a tapped paper condenser. Bob resolved to take a flyer at selling it; he put in his personal savings of $3,200, his father put in $10,000, and other relatives and friends brought the initial capitalization of the little enterprise up to $25,000.

Starting as a kitchen-table venture in Bob's Quincy home in June 1926, the venture began badly. In five months more than half the money had gone, and not enough of the tone controls were being sold to cover expenses. Then Bob's younger brother, Julian, joined the firm and asked a question: if the public couldn't be persuaded to buy enough tone controls, would there be a chance to sell the unusually compact and efficient condenser it contained directly to radio manufacturers? This was tried with almost the last of the little firm's cash, and it proved to be a roaring success. In less than three years the company had become a rapidly growing and highly profitable industrial enterprise. Weathering a couple of shaky years in the Depression, it continued to expand and prosper until now it is the country's largest maker of capacitors and a leading manufacturer of electronic components.

Frank Sprague played no direct part in his sons' success, aside from the initial $10,000 and some advice to Bob about his patents. But the investment was profitable to him in his final years and in his widow's subsequent ones. More important than that, it was a source of pleasure and pride to him to realize that the Sprague name would continue to be a respected part of the U.S. electrical industry.

Sprague slowed down very little in his last years. Still unwilling to stop working, he maintained an office and laboratory at 421 Canal Street in New York City, working there regularly in the early Thirties. There is a suggestion that he made a conscious effort to avoid the pitfalls of living too much in the past. He remained spry, cheerful, and inventive. (That last word, he once told an interviewer, annoyed him almost as much as the word "wizard." Both terms made the process sound altogether too mystical. Really, he insisted, most useful developments are not mystical in the least; they are just engineering solutions to freshly defined problems.)

Once Sprague invited a visitor into his office at the Canal Street laboratory. It was a comfortably-littered room with photographs on the wall from Richmond and the Alley L, and with his framed commission as an ensign, signed by Chester A. Arthur. Seated at a large, old-fashioned desk that was piled high with blueprints and technical papers, Sprague unearthed for his guest a peculiar-looking electric toaster. Although he didn't have the remotest intention of manufacturing appliances, he explained, he had designed and built this particular one. Why? Well, just about every toaster he had ever seen was an abomination, miserably clumsy and inefficient. So simply for fun he had sketched out and made one with some sense to it. "Works just fine," he added with a flashing grin.

More serious projects in his last years included an electric autopilot for aircraft and a new concept in animated electric signs. He had been fascinated by the moving electric sign that, a few years before, had been built in a narrow horizontal band around the New York Times Building in Times Square. It was clever but clearly inefficient, limited to the pace of the slowest readers, and unable to transmit anything but block letters. He saw how the idea could be vastly improved. He'd borrow a trick from movie titles: provide a giant rectangular panel of lights and make the words appear in lines that moved slowly up from bottom to top. That way he could put out five times as many words a minute, and he could use trademarks and animated displays, too.

He worked out the details, applied for patents, and built several large working models that, he felt, showed how superior the sign was to existing ones. "But it is always hard to convince the conservative element," he remarked to his visitor. "They won't believe anything they see in a laboratory. I will have to do with this what I have always done, set it up outside someplace, start it going, and then say to them, 'There it is.'" So Sprague did just that. A large moving sign that he designed was part of the Time-Fortune exhibit at the Chicago Century of Progress Exposition. And yet this was one final battle that Sprague could not fight out to a finish with the "conservative element." In October 1934 he caught a cold that quickly progressed to pneumonia, his third attack in two years. He seems to have had no inkling that this bout was any more serious than the earlier ones. He was exasperated that his doctor wouldn't permit aides from the laboratory to come to his bedside to talk over some circuit modifications that had occurred to him. Then, on the night of October 25, 1934 in his seventy-seventh year, he died.

Sprague was buried with full naval honors in Arlington National Cemetery. The outpouring of eulogistic newspaper editorials honoring the "father of electric traction" surprised most of his surviving associates, many of whom believed that Sprague had been too little recognized by the public, and still obscured by the posthumous shadow of Edison. But his death was extensively covered in the press, typically in editorials pointing out that, with the death of Alexander Graham Bell and Thomas Edison and now Frank Sprague, the three great pioneers of electricity had now all passed on. Sprague received editorial tribute in everything from the Milford (Connecticut) Citizen to the New York and London Times.

In a rather strange way, Sprague had been given the rare and perhaps even disquieting opportunity of listening to and reading his own eulogies. This came about, of course, at the unusual public birthday party (mentioned in Chapter I) that had been tendered him on his 75th anniversary. The idea of staging a public tribute to Sprague originated some months before the occasion among four of his oldest friends. They were Frank Shepard, then of Westinghouse; W. B. Potter, of GE; Frank Hedley, of New York's IRT subway system; and Guy Richardson, of the American Electric Railway Association. Meeting in secret, they had the pleasing notion of going beyond the conventional rites of a testimonial ceremony. Instead, they would write privately to everyone they could locate who had known or worked with Sprague from the earliest days, and to people from each of the other worlds that he had also moved in. Then, if they got enough letters of response, they would surprise F. J. with them on his birthday. This would give their old friend something more tangible than just the recollection of probably embarrassing public praise.

Shepard and his cronies, taking pains to keep the project secret, sent out letters to a master list they had compiled. The response was overwhelming. Almost five hundred replies of affectionate reminiscence and tribute came back. Some were from the great ones of the day, people like Herbert Hoover and Franklin D. Roosevelt, whose paths had happened to cross Sprague's in the past. Others came from associates who

XIII: THE HABIT OF A LIFETIME

had moved on to the upper slopes of great corporations and universities. A quite separate group were his "anti-engineering" friends, people like Booth Tarkington, Oliver Herford, Robert Bridges, Emil Ludwig, and Ossip Gabrilowitsch, who didn't know A.C. from D.C. but had become his friends in the mellower years. And a fourth group was also represented, unexpectedly renewed friendships from the distant past.

The letters, bound together in six volumes, were presented to Sprague at the climax of the birthday party at the Engineering Societies Building on that hot July night in 1932. They touched Sprague, and no wonder, for they make fascinating reading even today. Not unexpectedly, the ones that hold the most interest now are not from the movers and shakers but from the distant if unforgotten past. Classmates from '78 in the Naval Academy recalled the excitements of the trip to the Centennial, or of the time they had pitched in to help a sharp young instructor on the faculty, an ensign named Albert Michelson, make his first experimental measurement of the speed of light. One classmate recalled with awe the fistfight that Sprague had had over his unwillingness to send the black classmate to Coventry.

Then there were echoes of the earliest days in electricity. Bill Hammer wrote of the exciting months at the Crystal Palace in London, Charlie Clark reminded Sprague of the day in Brockton when he'd had to heave a treasured but badly-smoking experimental motor right through the boarding-house window.

From Richmond, from the first elevator jobs in New York, from the canal bank, and from the Alley L came a whole chorus of recollection. Carichoff remembered the control handles that whizzed so explosively into the Erie Canal. Sunny described his short-lived laugh about how some idiot director had been taken in by a "fellow with a military title who had built a dumbwaiter for cocktails." One man, himself now old, wrote of his first job as an anxious 16-year-old during the Alley L installation. He recalled how alarmed he had been when the great and dangerous Mr. Sprague, sighting a raised drawbridge down the track, had stuck his head from the cab to say coolly, "There's quite a hill ahead, but I think we can make it with a run." And Oscar Crosby whose subsequent career included being U.S. Commissioner of Patents and Assistant Secretary of the Treasury, wrote of 1888: "And out of the woods we emerged, flags flying, as we captured Richmond! Great days! Technical difficulties, financial difficulties, professional jealousies, nothing could daunt the man to whom the world owes more, in the matter of electric traction, than to any other ten men combined."

As Sprague got up to speak that July night, about the only ones out of the past who were not represented were those whom death had already taken—Edison, Villard, Ed Johnson, Coffin, Dana Greene, and Pat O'Shaughnessy. Sprague delivered a graceful and highly civilized speech of thanks. Quickly he summarized the ancient battles and trials, meticulously listing his associates on each occasion and skirting the conflicts and jealousies that had been passed. Only at the very last part of the talk did he allow himself a flash of emotion, couched in terms most of his audience would appreciate:

"And now I must say, not goodbye, although some of us may perhaps not meet again, but rather au revoir, for the current is still on the line, and the pantograph is up, and we are headed for another station."

FOR FURTHER READING

Harold C. Passer, *Frank Julian Sprague, Father of Electric Traction,* Reprint by permission of the publishers from *Men in Business*, edited by William Miller, Cambridge, MA: Harvard University Press, 1952, pp. 212 - 237

H. C. J. Sprague, *Frank J. Sprague and the Edison Myth*. New York: William-Frederick Press, 1947.

F. Dalzell, *Engineering Invention, Frank J. Sprague and the U.S. Electrical Industry.* Cambridge, MA: MIT Press, 2010.

W. D. Middleton and W.D. Middleton III. *Frank Julian Sprague, Electrical Inventor and Engineer.* Bloomington, IN: Indiana University Press, 2009.

P. Connor, "The underground electric train," *Underground News*, a series of five articles detailing F. J. Sprague's technology and its impact on the London Underground, vol. 523, pp. 270 - 273, July 2005; vol. 524, pp. 325 - 330, Aug. 2005; vol. 525, pp. 404

- 408, Sept. 2005; vol. 526, pp. 486 - 491, Oct. 2005; and vol. 527, pp. 534 – 539, Nov. 2005.

Frank J. Sprague Papers (1874-1939), New York City Public Library, Rare Books and Manuscripts Division, Accession number *88 M 28.

Frank J. Sprague Seventy-fifth Anniversary Books. Williamstown, MA: Chapin Library, Williams College, 1932.

Frank J. Sprague Seventy-fifth Anniversary Program. New York City, NY, 25 July 1932.

P. Israel, *Edison: A Life of Invention*. New York: John Wiley & Sons, 1998.

John L. Sprague and Joseph J. Cunningham, *A Frank Sprague Triumph, the Electrification of Grand Central Terminal*, IEEE Power & Energy Magazine, vol. 11(#1), pp. 58 – 76, January/February 2013

APPENDIX 1

Through the wonderful responses that make-up the six volumes of letter books referred to at the end of Chapter 13, it is possible to recreate Frank J. Sprague's life through the eyes of those who knew him, worked for him, competed with him, and knew of him. In this appendix, samples of those responses that dealt with his creative genius are presented as sequentially as possible by category, starting with the US Naval Academy at Annapolis, MD. The greatest number of salutations came from FJS' two largest competitors, GE (close to 30) and Westinghouse (nearly 40). The letter books for both Appendices now reside as part of the Frank J. Sprague papers in the Chapin Rare Book Library of Williams College in Williamstown, MA. The letters that follow are full digitized copies of the originals or shorter summaries of their content.

Annapolis/US Navy:

J. H. Glennon (Rear Admiral, USN <ret.>, Annapolis graduate, and close friend of FJS)

H. P. Huse (Vice Admiral, USN <ret.>, Annapolis roommate, and close friend)

H. E. Lackey (Captain, USN and friend)

Edison General Electric (EGE):

C. L. Clark (former EGE co-employee and close friend)

G. Pantaleoni (important Westinghouse engineer & founder; letter sent to FJS by his son, Guido Pantaleoni, Jr.)

Sprague Electric Railway and Motor Company (SERM)/Richmond:

W. Hammer (SERM founder, incorporator, and first treasurer)

N. Tesla (famous inventor and EGE associate)

Elihu Thomson (co-founder of Thomson-Houston that merged with EGE and became GE)

D. C. Jackson (MIT Professor; was early FJS associate at SERM, and close friend)

S. W. Huff (1890 summer employee at SERM; later president, N Y 3rd Avenue Railway System)

J. W. McCloy (Editor of American Electric Railway Association)
G. Marconi (famous inventor and scientist)

Sprague Electric Elevator Company (SEEC):

H. F. Gurney (Otis Elevator executive and former SEEC employee)
L. K. Comstock (tongue-in-cheek recall of 1893 inspection of SEEC NYC Grand Hotel elevator installation)

Sprague Electric Company (SEC) and MU:

W. H. Sawyer (amusing recall of early MU incident)
H. H. Westinghouse (Ch. Westinghouse Air Brake Co. lauds MU)
A. D. Campbell (amusing recall of industrial espionage by MU competitor)
J.W. Butt (recalls meeting FJS in Brooklyn and testing of MU system)
F. E. Case (one of most important MU endorsements by key GE engineer)
S. W. Childs (recalls importance GE president C. A. Coffin placed on acquisition of FJS MU patent)
E. W. Rice (another important GE endorsement)

Naval Consulting Board

E. G. Oberlin (thank you for FJS' endorsement of creation of the Naval Research Laboratory)
E. L. Beach (Captain, USN <ret.> recalls different FJS inventions including armor-piercing "depth bomb")

Dual Elevator: H. D. James (Westinghouse executive describes dual elevator installation)

General: S. S. Robison (Rear Admiral, USN <ret.> summarizes FJS' life and accomplishments)

APPENDIX 1

Jamestown, R.I., June 23, 1932
Dear Sprague,

Looking back from the three quarter mark some 58 years this September, I see walking in front of the Old Recitution Hall at the Naval Academy, a young man of your size in the uniform of some Massachusetts Military Academy. I heard later that it was you. You were not ashamed or afraid to face the hazards of the upper classes. You were going, as became a native of Massachusetts, to talk to the black cadet midshipman of our class, if you wanted to. Punishment was awarded by the upperclassmen and turnbacks. You were not much phased, persecution kept up, and finally a fight with a third classman was arranged. You have not the pug nose of a fistic champion, were a sorry sight after the battle, but you licked your man.

On the third class cruise you rode the port yardarm on coming into anchor. Rather a precarious position for anyone in bracing the yard square, but you stuck to it, holding on like grim death.

We, you and I, measured the horizontal magnetic force of the earth in the neighborhood of the Physics Building in our First Class year. Sampson I think gave us, all that took the Electric Course in Physics, perfect marks because we voted against an additional differential for elective work. Both you and I were cadet Ensigns at the time and poked fun at each other at the Staff Table as long as I remained an Ensign Cadet.

After your two years cruise you came back for final examination. The Board of practical men who orally examined you in Seamanship first stumped you with a mean question as to how to get a top or crosstrees over the mast, befuddled you with a compass question and gave you an unsatisfactory mark in Seamanship. Any of us could have fallen the same way. Though on re-examination you passed, the counting mark was the unsatisfactory one, and it reduced you from your four year position of seven in the class to nine or ten. Not long afterwards you resigned, probably in disgust.

Well you can look back over the years and see yourself gaining your number back, and going to the front. There are very few of the class left, but such as they are, I think they will all cheerfully accord you the honor position of #1. Personally, I consider you the greatest inventor of the day, and knowing your stubborn and honest characteristics, I am certain you have done it yourself, and that what is called yours is actually the product of your own mind and work. I wish you long life, health, happiness and all future success.

The sponsors limit one to one page. Maybe you can get a reduced copy of these three.

APPENDIX 1

Always with much regard
Your old classmate
J.H. Glennon,
(Rear Admiral USN (ret.)

James H. Glennon, Rear Admiral (ret)
(courtesy of Chapin Library)

3 June, 1932

My dear Sprague:

Yesterday I saw my grandson graduate at the Naval Academy. The ceremony was an enlargement of one which took place on a beautiful day in June 54 years ago when you and I received our diplomas. The past came back so vividly that it almost seemed more real than the ceremony that was actually being enacted. And my thoughts went even further back — to a day in September 1874 when you and I started, "housekeeping" together in a room on the second floor of Building No. 2 Stribling Row. You were wearing a cap which you said was part of the uniform of a boys' military organization in North Adams, Massachusetts. The memories remain, but the buildings are all gone; not one remains of those that stood when you and I entered the Academy 58 years ago except, in a modified form, the little guard-house at the gate on Maryland Avenue.

Do you remember how Ensign Michelson of 1873, who was an instructor in the department of Physics and Chemistry and taught our class, rigged up some curious looking mirrors in one of the windows of Commander W.T. Sampson's house in Blake Row and other mirrors in a window of the Physics department two or three hundred yards distant? We knew that he was seeking to measure the velocity of light through the deflection of a ray by a revolving reflector, but we no *more* realized the far-reaching and immense importance of his work than we did the fore-shadowed results of the work of a youngster of our own class who spent his recreation hours playing with gadgets in the physics Laboratory. If I remember right, one of these gadgets became a telephone; but we always suspected that the one you rigged up played little part in conveying the words we would yell into the receiver at one end of the line to be carried to the other end on the floor above.

Was it in the old line-of-battleship Minnesota in 1880 that you showed us the working model of an arc-light that you had designed? I remember that what pleased you was, not the originality of the device, but that you had been able to design a machine that actually operated as you intended it should. In other words, you had succeeded in giving material expression to an idea. This was doubtless the practical beginning of what became your life work.

We are very proud of you, Sprague, and we like to remark in a casual way, "Yes; Frank J, Sprague graduated in my class at the Naval Academy in 1878.

Sincerely yours,
Harry P. Huse
Vice Admiral, U. S. Navy

NAVY DEPARTMENT, BOARD OF INSPECTION
AND SURVEY, PACIFIC COAST SECTION,
100 HARRISON STREET, SAN FRANCISCO,
CALIFORNIA
17 June, 1932.

Admiral (ret.) Lackey summarizes his long time relationship with Frank J. Sprague, including the work Sprague did on deceleration spring safety fuses during World War I, and his June 1925 trip from Annapolis to Hawaii on then Captain Lackey's USS Memphis. They were close friends.

Always sincerely yours,
Henry E. Lackey

APPENDIX 1

1161 Parkwood Boulevard
Schenectady, NY
June 10, 1932

My dear Sprague:

So you are going to acknowledge 75 birthdays, since the original one, on July 25th. For which, as you are still active and in good bodily condition, I must and gladly do congratulate you — with the hope that you may continue on for a long time yet.

It is so well-known what you have done in electricity for the benefit of mankind, as expressed in one of many ways by the public honors you have received, that I forgo repeating even a part of your achievements. Instead, I will get at a few of the personalities of the case — there are heart beats and red blood in such.

Well what have the years done for you as one of the human family — all of them utterly self-willed at the start, coming into the world with a howl and kicking to the best of ability, sometimes to be kept up the lifelong?

Aside from your electro-mechanical talents, so universally recognized, an outstanding and particularly helpful trait has been a forceful, if occasionally required, very vocal rush, as evidenced by the energy with which you defended novel electrical plans to successful fruition in the face of normally discouraging objection — that they wouldn't work, or were impractical, or something else was better.

You early displayed that trait when you came with Edison in 1883 — and first to my attention in connection with calculation of cross-section for underground conductors of his electric lighting systems, about which you had very positive ideas as to how expeditiously to do it with practical accuracy, and which were energetically expounded by you in Spragueque fashion in a somewhat controversially similar Edisonian atmosphere.

And can you recall the time when you were in Brockton, Massachusetts, in 1883, in connection with the installing of an Edison plant there; but with plans for developing a superior electric motor disturbing your mind, the outcome of which was the later extensively used Sprague motor?

Of course you must remember it — and how, after laboriously winding a small experimental machine and filling the coils with shellac, you put it to test before being thoroughly dried out, in line with your pushing trait, with the result of a prompt burn out, instantly followed by swift ejection of the offending rascal through a window; glad nevertheless to get out of hearing of the vocal storm chasing in its wake. It did the motor no immediate good; but its sedative effect upon the parent's nerves led to recovery, rewinding, reshellacing and this time thorough drying out, whereby the machine was in proper condition to do its duty — and did it.

APPENDIX 1

The foregoing are early examples of one feature of the Sprague complex, that served you a good turn in after years, and has become a great good for the people in a number of ways, which are part of the history of technical progress.

But how about that same feature of the Sprague complex at 75 years of age? I warrant that time has not worn it out or markedly diminished its efficiency for useful results; but that it has become mellowed with the response of experience to the conserving of vital forces in the doing of things.

Frank: in the inexorable order of Nature, we are getting toward the west. By and by, the twilight of life will be abundantly apparent to our senses; and when that time comes let us hope it may be illuminated with all the memory colors of a glorious sunset, to sustain a faith in a better life to come.

Well have you done your work for this world,

              Your fifty-year friend,

Chas. L. Clarke (Consulting Engineer, GE <ret.>)

            Frank J. Sprague, Esq.
              New York City

G. PANTALEONI
BANK OP COMMERCE BUILDING
ST. LOUIS. MO.

My dear Guido;

The work of Frank J. Sprague in the development of Electric Science in all of its branches has been so far reaching that it is not even necessary to refer to it in an occasion like the present one, as not only all technicians, but even all civilians of Education know of it.

I first heard of him in the early days in a matter that is perhaps not generally known, and yet is as indicative of the man's character and far sightedness as any minor thing can be.

You must remember that in the early days of electric development, real scientific points of view were entirely obscured by the unbelievable mutual hatreds and jealousies of the parties engaged in the financial promotions; each group had their special "Wizard", to whom everything good was attributed, and nothing could have any good in it unless endorsed by this leader.

When the Westinghouse people began to push and recommend the use of alternating currents, a perfectly unbelievable storm of opposition was started, going so far as to cause a special bill to be introduced and put through the Legislature of the

State of New York, substituting the death penalty by the use of alternating currents (as recommended by the Westinghouse interests)for all other methods theretofore in use.

Sprague was then on the staff of the Corporation (Edison General Electric) that was more bitter in its antagonism to alternating currents than any of the many.

I do not know how it happened or was brought about, but Sprague was directed to study the entire question, with the implied intention of definitely burying alternating currents, by rendering it improbable that financiers would invest in a thing so condemned.

Sprague's report was an exhaustive one, and a remarkable one when you remember the atmosphere of hate then existing; his analysis of the very crude state of the art as it then was, the immense possibilities of the use of alternating currents could not have been bettered today. He strongly recommended to his particular wizard that immediate steps be taken to develop any possibilities that there might be in this new departure; fortunately I may say, for the interests with which I was then connected (Westinghouse), his principals suppressed the report; I had an opportunity of seeing it at about the time it was written, and mentioned it to Mr. Westinghouse. It has always been a matter of regret to me that we did not see our way then to approach Sprague and inveigle him into our camp; we would have advanced very much faster in all the art.

I do not know whether Sprague himself can remember these little details of his early life, because he has accomplished so much that it must be difficult for him to remember all he did; personally I am sure of the above being an exact statement of a small episode probably unknown to the world at large.

G Pantaleoni

APPENDIX 1

527 Lexington Ave., New York City, NY July 25, 1932

My dear Sprague,

I esteem it a privilege to join with your other engineering friends and associates in this well merited tribute to you upon your 75th Birthday.

Perhaps the writer may claim to have been one of your earliest and most intimate associates, for with the late lamented Edward H. Johnson and your good self I was privileged to act as an Incorporator of the Sprague Electric Railway and Motor Company in 1884 and serve as one of the Sprague Board of Trustees and the company's first secretary & there were other intimate points of contact which you will doubtless recall, notably the 98 stationary Sprague motors which, in cooperation with the local Sprague agents, I installed upon the overhead and underground circuits of the Boston Edison Co., of which I was Genl. Manager and Chief Engineer in 1886 & 1887. This was a very early & extensive use of electric power.

Our first meeting was at the Int. Electrical Exhibition at the Crystal Palace England in 1882. You at the time an Ensign in the U. S. Navy, had been sent by Uncle Sam to report upon the Exhibition, and here it was that you as Secretary of the Test Jury made your elaborate report, which was a model of its time and it was during this period that you, Johnson, and I were thrown together and we formed our lasting friendship.

In 1881 Mr. Edison had sent Mr. E. H. Johnson, one of his ablest associates, and myself to London to form the English Edison Company. We built the historic Holborn Viaduct Central Station, the first central station in the world for supplying the Edison incandescent light. The Station, of 2 & later 3 30 ton "Jumbo" Edison dynamos and 3,000 Edison lamps, was started upon Jan. 12th, 1882.

At the same time we installed a smaller station at the Crystal Palace Exhibition employing 12 – 60 light – bipolar Edison dynamos together with the exhibit of Mr. Edison's inventions which had previously been shown at the first Electrical Expo. at Paris in 1881 & was sent over to us.

Among my valued Sprague memorabilia is an autographed copy of your Crystal Palace Exhibition report which you gave me, a description of your "Multiple Unit System of Motor Control" which you sent to me in Berlin, Germany in 1883 – at the time I was Chief Engineer of the German Edison Co. (A.E.G.) (there is a problem with Hammer's date since MU wasn't developed until the mid-1890s), and a formula which you had later devised for calculating the copper for the Edison 2 and 3 wire systems of Light & Power, this latter is in your own handwriting.

APPENDIX 1

I recall that upon your frequent trips to and from London & the Crystal Palace we discussed the various problems which would have to be met in the ultimate electrification of the London Underground Railway System and I remember how encouraged you were, even at this early period with the Electric Motor and its commercial possibilities to which you have since contributed so materially.

Very truly yours, W. J. Hammer

THE BIRTH OF ELECTRIC TRACTION

Hotel Governor Clinton, 31st Street & Seventh Ave, New York, N.Y.
June 13, 1932

Mr. Frank J, Sprague,
421 Canal Street New York, N.Y.

Dear Sprague:

It gives me great pleasure to join your many friends and admirers in congratulating you and expressing appreciation of your achievements on this fortunate occasion.

At the very beginning of our acquaintance in 1884 you impressed me as a man of great force, tenacious of purpose, eloquent, strong in argument and thoroughly permeated with practical sense. These qualities would have enabled you to succeed under the most adverse circumstances.

In your important contribution to the electrical industries you have proved yourself an original, resourceful and painstaking worker. Your electric trolley railway, put in operation in 1887, was a true pioneering enterprise inaugurating a new epoch. As a business venture it was an amazing feat demonstrating to the incredulous world the soundness and value of your ideas and improvements which have stood the test of time. The credit for them was often given to others, but posterity cannot be deceived and will assign to you a distinguished place in the history of electrical arts and industries.

    Wishing you heartily many happy returns of your birthday and continued success, I remain

> Sincerely yours,
> Nikola Tesla

THE BIRTH OF ELECTRIC TRACTION

Elihu Thomson, Director
Thomson Research Laboratory
General Electric Company
Lynn, Mass.

May 24, 1932

My Dear Sprague:

It gives me great pleasure to join with your many other friends of long past in writing you and sending my congratulations on your attainment of the age of seventy-five years. I remember well the time we first met at the Franklin Institute Electrical Exhibition in Philadelphia in the fall of 1884, when you explained the work in which you were engaged, in the design of advanced types of electrical motors for direct current work. Now I have been more or less familiar with your subsequent work and career and take this occasion to emphasize the fact of its great importance, especially to the art of electric railway control and propulsion. I think it can be truly said that your trials of the trolley system in Richmond, Virginia were a definite starting point in the development of trolley systems in the United States. I feel sure that it was this work of yours which led Mr. Henry H. Whitney of the West End road in Boston to look favorably upon the adoption of electric traction for that city, as a substitute for horses. Needless to say, the subsequent electrification of the whole of the street car lines itself followed and created a profound impression which led to the rapid extension of the electric railway systems throughout the country.

It is also my privilege to point out that the first actual demonstration of the multiple unit operation of electric trains, so far as I know it, was worked out successfully by yourself and applied to the elevated road trains in cities such as Boston.

Better than all of this, I have appreciated the many years of sympathetic acquaintance and friendship which it has been my privilege to have had with you, and in closing this brief letter, I wish you many future years of life and activity.

                    Very truly yours,
                    Elihu Thomson

Mr. Frank J. Sprague
c/o Frank J. Sprague Anniversary Committee
Room 1613 – 150 Broadway
New York, NY

MASSACHUSETTS INSTITUTE of TECHNOLOGY
DEPARTMENT of ELECTRICAL ENGINEERING
CAMBRIDGE, MASSACHUSETS

May 13, 1932

MIT Professor Dugald C. Jackson remembers his early 1886 employment by Frank Sprague at SERM, Sprague's success at Richmond, followed by his electric elevator work and then MU.

He then goes on to "bespeak a special thought for Mrs. Sprague and her rose garden into which she <shunts> you of summers."

Sincerely yours,
Dugald C. Jackson

APPENDIX 1

OFFICE of the PRESIDENT
Third Avenue Railway System
2396 Third Avenue, New York

July 25, 1932

S. W. Huff recalls "The summer of 1990 I spent as a pit hand in your old street railway shops at 29th and P Streets in Richmond", adding a colorful comment about Pat O'Shaughnessy.

He then goes on to describe problems they had with the early electric motors, because parts weren't interchangeable and a sledge hammer sometimes was required to hammer together the fields and pole pieces.

Yours very truly,
S. W. Huff

June 14, 1932

Mr. Frank J. Sprague, President,
Sprague Safety Control and Signal Corp.
421 Canal Street,
New York, New York.

Dear Mr. Sprague:

    It is at once a pleasure and a privilege to join with your host of friends in extending my best wishes on the occasion of your seventy-fifth birthday.

    When the first commercially successful electric street railway line was opened to service under your direction in Richmond, someone is said to have remarked that Frank Sprague had finally freed the mule.

    You did much more than this. You and those others who followed along the path which you traced freed the city dweller from the bondage of horse-drawn transportation. What this has meant to our present-day civilization in terms of comfort, convenience and health no man can measure. Certainly, it was one of the most notable and significant advances in civic development that has taken place in our day and generation. And in spite of all the changes that time has brought, organized transportation, with the electric car as its primary basis, is today one of the most important and essential elements in city life.

APPENDIX 1

So here's to your good health, and may you enjoy many more birthdays in the future.

> Sincerely your friend,
> James McCloy
> Editor of AERA

Marconi House, Strand
London, W. C. 2

May 6. 1932

Frank Julian Sprague, Esq.,
Dear Mr. Sprague,

    This is just a line to congratulate you very heartily on the occasion of your seventy-fifth birthday, and to wish you Many Happy Returns of the 25th of July.
    Several of your friends in America assure me that you are as young and as energetic as ever - which I readily believe and am delighted to hear - and I trust that the future holds for you many more years of health and happiness.
    I often recall with pleasure my early days in America, when your friendship and kindly interest were an unfailing source of encouragement to me in my work. And earlier still, when I was quite a boy, I remember the enthusiasm throughout Italy when the first electric tramway - built after your design - was inaugurated at Florence.
    In memory of those early days, and, as a token of my enduring esteem and regard, I am sending

APPENDIX 1

you my photograph, together with every good wish for your continued prosperity and happiness. Believe me, dear Mr. Sprague,
Very sincerely yours,

G Marconi

Otis Elevator Company
June 12, 1932

Frank J. Sprague, Esq.
New York City

My dear chief,

I cannot realize you will soon be seventy five years old because you still appear as youthful and as full of pep as you were in 1893 when you demonstrated to me what a human dynamo really was. The energy and "sticktoity" you displayed were a lifelong example for me.

You originated and developed the high speed electric elevator at the time and not only that, but you drove the hydraulic elevator out of business and put the Electric in its place.

I am and shall always be proud of my working with you at that time. Wishing you continuing success and happiness, I am Sincerely Yours,

Howard F. Gurney

L. K. COMSTOCK & COMPANY INCORPORATED ELECTRICAL CONSTRUCTION
16 East 52 Street New York City

In this amusing anecdote, electrical contractor Louis Comstock describes the sales job he was given on an 1893 visit to the Sprague elevators in the NYC Grand Hotel.

"Dr, Sprague assured me that 'the travelling nut would not over-run its travel because it was the physical concept of the square root of minus one'; whereupon Dr. Pratt, leaning heavily on Charlie Benton, gravely said, 'these case hardened steel balls perform the function of the differential co-efficient of the speed of the screw times the radius of gyration of the unknown quantity raised to the nth power'. And Benton said, 'L'enfant dit vrai'". Armed with this information Comstock was able to wow his clients.

Louis Comstock

Willits H. Sawyer
EXECUTIVE ENGINEER
As of July 25, 1932.

To Him Who Is All Things Wonderful To All Engineers but is Specifically and Rightfully Claimed as Father, Dad, Mentor, and Most Inspiring Exemplar to Electric Traction Devotees, - My Honored friend, Frank J. Sprague:

    It was in the late eighties that I first read about Frank Sprague and his accomplishments and inventions. For a period of something like ten years, I had a feeling akin to reverence for you. I ascribed to you at that time the attributes of the scientist and looked up to you in wonderment and awe at your many achievements. Time has but added to and multiplied my respect and admiration for those achievements which were, in effect, but the beginning of your most successful career. It was, however, in the latter part of the nineties that I first met you and was brought to an appreciation that, in addition to your accomplishments as savant and scientist, you were a most human individual and a very definite "he man" who said what he had to say in unmistakable understanding language.

    That was my first personal contact reaction. My close second reaction at that time was of your everlasting, indomitable, energy. You were most alive and alert both mentally and physically. You delighted in achieving the impossible. Nothing daunted you and it was also particularly noticeable how you transmitted your enthusiasm to your immediate associates. As time has gone on, my profound respect has rightfully and properly increased for your achievements in many and diverse fields. Perhaps I should be content, at such a time as this, to speak only of those record achievements but, when I get to reminiscing, there is one particular picture of you which stands out most plainly. It was on the berme bank at Schenectady. The test car was out for your inspection and approval. The mechanism failed to work properly, your normal restraint broke bounds. There issued from your lips a flow of language that burned, sizzled, and would have withered a longshoreman. As I remember it, the controller handle went over into the canal. I certainly had an appreciation that day that you wanted what you wanted when you wanted it and were going to get it.

Frank, for your contribution to the world's welfare, you have the respect, gratitude, and admiration of a vast multitude. In addition you have a host of close friends who also hold a deep personal affection for you. I trust you will think of me in this letter class.

Most sincerely yours,
Bill
W.H. Sawyer

150 BROAD WAY, NEW YORK

July 25, 1932

Dear Frank,

    Having been reliably advised that July 25th registers the 75th anniversary of your birth, I trust I may be permitted to join with your many friends, in expressing to you my sincere congratulations upon the event and wishing you a long period of continued good health and usefulness in your chosen field of activity.

    During the extended period of our acquaintanceship, we have had many pleasant contacts, some of which I recall more definitely than others. One in particular (among your many achievements) which I know most about, has remained with me as outstandingly meritorious, being the development of the Multiple Control System, so successfully adapted to transportation problems. Not only did the apparatus employed exhibit a high order of inventive genius, but also the capacity of the inventor to establish its practicability. Its prompt and extensive adoption clearly demonstrated its great utility, and I regard it as a major contribution to the art of electric railway transportation.

    When in what may be classified as a retrospective mood, I find that one of the chief satisfactions in life is the contemplation of the friendships and pleasant memories attached to such relations as have existed between us - which I trust may be indefinitely continued. Were my brother still with us, I am sure it would have given him great pleasure on this occasion to express his admiration of your achievements and the high regard in which you were held by him.

    Very sincerely,
                Very Sincerely,
                H H Westinghouse

THE CITY OF SEATTLE
DEPARTMENT OF PUBLIC WORKS

June 7, 1932.

Former Sprague employee Campbell describes attempted industrial espionage by two employees of an unnamed competitor in the late 1890s.

"They came out one early morning and were sitting in the dirt under the MU street car counting the new cast iron grids and making notes. When I appeared and said 'Good morning', they lost no time in taking their departure."

Very truly yours,

A. D. Campbell

Supt. of Equipment

APPENDIX 1

The New York Central Railroad Company
466 Lexington Ave., N Y
Mr. Frank J. Sprague,
New York, N. Y.

My dear Mr. Sprague:

Kindly accept my sincere congratulations upon the *75th* anniversary of your birthday. I feel honored that I have this opportunity and that I had the good fortune to meet you during the early days of multiple unit control application to the elevated railroad oars in Brooklyn, New York,

Your vision, courage and energy, also your brilliant career are very inspiring.

Your many *notable* accomplishments are benefactors of mankind.

Since the time I met you in Brooklyn, I have been engaged in the development, application and operation of one of your notable inventions, namely, the multiple unit system of control for electric locomotives and multiple unit cars.

Well do I remember the many difficulties encountered in your endeavor to place the multiple unit system in operation on the cars of the Brooklyn Elevated Railroad.

One of the tests of operation of the multiple unit system which I feel sure convinced all persons who witnessed it, was the running of two cars on the middle track of the Broadway Division with the coupling link and pins removed from between the cars. With air brake hose coupled, safety chains hooked and electric jumper cables in place, the two cars were considered ready for the run. Witnesses were assembled on the two adjacent platforms of the cars where they could note the variation in the space between them as they proceeded along the track. The two cars started at practically the same instant. During acceleration and up to the time the air brakes were applied, there was but a small variation in the width of this space. This demonstration gave me a better understanding of the operation of the multiple unit control system than I had before the run and the information obtained was of value in the layout and other drafting work in which I was engaged at the time in connection with the application of electrical equipment to the cars of the Brooklyn Elevated Railroad.

I wish you the best of health, happiness and success, also the continuance of your brilliant career.

Yours very truly
J. W. Butt

APPENDIX 1

General Electric Company

East Lake Road
Erie, Pennsylvania

April 22, 1932

Dear Mr. Sprague:-

Although your engineering accomplishments were known to me, it was not until the summer of 1897, during the trials of your multiple-unit control on the Berme Bank in Schenectady, that I first met you. I had had an humble part in the preparations for the demonstration as the designer of the drum controllers which you purchased from the General Electric Company and to which you added pilot motors for permitting synchronous remote operation.

The immediate success of the South-Side Elevated cars the following year compelled both of the large electrical manufacturing companies to attempt to produce alternative systems. However, the thoroughness with which you had supervised the preparation of your patent application effectively thwarted every endeavor.

Multiple-unit control was one of the most important developments in the electric railway field and one which was chiefly responsible for the rapid expansion of elevated railways and for their increased carrying capacity; for the introduction of underground railways; for rapid transit lines; for electrified steam railroad terminals; and finally for the increase in size of electric locomotives.

I have often recalled the time when you, W. J. Clark,

W. B. Potter, and I had lunch at the Hardware Club in New York not many years later, and it developed during the conversation - first, that you and Mr. Clark came from the same section of Connecticut, and finally that Mr. Potter and I also were born in the good old Nutmeg State.

May the collection of letters, of which this is to become a part, be a source of many happy reminders of a busy and fruitful life.

Sincerely yours,
   F. S. Case

APPENDIX 1

Starling W Childs
One Wall Street,
New York

May 23rd, 1932.

In writing to Frank J. Sprague financier Starling Childs recalls the importance his father-in-law, GE president Charles A. Coffin, placed upon the Sprague MU patent which GE had acquired in 1902.

"He looked upon your 'Multiple Unit' control patent as about the most valuable of its patent rights." Continuing, "GE felt that in your work there was a definiteness and practicality which had never been equaled, even by the 'Wizard of Menlo Park'."

Yours sincerely,
Starling W. Childs

General Electric Company
Schenectady, N. Y.
Office of the Honorary Chairman
Schenectady, June 10, 1932

Mr. Frank J. Sprague,
Sprague Safety Control & signal Corp.
421 Canal Street
New York, N.Y.

My dear Sprague

I rejoice to send you my warmest greetings on your seventy-fifth birthday, although I cannot associate such a vigorous young man with so many years. Unfortunately for me I have seen less of you recently than in former times, yet I carry with me constantly the impression of the virile and aggressive person I met first some forty years ago.

When I think of the enormous amount of work you have done, the years seem all too few for each a marvelous record. It must be a source of satisfaction to you, not only to realize what the world has been greatly benefited as the result of your contribution, but that your genius and creative ability has been highly appreciated by your fellow men.

APPENDIX 1

I feel proud to be included among your many friends and admirers and wish you the best of health and real happiness for many years to come.

Sincerely yours,
E Wilbur Rice, Jr.
EWRice, Jr

Naval Research Laboratory
"BELLEVUE" ANACOSTIA, D. C.
25 July 1932

Dear Mr. Sprague:

Captain Oberlin recalls one of Frank J. Sprague's most important roles on the Naval Consulting Board.
"I remember the resolution you presented that resulted in the establishment of the Naval Research Laboratory."

Cordially and respectfully yours,
B. G. Oberlin

APPENDIX 1

Edward L. Beach
Palo Alto, California
June 18, 1932

My dear Frank Sprague:

I have been rummaging through old boxes of ancient relics hoping to find an old photograph of myself that you would instantly recognize. I hope still to find one to send you later, just to remind you of the Torpedo Station days of 1917 – 1918. You would not recognize the clean shaven white haired old gentleman.

I so often think of our temporary, but very close association; of your marvelous invention of that depth bomb mechanism of the shell that would explode, not when it struck a ship's armor, but after it had passed through that armor. And of the long talks we had when the day's work was done and we were at ease.

And in all the years since then you have been so often in mind. I first heard of you in the early '80s as a midshipman aboard the Trenton, who before 1880 had amazed the world by inventing the constant speed motor (Beach's date is a little early), which so soon revolutionized many of the world's methods. The Richmond Va. trolley cars have been duplicated in all parts of the world. Electric train control, elevator control, and thousands of things followed based upon your inventions.

I first saw you at Annapolis in 1887 when you delivered a lecture to my class. In 1907 I was asked by a city magazine to write an account of your contributions to world progress. This was for me a privilege, and a most interesting one. And to cap it all came the joy of associating with you at Newport.

You, of course, early gained your place of one of the great electrical leaders of the world's history. Your contribution to world progress is part of the world's record of advancement. And the world is richer because of your life.

With much affection, E. L. Beach

APPENDIX 1

Westinghouse Electric & Manufacturing Company
May 12, 1932

Mr. Frank J, Sprague
150 Broadway, NYC

Westinghouse engineer, H. D. James notes Sprague's electric elevator work, and in particular the dual elevator installation at East Pittsburg known as the "Westinghouse-Sprague Dual Elevator".

Yours very truly,
H. D. James

THE BIRTH OF ELECTRIC TRACTION

Frederick, Maryland, June 18th, 1932.
To Frank J. Sprague:

It is with a great deal of pleasure that I take this opportunity to pay tribute to you, a fellow graduate of the Naval Academy, and a distinguished Engineer, whose fame is world-wide.

A leader in the electrical art for half a century, seventy-five and still marching on.

I like to recall the times my path as a naval officer has crossed yours. I remember you as a young man of thirty, coming to the Naval Academy, to tell us - the first class - of your trials and triumphs with your street-car motor; the first successful one of its kind. This was at a time, forty-five years ago, when all that was known of electricity - static and current - was found in the pages of Ganot or Thompson's Elementary Lessons. Silvanus Thompson's "Dynamo Electric Machinery" was recently off the press. Fiske's Electrical Engineering in advance of the time.

Motors were mysteries and measuring instruments unknown.

Later, I read of your special service, while still in the Navy, at Crystal Palace in London and at the Electrical Exhibition in Paris and of your cruise in the "Trenton", the first electrically lighted man-of-war.

Tour work in the succeeding years, after establishing the electric street-car industry, is an important part of the electrical history of America, crowned, it would seem, by the electrification of the New

York elevated railways and your invention of multiple control.

Some twenty years ago it was my good fortune to read here a brief history of your naval career, on the occasion when your achievements in electricity and your services to your country were recognized by the presentation of the Edison medal.

Again, in the World War, we met, when you were a member of the Naval Consulting Board and I was in command of Submarines and President of the Special Board on Anti-Submarine Devices, a strenuous period for all.

About three years ago I saw you at the Annual Dinner of the Naval Graduates Association, over which you, as President, presided gracefully, honored by all, mellowed by the years - already more than three score and ten - which had passed lightly over you.

Later, before a Scientific Society, I heard you give an outline of your busy life since the War.

Active, forceful and devoted to your life's great hobby - Electricity in the Service of Man.

> Most Sincerely yours, S. S. Robison,
> Rear Admiral USN (ret.)

APPENDIX 2:

These are samples of the "Birthday Book" letters (and some photos) from FJS' "anti-engineering" friends & family

<u>Friends</u>
    Ossip & Clara Gabrilowitsch (Clara, the daughter of Samuel Clemmens <Mark Twain>, was a close friend of Harriet before she married FJS)
    A. B. Paine (author)
    W. C. de Mille (movie producer)
    C. Hamilton (author & drama critic; very touching tribute)
    Robert Bridges (former Scribner's editor)

<u>Family</u> (Included are two photos, one of brother Charles and a 1932 group photo of entire family <except Robert's wife Florence>). It should be noted that FJS' three sons all ended up being employed by the electronic components company that Robert formed in

1926 and which became the second Sprague Electric Company. So did Althea's husband, Bud Tucker. Although there was no letter from Althea, Bud sent a nice note saying what a good father-in-law FJS was)

Charles Sprague (younger brother)
Desmond (son by Mary Keatinge)
Robert (son by Harriet)
Julian (son by Harriet)

1932 Sprague family photo, standing left to right: Julian's wife Helene, Julian, Robert, Desmond, Desmond's wife Ruth, Althea's husband Bud Tucker; seated left to right: Harriet, Frank, Althea; missing: Robert's wife Florence (courtesy of John L. Sprague)

APPENDIX 2:

Detroit Symphony Orchestra
OSSIP GABRILOWITSCH Director

TO FRANK J. SPRAGUE FOR HIS
SEVENTY-FIFTH BIRTHDAY (July 25, 1932)

This delightfully low key poem by close friends Ossip and Clara (Mark Twain's daughter) Gabrilowitsch celebrates Frank Sprague's many accomplishments with such timeless prose as:

"To his amazing, brilliant brains
We owe our rapid transit trains,
and ai'nt he also the creator

of the electric elevator?

"Of the perfected modern motor
He's the inventor and promotor."

Ossip and Clara. Gabrilowitsch

425 East 51st Street
Beekman Hill
New York City,

April 24, 1932

Dear Frank Sprague,

    It is my great pleasure to congratulate you on your approaching seventy-fifth birthday. In my mind is a very clear picture of Mark Twain and you and I, sitting on a couch in his billiard room at Stormfield, the while you explained to us certain curiosities of mathematics. Unhappily I forgot them, long ago; but I remember that I regarded you as a kind of wizard, and I feel certain that Mark Twain had the same idea, for figures to him were always associated with magic, black magic, I suspect. Perhaps he has solved certain mysteries, now, for it is just twenty-two years since Halley's Comet bore him from our orbit, as he always hoped, and believed, it would. "I came in with Halley's Comet," he said to me, one day, "and it will be the greatest disappointment of my life if I don't go out with it." He did exactly that; Halley's Comet appeared in the sky on the night he died. And it was twenty-two years ago to-day that we laid him to rest, at Elmira.

APPENDIX 2:

Again congratulations. I rejoice in your long and useful life. My wish is that you may live as long as you find life desirable;

                                        Faithfully yours,
                                  Albert Bigelow Paine

William C. DE Mille Productions, INC.
7046 Hollywood Boulevard
Hollywood
California

Office of
William C. DE Mille

Movie producer de Mille comments on the wonder of "Sunday evenings at Brander's", a recurring theme of many of Frank J. Sprague's social friends.

Faithfully,
July 25th, 1932 William C. de Mille

APPENDIX 2:

Clayton Hamilton
July 25, 1932
The Players – New York City

Frank Julian Sprague, D. Eng., D. Sc., L.L.D.

Author and drama critic Clayton Hamilton pays tribute to a little known side of Frank Sprague's character.

For more than half a century, Brander Matthews had known every man of letters, every man of the theatre, every artist who was worth knowing, in New York, London, and in Paris. Yet, when he was ultimately incapacitated, the one friend upon whom he relied absolutely to look after him in his declining years was not an artist but an engineer, Frank Julian Sprague.

Ever yours affectionately,
Clayton Hamilton

CHARLES SCRIBNER'S SONS
PUBLISHERS - IMPORTERS - BOOKSELLERS 597
FIFTH AVENUE NEW YORK

TO FRANK J. SPRAGUE

On His Seventy-Fifth Birthday

I am not an engineer but, as you know, I am allowed to sit with them at the table because I "listen". This has been denied by several eminent scientists who play backgammon.

However, one of my privileges has been to meet you for forty years and you never oppressed me with technical language that I could not pretend to understand. There has always been an element of humor and pleasure in the days when you were with the engineers and I want to be included among your old and best friends.

Faithfully yours,

Robert Bridges

Englewood Golf Club
Englewood, N. J.

APPENDIX 2:

*Frank J. Sprague's younger brother Charley
(courtesy of John L. Sprague)*

July 25, 1932
Mr. Frank J. Sprague
New York City

Dear Frank,

With the many others paying you tribute this day, permit me to offer hearty congratulations upon you reaching the 75th milestone in life's eventful journey, a life crowded with strenuous efforts and wonderful accomplishments, and, above it all, gracious and kindly consideration of your fellows.

Many happy returns of the day and with it still greater achievements.

Very Sincerely,
Chas. M. Sprague

APPENDIX 2:

Sprague Specialties Company

Dear Dad:

It is a rare privilege to be able to join this notable company who gather to do you honor on your birthday, and express their appreciation of your technical achievements and world recognized contributions to applied engineering.

Many more able will have commented in detail on these outstanding developments, but it is interesting to realize that my own advent into this complex and unstable civilization was practically coincident with the birth of the trolley, and that I have grown up side by side with that art of electric transportation which you created, from the mule to the Milwaukee.

While my recollections of the mule are rather hazy, I distinctly recall your difficulties when you decided to turn the trolley on end, for the glorification of New York real estate. Many a time as a very small boy, I sat in the engine rooms of the Postal Telegraph, or the old Waldorf, making collections of the cracked steel balls that came as a steady stream from the bearings of the old screw elevator machines. And the highlight of the proceedings was when you fell down the shaft at the gala opening.

However, the most vivid of my youthful memories were when you took me to Chicago in '97, on a forty-eight hour trip that lasted a month. I believe we had rooms at a hotel, but they were seldom used, as we slept and ate on the "loop line" most of the time. You had many problems; sometimes the motor cars wouldn't go; then someone would mix the jumpers and the respective halves of the train would start in opposite directions. But to me these were minor annoyances. It was very hot, and the real problem was whether the subsidized Italian fruit vendor would have the bucket of iced lemonade ready when we reached the Van Buren Street spur.

But recollections take a more serious turn years later, during the war, into channels little known to most of your associates - the shrapnel tests at Sandy Hook, the isolated fulminate sheds at Indian Head, depth charges off Newport, - where you daily risked your life experimenting for the general cause.

And later it was my privilege to work with you on train control, on which you spent your personal fortune and many valuable years, in establishing the general principles now considered fundamental in trunk line cab signaling.

That these many pioneer achievements be amplified is the most sincere birthday wish of your many friends, and of your family.

Desmond

APPENDIX 2:

SPRAGUE SPECIALTIES COMPANY
NORTH ADAMS, MASSACHUSETTS
June 1932

Mr. Frank J. Sprague,
Sprague Safety Control & Signal Corporation,
421 Canal Street,
New York City

Dear Dad:

    It is with a feeling of great pride that I join in this tribute to your accomplishments on the occasion of your seventy-fifth birthday.

    You have left a group of accomplishments and engineering achievements benefiting practically everyone. This is an extremely difficult heritage for your sons to continue with the same measure of success. Over and beyond these accomplishments, and responsible for many of them, is a fighting spirit which has carried you through many difficult periods, and is in strongest evidence today in your seventy-fifth year, when most men would have "taken the count". In this you have set an example which is up to us, your sons, to carry on.

    With a great deal of pride, love and affection

Your son,
Robert

SPRAGUE CONDENSERS Sarnia- Ontario
LIMITED
June 14, 1932
Frank J. Sprague, Esq.
40 West 55th Street,
New York City, N.Y.

Dear Dad:

It gives me a tingling sensation of pride and pleasure to be allowed to join the host of your great friends and admirers in doing honor to your life's work and in wishing you many happy returns of the day on your Seventy-fifth Birthday.

It is hard for me to realize that you are three-quarters of a century old, for your activity and work today is just as brilliant, just as progressive and just as exhausting as it ever was. Others will recollect in this book your early struggles, trials, tribulations and courageous success. They will recount your many brilliant achievements — the Richmond Trolley, the Multiple-Unit System, the Sprague Elevators and the Sprague Industrial Motors — to bring about which you worked against seemingly insurmountable handicaps and misfortunes.

Unfortunately, I did not have the opportunity of following these developments first hand. I can, however, speak of the indomitable willpower, fortitude and ceaseless energy with which you worked for years in the perfection of automatic train control, your war-time developments and your present sign. I have never known anyone else, and never expect to, who, when faced with the odds with which you have had to cope, could have carried through. All this record of your life is tangible and will go down in history as one of the greatest human epics.

The part of your life which possibly is not so well known is your kindliness and unselfish devotion to those you held dear. It brings a lump to my throat to think of all the sacrifices that you have made for your children and to realize that, in all probability, I will be unable to in any way repay what you have done, or even to adequately show my appreciation for the innumerable fatherly kindnesses which you have shown. I only hope that I, by my work and life and human relationships, can in some small measure hold your faith and justify all you have done, I know that Bob, Althea and Demmie will do the same.

Helene joins me in once again wish you a happy Birthday, Dad

> Devotedly,
> Julian K Sprague

INDEX

Page references in *italics* indicate photographs.

A

accidents: elevator, 170; railroad, 258–259; trolley, 138–139

accounting systems, 182

accumulators, 46

AEG (Allgemeine Deutsche Elektrizitaets-Gesellschaft), 138–140, 150

aesthetics, 7

AIEE. *see* American Institute of Electrical Engineers

Alley L (South Side Elevated Railway), 264, 280; electrification of, 205–213, 215, 217–228, *228,* 233; five-car MU train, *228*; net earnings, 228–229, 236; stock, 229

Allgemeine Deutsche Elektrizitaets-Gesellschaft (AEG), 138–140

alternating current, 232–233, 240, 256–258

aluminum, 143

American Electric Railway Association, 278
American Institute of Electrical Engineers (AIEE), 123–124, 187, 220
"Ampere" locomotive, 74
animal railways, 119
animated electric signs, 276–277
"anti-engineering" friends, 279, 335–349
arc lamps, 29, 40, 46
Arlington National Cemetery, 277
Armington-Sims steam engine, 57
Arthur, Chester A., 276
ATC (automatic train control), 251–252, 262–263, 272
automatic control circuits, 233, 260–261
automatic train control (ATC), 251–252, 262–263, 272
automatic watertight doors, 181, 263–264
autopilot, 276

B
Baker, Benjamin, 214–216
Baltimore & Ohio, 191
Bank of England, 204, 213–214
Beach, Edward L., 329–330
Beauregard, P. G. T., 235
Bell, Alexander Graham, 29
belts, 76
Bentley and Knight, 75, 120, 150
Bickford, J. H., 134–135
Bobbs-Merrill Company, iv

Boston Elevated Company, 239, 241
Boston Herald, 36
Boston-to-Lowell car line, 144
Bridges, Robert, 279, 335, 342
Brill, 138
Brockton, Mass. electric light installation, 59–62
Bronx NYC trolley cars, renovated, *133*
Brooklyn Elevated, 238
Brooklyn Navy Yard, 38–39
Browne & Sharp, 100
Brush Arc Light Company, 132
brushes, 114–115
Butler, Nicholas Murray, 9
Butt, J. W., 321–322

C
cable and insulation business, 180
Campbell, A. D., 320
Carichoff, E. R., 217–218, 221, 225, 280
Carnegie, Andrew, 70
Carter, Leslie, 205–210, 212, 219–220
Case, F. S., 323–324
cast-iron grids, 171
Centennial Exposition (1876), 10, 29, 34–35, 279
Central Committee for Electrification, 253–254
Central London Railway, 204–205, 214–216
Century Magazine, 68–69, 81–83
Chicago, Milwaukee & St. Paul railroad, 258
Chicago Century of Progress Exposition, 277
Childs, Starling W., 325

Christmas tree lights, 193
Clark, Charles, 61–62, 235–236, 279
Clark, William J., 206, 215
Clarke, Chas. L., 295–297
Class I railroads, 263
Clemmens, Clara, 248–249
Clemmens, Samuel (Mark Twain), 248–249
Cleveland, Ohio, 138
Coffin, Charles, 132–134, 156–157, 188, 236–240, 243–245
Columbia University, 123–124
compressed-air dynamite guns, 264
Comstock, Louis, 315
constant speed motors, 70
contract issues, 150
control systems: automatic control circuits, 233, 260–261; automatic train control (ATC), 251–252, 262–263, 272; "dead-man's control," 178, 260; series-parallel motor control patents, 240; speed control, 192, 194; Sprague General Electric Multiple-Unit Control, 244; tone controls, 273–275
Cook, WIlliam W., 265–266
Coolidge, T. Jefferson, 134
Cooper-Hewitt, 268
Corliss steam engine, 34–35
Cornell University, 195
Cox, William, 247–248
Crawford, John, 79–80
Crosby, Oscar T., 90, 112, 128, 235, 280

Crystal Palace Electrical Exhibition (London, England), 42–46, 186, 279; Report on the *Exhibits at the Crystal Palace Electrical Exposition, 1882* (Sprague), 46–47

Cunningham, Joseph C., viii

D

Daft, Leo, 74
Dalzell, F., vii
Daniels, Joseph, 267–268
Davenport, Thomas, 25
Davidson, Robert, 25–26
"dead-man's control," 178, 260
de Mille, WIlliam C., 340
Depression, 179, 190
depth charges, 270
Diesel, Rudolph, 46–47
direct current, 256–257
Dougherty, Paul, 262–263
Drexel, Morgan & Company, 144–145
Drury Academy (North Adams, MA), 21
dual elevators, 273, 288
dumb waiters, 209–210, 280
Duncan, Louis, 161
Dunn, Gano, 3, 8–9
Durant Sugar Refinery (New York City, NY) trials, 79–81
Dyer & Seeley, 150
dynamite gun, 160–161, 264–265

dynamos, 28–29, 31, 35, 59–61; series-parallel, 193; with series-parallel armature circuits, 40; Sprague on, 46

dynamo windings, 46

E

E. Parson & Sons, 205

Eaton, Major, 150

Edison, Thomas, iii–iv, 29, 35, 267; anti-alternating current campaign, 257; as "chief," 50–51, 57; correspondence with Sprague, 35, 38–39, 62–66, 129–130; electric railroad efforts, 51–54, 74; lawsuits, 53; Menlo Park facility, 49–66, 189; on Naval Advisory Board of Inventors, 267, 267–269; patents, 53, 132, 237; relations with Johnson, 130; relations with Sprague, 4, 35, 47, 49–66, 129–130, 147, 153–156, 235, 256–257; sale of Edison General Electric, 157; on Sprague, 70; Sprague stockholdings, 144–145, 235; Sunbury, PA lighting system, 54–55; three-wire system, 43

Edison-Eickemeyer armature, 154–155

Edison fetish, 154

Edison General Electric (EGE or Edison-GE), iii, 147–152; 1889 annual report, 148–149; acquisition by General Electric, 157, 188, 194; acquisition of Sprague Electric, 147–149; competition from Thomson-Houston, 133–134, 151–152; competition from Westinghouse, 151–152; earnings ratio, 156; letter books, 286; merger with Thomson-Houston, 243

Edison Machine Works, 90, 128–130, 145; espionage on, 136–137; stockholders, 131
egalitarianism, 32–33
EGE. *see* Edison General Electric
Eickemeyer, Rudolf, 151, 153–155
electrical call systems, 42
electrical distribution circuits, 46
electric arc lamps, 29, 40, 46
electric autopilot, 276
"electric candles of Jablochkoff," 29
Electric Club, 187
electric elevators, 72, 150, 153, 159–183, *166*
electricity: development of, 24–25, 29, 49–66; early, 28–29, 35; Edison on, 53; mid-19th Century, 17–18; practice of, 49–66; war of the currents, 257
electric motors, 192–193, 195; dynamos, 28–29, 31, 35, 40, 46, 59–61, 193; history of, 25; series-parallel, 193–194
electric railroads, 40, 185–202; Edison's efforts, 51–54, 74; Richmond, Va. street railway, 85–102, 105–109, 120–123, 129; South Side Elevated Railway (Alley L), 207–213, 215, 217–229, *228*; Union Passenger Railway Company, 119; from Washington to Bladensburg, MD, 26–27
Electric Railway Journal, 258
electric signs, animated, 276–277
electric toasters, 276
electric traction, iii, vi, 272, 277, 280
electric transportation: Durant Sugar Refinery trials, 79–81; early electric cars (electrics), 26; early

history, 25–26, 74–75; Edison's efforts, 51–54, 74; mainline electrification, 137–138, 190–191, 252–253, 257–258; multiple unit (MU) system, 197, *198,* 198–200, 203–229; railroads, 40, 185–202; Richmond, Va. street railway, 85–102, 105–109, 120–123, 129; search for railroad for, 185–202; "The Solution of Municipal Rapid Transit" (Sprague), 123–124; Sprague's dream and work, 44–45, 72, 191; from Washington to Bladensburg, MD, 26–27. *see also* trolley cars

electrification: of Alley L, 205–213, 215, 217–228, *228*; Central Committee for Electrification, 253–254; mainline, 137–138, 190–191, 252–253, 257–258

electromagnetic engines, 7, 25–28

elevated railways, 195–197, 231; Alley L (South Side Elevated Railway), 205–213, 215, 217–229, *228,* 233, 236, 264, 280; Brooklyn Elevated, 238; Manhattan Elevated Railroad, 76, 80–82; Metropolitan Elevated, 196, 225–227

elevators, 204; "dead-man's control," 178; dual elevator, 273, 288; electric, 72, 150, 153, 159–183; Grand Hotel, 169, 171, 173; gravity, 162; hydraulic, 163–164; modern features of, 177–178; passenger, 162; Postal Telegraph Company, 172–173, 175–177; *Shepard's Bush* Elevator, 204, 208–209, 213–216; Sprague-Pratt Elevators, 167–168, 170–171; steam, 162–163

empiricism, 57

Engineering Societies Building, 2–3, 8–9, 279

Erie Canal, 219
espionage, industrial, 134–137, 241, 320
Essex Terraplane, 2
esthetics, 7
Ewing, Thomas (Tom), 234, 237, 243

F
"Faraday" locomotive, 74
Farmer, Moses, 26, 29, 31, 35, 39–40, 76
Farmer, Sarah, 220
Farrant, Richard, 214, 216
"The Father of Electric Traction," iii
The Father of Electric Traction (Passer), vi
Field, Cyrus W., 82
Field, Stephen D., 53, 74
Fiesole, Italy, 138
Finley, John H., 3, 9
Fiske, Bradley, 67
Florence, Italy, 138, 142
Flynn, Maurice B., 87–88, 101, 119, 123
Frankfurt, Germany, 142
Frank J. Sprague and the Edison Myth (Sprague), iii–iv
Frank J. Sprague and the U. S. Electrical Industry (Dalzell), vii
Frank Julian Sprague, Electrical Inventor and Engineer (Middleton and Middleton), vii
Franklin Institute Exposition, 67, 70–71

G
Gabrilowitsch, Clara, 335, 337

Gabrilowitsch, Ossip, 249, 279, 335, 337
gas engines, 43; Report on the *Exhibits at the Crystal Palace Electrical Exposition, 1882* (Sprague), 46–47
GE. *see* General Electric
gear drives, 76
General Electric (GE) Company, iii, 4, 148, 191, 206, 215, 227–228, 235; acquisition of Edison-GE, 157, 188, 194; acquisition of SEC, 244; competition with SEC, 238–241, 243–244; competitive MU system, 236–237; elevated locomotive, 195–196; formation of, 157; letter books, 323–324, 326–327; patents, 194
Germany, 139–140, 150
Glennon, James H., 289–291, *291*
Gooch, 144, 146–147
Gould, Jay, 80–81, 186–187, 196
Gramme, Zenobie Theophile, 28
Grand Central Station (New York City, NY), 252–253
Grand Hotel (New York City, New York), 169, 171, 173
gravity elevators, 162
Great Blizzard (1888), 116
Great Epizootic, 119
Greene, S. Dana, 90, 93, 235–236; and Richmond, Va. electric street railway, 96–101; salary, 128; Sprague stockholdings, 235; Union Passenger Railway Company trolley system work, 111, 113, 116
grids, cast-iron, 171
guns: dynamite gun, 160–161, 264–265; Krupp guns, 35; naval, 160–161

Gurney, Howard F., 314

H
Halle, Germany, 138
Hamilton, Clayton, 250, 335, 341
Hammer, William J. (Bill), 43–44, 49, 279, 301–303
Hartford railroad, 252–253
Hedley, Frank, 278
Henry, John C., 75–76
Herford, Oliver, 249, 279
Higginson, Henry Lee, 134
Hitler, Adolf, 2
Hoc web press, 35
Holden, James W., 251
Hoover, Herbert, 1, 278
Hotel Cecil, 214
Houston, Edwin J., 131–132
Howells, William Dean, 248
Huff, S. W., 309
human failure accidents, 258–259
Huse, Harry P., 292–293
Hutchinson, Cary T., 161
Hyatt, HCarles E., 218
hydraulic elevators, 163–164

I
incandescent lamps, 46
industrial espionage, 134–137, 241, 320
industrialism, 181, 183, 240
Ingersoll jackhammer, 35

Insull, Samuel (Sammy), 52, 150, 235
intelligence reports, 134–136
Interstate Commerce Commission, 263
interurbans, 6–7
IRT subway (New York City, New York), 259, 278
Italy, 138

J
J. G. White Company, 3
Jablochkoff: "electric candles of Jablochkoff," 29
Jackson, Dugald C., 308
Jacquard power loom, 34–35
James, H. D., 331
Johnson, Edward H., 43–44, 47, 233; cable and insulation business, 180; correspondence with Sprague, 143; Edison stockholdings, 131; electric elevator work, 161; and Pratt electric elevator, 153, 167; relations with Edison, 130; relations with Sprague, 68–69, 147–148; and Richmond, Va. electric street railway, 91, 96–101, 120; salary, 128; and Sprague Electric Elevator Company, 180; at Sprague Electric Railway and Motor Company, 67–70, 76, 82, 120; Sprague stockholdings, 69–70, 144–145, 234–235
Johnson bar, 260
Jones, Harriet C., 245–246, *246*

K
Keatinge, Mary Harned, 72, *73*
kedges, 111

Kodak, 249
Kreusi, John, 50, 151, 235
Krupp guns, 35
Krupp works (Essen, Germany), 42

L

labor strikes, 181, 215
Lackey, Henry E., 294
Le Sprague, vi
letter books, 285–288
Libby, S. H., 218, 221
lighthouses, 29
Lincoln, E. S., iv
litigation, 150, 272
locomotives: "Ampere," 74; electric, 74; elevated, 195–197; "Faraday," 74; "Ohm," 74; steam, 196–197; "Volta," 74
Lowry, Malcolm, 85
Ludwig, Emil, 279
Lundy, 207–208, 210, 241

M

magnetic engines, 26–27
mainline electrification, 137–138, 190–191, 257–258; first, 191; technical problems of, 252–253
Manhattan Elevated Railroad, 76, 80–82
Manhattan Hotel, 217
Manhattan Railroad Company, 200–201, 204
Manhattan Railway, 238
Marconi, G., 312–313

Mason, Dave, 89
Massachusetts Institute of Technology, 308
mathematics, 56
Matthews, Brander, 249–250
Matthews, Edith, 250
Maxim, 268
McCloy, James, 310–311
McIver, Alex, 218, 225
McKay, L. W., 212–213
Melbourne, Australia, 138
Menlo Park: electric railroad, 51–54, 189; Sprague at, 49–66
Mesmerism, 18
Metropolitan District Railway, 44–45
Metropolitan Elevated, 196, 225–227
Michelson, Albert, 279
Middleton, W. D., vii
Middleton, W. D. III, vii
Milford, Connecticut, 18–19
Moir, Willian, 205
Morgan, Helen, 2, 157
Morgan, J. Pierpont, 50, 59, 131, 133–134, 148, 188; Sprague stockholdings, 144–145, 235
moving signs, 276–277
multiple unit (MU) system, 197, *198,* 198–200, 203–229; Alley L (South Side Elevated Railway), 205–213, 215, 219–229, *228*; benefits of, 228–229, 236; Boston Elevated, 239; competitive systems, 236–237, 239; letter books, 287; patents, 220–221, 234, 237, 240; rights, 234; Schenectady test runs, 220–225;

Sprague General Electric Multiple-Unit Control, 244; Sprague patent, *242,* 243–245; success of, 232

N
National Electric Light Association, 127
National Socialist Party (Nazis), 2
Naval Advisory Board of Inventors, *267,* 267–270, 288
naval guns, 160–161
Naval Research Laboratory (NRL), 269–270, 328
Newcomen engines, 24
New Haven Railroad, 252–254, 256–258
New Orleans, Louisiana, 138
Newport Torpedo Station, 39–41, 76
New York Central Railroad, 252–253, 256, 258, 263, 321–322
New York City, New York: Central Committee for Electrification, 253–254; mainline electrification, 252–255; renovated Bronx NYC trolley cars, *133;* Sprague on, 23; underground railways, 161, 187, 255–256
New York Edison, 4
New York Post, 187
The New York Times, 1–3
The New York Times Building, 276
New York World, 109–110
Niagara Falls, 241
North Adams, Massachusetts, *16,* 20–21
North American Company, 189–190
Northern Pacific Railroad, 52–53, 188–191

NRL. *see* Naval Research Laboratory

O

Oberlin, B. G., 328
"Ohm" locomotive, 74
Omaha, Nebraska, 138
O'Shaughnessy, Pat, 107–109, 119, 171, 218–219, 221, 225
Otis Elevator Company, iii, 162, 183, 233, 314

P

Page, Charles G., 26–28
Paine, Albert Bigelow, 248, 338–339
Pantaleoni, G., 298–301
Paris, France, vi, 29
Paris Electrical Exhibition, 40–42
Paris Exposition, 139–140
Park Avenue tunnel, 253
Passer, Harold, vi, 231
Passer, Harold C., 201–202
Passer, Harold K., 1
patent litigation, 237, 240
Patent Office, 234
patents, 144, 156, 185, 194; lawsuits, 150; sales, 7; series-parallel motor control, 240; Sprague MU patent 660,065, *242,* 243–245; Sprague structure, 220–221; trolley, 115–116, 132, 221
Pearl Street Central Station, 81
Pemberton Mills (Lawrence, Mass.), 72, 165
Pennsylvania Railroad, 71

Pittsburgh, Pennsylvania, 138
pneumatic dynamite guns, 264
poetry, 337
Pommer, Eugene, 104
postal mail, 13–14
Postal Telegraph Company (New York City, NY), 172–173, 175–177, 197, 203–204
Potter, W. B., 278
Pratt, Charles, 150, 161, 167, 178, 180
Pratt electric elevator, 153
problem method, 34
psychological warfare, 243
public relations, 109–110, 123
public transportation: early, 15–16; "The Solution of Municipal Rapid Transit" (Sprague), 123–124. *see also* electric transportation
Pupin, Michael, 9

R

race relations, 32–33, 279
railroads, 15–16; city, 15–16; early, 15; electric, 40, 185–202; multiple unit (MU) system, 197, *198,* 198–200, 203–229; self-propelled cars, 197, 209; underground, 161, 187; vertical (*see* electric elevators). *see also specific lines, railroads*
rail safety, 258–259
RATP, vi
Reconstruction period, 32–33, 85
Report on the *Exhibits at the Crystal Palace Electrical Exposition, 1882* (Sprague), 46–47

ribbon communities, 5
Rice, E. W., 236–237, 245
Rice, E. Wilbur, Jr., 326–327
Richardson, Guy, 278
Richmond, Virginia: electric street railway, 85–102, 105–109, 120–123, 129, 280; telephone service, 105, 110–111
Richmond Dispatch, 86, 94–95
Richmond Grade, 94
Ritchie, Miss, 128
Robeson, Paul, 2
Robison, S. S., 332–333
Roosevelt, Franklin D., 1, 3, 268, 278
Roosevelt, Theodore, 264, 266
Rough Riders, 266
Rowsome, Frank, Jr., iv, iv–v, vii–viii

S
safety, 258–259
"safety catch," 79–80
Sargent, Fred, 206–208, 210
Sargent and Lundy, 206, 210
Sawyer, Willits H. (Bill), 316–317
Schenectady factory, 151, 215; South Side Elevated Railway test runs, 220–225
Schwab, Charles M., 9
science, 17
SEC. *see* Sprague Electric Company
self-propelled trains, 197, 209
series-parallel armature circuits, 40

series-parallel electric motors, 193–194
series-parallel motor control patents, 240
series system, 75
Sharon, Connecticut, 247–248
Shepard, Frank, 10, 206, 236, 278–279
Shepard's Bush Elevator, 204, 208–209, 213–216
Shore Line Trolley Museum (Branford, CT), vii
Short, Sidney, 75
Short Electric Railway Co., 143
Shove, Susan Amelia, 19
Siemens, Werner, 74, 140, 142, 164–165
signs, moving, 276–277
simplicity, 75–77
Sims Dudley Defense Co., 264–265
skylines, 15–16
skyscrapers, 272–273
Snowflake, 109
solenoids, 27
"The Solution of Municipal Rapid Transit" (Sprague), 123–124
South America, 138
Southern Pacific railroad, 258
South Side Elevated Railway (Alley L), 264, 280; electrification of, 205–213, 215, 217–228, *228,* 233; five-car MU train, *228*; net earnings, 228–229, 236; stock, 229
Spanish-American War, 264
special service motors, 180–181
speed control, 192, 194
Sperry, 268

Sprague, Althea, *246, 247, 336*
Sprague, Charley, 9, 18–21, 182, *343*
Sprague, Chas. M., 344
Sprague, David Cummings, 18–19
Sprague, Duncan, & Hutchinson, 189–190
Sprague, Elvira Ann, 19, *20,* 20–21
Sprague, Frances Julia King, 18
Sprague, Frank d'Esmonde (Desmond), 139, 173, 219–220, 269–270, *336*; birth, 116; birthday book letter, 345–346
Sprague, Frank J., *8, 267, 271, 336*; accounting systems, 182; on alternating current, 256–257; as Anglophile, 214–215; "anti-engineering" friends, 279, 335–349; on arc and incandescent lamps, 46; birth, 13, 18; "Birthday Book" letters, 335–349; cable and insulation business, 180; as cadet midshipman, 37–38; Canal Street office and laboratory, 275–276; career, 185–186; Centennial Exposition (1876), 34–35; childhood, 18–21; Coffin on, 245; college years, 31–36; commercial success, 127–157, 229, 232; constant speed motors, 70; as consultant, 149, 245, 257–259; correspondence from Paris Exposition trip, 140–143; correspondences, 131, 285–334; correspondence with Bickford, 134–135; correspondence with Cook, 265–266; correspondence with Edison, 35, 38–39, 62–66, 129–130; correspondence with Gooch, 146–147; correspondence with Hammer, 49; correspondence with Johnson, 143, 145; death, iii, 277; description of, 22–23, 58, 88, 91–92, 128; as director of

Edison General Electric, 149; divorce from Mary Harned Keatinge, 178–179; dream for electric transportation, 44–45, 191; on dynamos and dynamo windings, 46; Edison on, 70; education, 21–22; electrical work, 39, 49–66, 72, 232–233; electric transportation work, 44–45, 72, 191; as engineer, 7, 51; as engineer-entrepreneur, 1; as Ensign, 38–47; esthetics, 7; European tours, 247; eye injury, 266; as 'father of electric traction,' iii, 272, 277; first company, 67–83; first inspection of New York City, 23; Franklin Institute Exposition, 71; health, 203–204, 277; honors, 36, 275; ideal control system, 261; as industrialist, 181, 183, 240; inventions, 36–38, 192, 263; as inventor, 4–5, 7, 36–37, 51, 192; as journalist, 36; leadership, 272; letter books, 285–288; as lieutenant, 46–47; manner, 113; marriage to Mary Harned Keatinge, 72, 91–92, 100, 116, 173–174, 178, 186; as mathematician, 36, 56; Menlo Park interlude, 49–66; as midshipman, 31–36, *33*; modesty, 127–128, 139; multiple unit (MU) system, 197, *198,* 198–200, 203–229; multiple unit (MU) system patent, *242,* 243–245; Naval Advisory Board of Inventors, *267,* 267–270; new courses, 231–250; notebooks, 36–38; Paris Exposition, 139–140; partnership with Johnson, 68–69; patents, 7, 185, 194, 198–199, 220–221, *242,* 243–245, 276–277; personality, 173–174, 248–249; as pioneer of electricity, 277; Postal Telegraph testimonial, 176–177; and Pratt electric elevator, 153; as propagandist, 187;

rawhide tongue, 108; recurring life patterns, 203–204; relations with Coffin, 237–238, 245; relations with Edison, 4, 35, 47, 49–66, 129–130, 147, 153–156, 235, 256–257; relations with Edison General Electric, 150–155; relations with Johnson, 147; relations with Mary, 178–179; relations with Matthews, 250; Report on the *Exhibits at the Crystal Palace Electrical Exposition, 1882*, 46–47; resignation from EGE, 151–155; resignation from U.S. Navy, 47; Richmond, Va. electric street railway, 85–102, 121–123; salary, 51, 128, 149, 213; as scientist, 7; second marriage, 232, 245–246; Sharon, CT house, 247–248; "The Solution of Municipal Rapid Transit," 123–124; as Sprague stockholder, 144–145; taste for simplicity, 75–76; technical education, 21–22, 34; testimonials, 2–3, 8–10, 176–177, 278–280; thanks from, 280–281; tributes to, 277; trolley mechanisms, 104; trolley patent, 115–116; Union Passenger Railway Company trolley system work, 111–114, 116–118; U.S. Naval career, 31–36, *33,* 37–47, 279; on *U.S.S. Minnesota,* 38–39; on *U.S.S. Richmond,* 36–38; vertical railway work, 159–183; Volunteer Electrical Corps recommendation, 264–265; wealth, 7; "wheelbarrow" mounting, 77; work for Edison, 49–66; as youngster, 22–23

Sprague, Harriet, iii–iv, vi, 9–10, 245–246, *246,* 247, 250, *336*

Sprague, Helene, *336*

Sprague, John L., v–viii

INDEX

Sprague, Julian K., iv, 247, 274, *336,* 348–349
Sprague, Mary, 72, *73,* 91–92, 100, 116, 173–174, 178–179
Sprague, Robert (Bob), iii, iv, *246,* 247, 273–275, *336*; birthday book letter, 347
Sprague, Ruth, *336*
Sprague Condensers, 348–349
Sprague Electric Company (SEC), 233–234, 239, 264; assets, 234; competition with GE, 238–241, 243–244; letter books, 287; sale to GE, 244, 252; stockholders, 234–235
Sprague Electric Company (second), 335–336
Sprague Electric Elevator Company (SEEC), 167–169, 172–173, 204–205, 233; acquistion by Otis Elevator, 183; billings, 179; letter books, 287
Sprague Electric Railway and Motor Company (SERM), 125, 243; acquisition by Edison-GE, 147–149; capital stock, 83; competition from Thomson-Houston, 133–134; contract with Union Passenger Railway Company, 88–90, 101–102, 123; electrification contracts, 137–138; factory, 128–129; formation of, 67–83; letter books, 286–287; offices, 128–129; payroll, 128–129; public relations, 109–110, 123; Richmond, Virginia electric street railway, 85–102, 105–109, 120–122; stockholders, 131, 144; Union Passenger Railway Company trolley system, 110–111
Sprague General Electric Multiple-Unit Control, 244
Sprague-Pratt Elevators, 167–168, 170–172
Sprague Railway Motor Truck, 77, *78*

Sprague Safety Control and Signal Corporation, 262
Sprague Screw-type Electric Elevator Patent, *166*
Sprague Specialties Company, 345–347
Sprague-Thomson rolling stock, vi
St. Joseph, Missouri, 87–90, 92
Stadelman, W. A., 135–136
Standard Third Rail Company, 256
Stanley Electric Company, 240
steam cars, 15
steam elevators, 162–163
steam engines, 15–16, 24, 57
steam locomotives, elevated, 196–197
Steger, H. B., 218, 221–225
Steinmetz, Charles, 132
street cars, 231; "The Solution of Municipal Rapid Transit" (Sprague), 123–124; Yonkers, NY system, 151. *see also* trolley cars
Street Railway Journal, 119–120
submarine detection, 270
subways. *see* underground railways
Sulzberger, Carl, viii
Sunbury, Penn. lighting system, 54–55, 58–59
Sunny, B.E., 203, 209, 280
Swope, Gerard, 9

T
Tarkington, Booth, 279
technology: development of, 23–24; mid-19th Century, 13–18
telegraph, 28–29, 35

telephone service, 105
Tesla, Nikola, 57, 152, 304–305
Teutonic, 161
Third Avenue Railway System, 309
Thompson, Sylvanus, 71
Thomson, Elihu, 131–132, 306–307
Thomson-Houston Co., 116, 127, 131–132; competition from, 133–134, 136–137, 143–144, 151–152; earnings ratio, 156; equipment, 151; espionage on, 134–136; lawsuits, 150; merger with EGE, 243
three-wire systems, 43, 54–55
Time-Fortune exhibit (Chicago Century of Progress Exposition), 277
toasters, electric, 276
tone controls, 273–275
traction, electric, iii, vi, 272, 277, 280
trains. *see* railroads
transportation: city-wide, 88; mid-19th Century, 13–17; restricted, 15–16. *see also* electric transportation
Tremont House, 167
trolley: invention of, 103–125
trolley cars, 5, 125, 193; accidents, 138–139; Dayton, Ohio cars, *115*; first system, 88–89; importance of, 5–6; renovated Bronx NYC cars, *133*; "The Solution of Municipal Rapid Transit" (Sprague), 123–124; Union Passenger Railway Company, 110–114, 116–118; Yonkers, NY system, 151
Trolley Dodgers, 6
trolley mechanisms, 104
Trolley Park, 5

trolley patents, 115–116, 132, 221
Tucker, Bud, 336, *336*
Twain, Mark (Samuel Clemmens), 248–249

U
underground railways, 161, 187
Union Passenger Railway Company (UPR), 85–102, 105–109, 120–122; contract with Sprague Electric Railway & Motor Company, 88–90, 101–102, 122–123; opening day, 107; trolley system, 110–114, 116–119
UPR. *see* Union Passenger Railway Company
upside-down rail, 255–256
Upton, Francis R., 50–51
U.S. Naval Academy, 21–22; race relations, 32–33, 279; during Reconstruction, 32–33; Sprague at, 31–36, *33*
U.S. Navy, 22, 38–39; Advisory Board of Inventors, *267*, 267–270, 288; Atlantic Fleet, 268–269; automatic watertight doors, 263–264; Brooklyn Navy Yard, 38–39; dynamite gun, 160–161; dynamos, 31; electrical call system, 42; letter books, 286; Newport Torpedo Station, 39–41, 76; Volunteer Electrical Corps, 264
U.S.S. Lancaster, 41, *41,* 42
U.S.S. Lexington, 274
U.S.S. Minnesota, 38–39
U.S.S. Richmond, 36

V

Van Depoele, Charles J., 74–75, 115–116, 132; Dayton, Ohio trolley cars, *115*; trolley patent, 221

vertical railways. *see* electric elevators

Vevey, Switzerland, 140–141

Villard, Henry, 52–54, 131, 148, 154, 188–189, 191; as Edison G.E. president, 156–157; relationship with Sprague, 189–190; Sprague stockholdings, 144–145, 235

Volstead Act, 1

"Volta" locomotive, 74

Volunteer Electrical Corps, 264

W

Waldorf-Astoria Hotel (New York City, NY), 204

Wallace, William, 40

war of the currents, 257

watertight doors, 181

Watsessing, New Jersey plant, 180–181, 198–200, 216, 238

Wells French Car Works, 225

West End Railway (Boston), 119

Western Union, 35, 211

Westinghouse (verb), 257

Westinghouse, George, 129, 132, 152, 236

Westinghouse, H. H., 318–319

Westinghouse Electric & Manufacturing Company, 4, 235, 239–241; competition from, 151–152;

competition from Thomson-Houston, 133–134; competitive MU system, 236–237; dual-elevators, 273; letter books, 331
"wheelbarrow" mounting, 77
Whitney, Henry M., 119–122, 134, 268, 270
Whittier Machine Company, 167
Wilgus, Williams J., 253–256
Wilson, Woodrow, 179
Winton, 247, 249
Wise, John S., 128, 144–145, 150
World's Fair, 195
World War I, 267–270
Wright, Wilbur, 267–268
"wyes" (forks), 104

Y
Yonkers, NY street car system, 151
Young, Owen D., 9

Made in the USA
Middletown, DE
29 May 2015